from the School of Natural Cookery

Intuitive Cooking

JOANNE SALTZMAN

BOOK PUBLISHING COMPANY

Summertown, Tennessee

Library of Congress Cataloging-in-Publication Data

Saltzman, Joanne, 1948-
    Intuitive cooking from the school of natural cookery / by Joanne Saltzman.
        p. cm.
    Includes index.
    ISBN-13: 978-1-57067-194-4
    ISBN-10: 1-57067-194-X
1. Cookery (Vegetables)   2. Cookery (Cereals)   3. Vegetarian cookery.   I. Title.
TX801.S24 2006
641.6'5—dc22   2006021148

15 14 13 12 11 10 09 08 07 06   1 2 3 4 5 6 7 8 9

© 2006 Joanne Saltzman

Illustrations: *Cy Hundley*
Cover: *Warren Jefferson*
Design: *Aerocraft Charter Art Service*

Printed in Canada.

Book Publishing Company
P.O. Box 99
Summertown, TN 38483
888-260-8458

ISBN 10: 1-57067-194-X
ISBN 13: 978-1-57067-194-4

The Book Publishing Co. is committed to preserving
ancient forests and natural resources. We have elected to
print this title at Transcontinental on Enviro Offset, which
is 100% postconsumer recycled and processed chlorine
free. As a result of our paper choice, we have saved the following natural resources:

32 trees
1,517 lbs of solid waste
13,763 gallons of water
2,981 lbs pounds of greenhouse gases
5,535 kw hours of electricity

We are a member of Green Press
Initiative. For more information
about Green Press Initiative visit:
www.greenpressinitiative.org

BOOK PUBLISHING COMPANY

CONTENTS

*J*oanne Ellen Saltzman is the author of *Amazing Grains* and *Romancing the Bean* (H. J. Kramer, Inc., 1990, 1993). A former choreographer and dancer, and a mother of four, she founded the School of Natural Cookery in 1983. The school's unique program teaches the art of whole food preparation using "The Language of Cooking." The language allows students to rely on their intuition and connection with the food, rather than recipes. Joanne is passionate about creating an atmosphere that empowers students to explore and define themselves as culinary artists. In addition, she helps natural food companies bring their ideas for products into form and designs them for production.

ACKNOWLEDGMENTS

*My father once said, "Nothing is absolutely original."
As he carried on with this thought, I got the impression that although as artists we thought perhaps we were significantly original, the truth is: somewhere, someone else is probably having a similar idea.*

guess I should thank the unknown spirits that woke me up at three in the morning to tell me that I would be writing this book. It has taken me almost 15 years to feel complete with that agreement. I had rebelled at the idea of writing yet another cookbook, because who really needed another cookbook, there are so many. They said, "No, you are going to write about the process." That idea caught my attention, and in exploring how to communicate what I knew about inventing dishes without recipes, I realized it took all the pieces of my life to do it. Curious . . . where to begin a gratitude page for a lifework? At the beginning, before I chose my parents, who are artists and who instilled principles of art and design, music, and rhythm? Or do I begin today, with my son's in-laws, Mary and Jerry Lametti, who have offered a place in their mountain home for me to write and cook while they throw and glaze pots? Then there are my teachers, the late Nancy Hauser, Aveline Kushi, and Cornelia Aihara; and my sister, Barbara Jacobs, who rescued me in the hospital with George Ohsawa's skinny little book *Zen Macrobiotics;* and Elizabeth Frediani, who taught me about the energy of knowing how to trust myself, to make the invisible visible.

I wouldn't like any of the dishes that I make if it weren't for the farmers who strive for quality soil and products. There is no way to make that statement big enough. I also owe much gratitude to the people who have come to study with me, who have gone into the world as natural food chefs, proving that this approach works; students who become teachers, and their students who have confirmed that this work makes a difference in people's lives. This work grows because of teachers at the School of Natural Cookery— Michael Thibodeaux, whose classic culinary training intertwined with my work brings collaboration, never forgetting his gifts of exquisite herbs and spices from France, Spain, and Mexico, and my first introduction to proper paella, pimenton (smoked paprika), and the magic of yucca root; Omid Roustaei, who reflects the work back to me in Persian cuisine, keeping me sharp, and full of saffron; Maia Cunningham, who offers proof that this is a living language by integrating it with meat, fish, and foul; and Tyua Jenkins, who has traveled from Hawaii, bringing her gift of teaching to the language of living food.

I am grateful to authors I respect who either teach here or have validated my observations, like Susan Jane Cheney, author of *Breadtime* (Ten Speed Press, 1998), for her great presence and mastery with bread; Harold McGee, author of *On Food and Cooking* (Scribner, 1984), for his definitive explanation on the transformation of ingredients; Linda Ziedrich, author of the master work on pickles *The Joy of Pickling* (Harvard Common Press, 1998); Scott Ohlgren, author of HowHealthWorks.com, who lives his teachings on how healing food works in the body; and George Ohsawa, author of *Zen Macrobiotics* (The Ohsawa Foundation, 1965), which motivated me to leave the hospital, without being discharged, to heal myself with dancing and whole food.

Many thanks to Ron at nutritiondata.com, who thoroughly answers my difficult questions, and Christina Wilson who put hours of research into the nutritional values. Thanks to the musicians whose music accompanies me while I cook, while I write: Jesse Cook, Afro-Cuban All Stars, Sade, Cirque du Soliel, Daniel Day Lewis, Karen Matheson, Gustavo Santaolalla for *The Motorcycle Diaries* soundtrack; Mozart, Pachelbel, Beethoven, Bach, Regina Carter, Andrea Bocelli, and Loreena McKennitt, to name only a few.

The information of this book evolved because of the wisdom and courage of Linda and Hal Kramer and Jay Harlow, who published my first two books, *Amazing Grains* and *Romancing the Bean* (H. J. Kramer, Inc., 1990, 1993). I deeply appreciate the personal support I've received from friends and relatives who reminded me I had flower essences in the drawer and who were tired of hearing about what I call the four letter word that took eight years of my attention; my children Maia, Joe, Jake, and Ryan, who have become my biggest cheerleaders even though they think my cooking is way too "healthy" for most people. Thanks to my cousin Val for the commitment ring that kept me going, and for the honest feedback from Jennifer Martin and Walter Katz, who took time to view this work with fresh eyes. Endless gratitude goes to my mother, Muriel Saltzman, whose critical eye for language and words is just what I needed many times, and my father, William Saltzman, whose passion for "visual energy" unknowingly transmuted from him to me.

There are hundreds of precious people who have come to learn this language and share their creativity. The following helped shape the recipe sketches in this book during their improvisation class: Casey D'Antonio, Lisa Ehlers, James Check, Ashley Thornton, Amanda Lawrence, Becky Boutch, Junko Kombayshi, John Bayley, Michael Wood, Ben Adams, Ben Hastings, Cindy Gawel, Misuzu Haruna, Mary Martha Shaw, Joe Herman, Amy Thayert, Harry Capulong, Beatrice Zukowska, Alina Langford, Jennifer Adler, Heidi Boverman, Jill Cirvillo, Erica Czahor, John Farley, Chris Fiola, Suzanna Foretich, Debbie Haynes, Sara Mandell, Lori Hewitt, Susan Hilliard, Kia Hoeltzel, Bree Hopman, Deb Hoverman, Nicole Idol, Sharon Jobes, Adam Kemna, Rachel Kesley, Monique Loushin, Elise Summer, Jessica Wallis, Sara Mickler, Lauren Gennett, Matt Kime, Tony Mroczek, Pam Ikerd, Jeff Dec, Jack Wilson, Christy Brennand, Gwen McCloskey, Lana Hughes, Dan Manders, Carisa McNamee, Dawn Rosiello, Jennifer Gherke, Shepherd Faught, and Christina Wilson.

It is difficult to express enough gratitude to Laura Kephart for editing the recipe sketches and to Jo Stepaniak for masterminding my creativity with words into a worthy piece of English language. I am grateful that working with Cy Hundley, the artist who illustrated my ideas, was full of grace and accuracy. And one doesn't really know until the book is just about done how amazing it is to have a publisher and managing editor who have compassion for the birthing process and the pain of life, and who know how to be supportive with wisdom, patience, and humor. I am honored that Bob and Cynthia Holzapfel agreed to publish this uncommon cookbook.

I fell in love with plants through this process, using the language of cooking. I'm grateful others are also interested and that the School of Natural Cookery has become a place to explore these cooking realities.

My real gratitude is that it is done.

 am one of those people who sees patterns in shapes, rhythm, and the dynamics of energy moving. I became aware of this system for cooking experientially, in the state of mind where science and art meet—observation.

Cooking has been part of my life since I was tall enough to reach the sink. Before I could hold a knife, my dolls would stack soup cans and play with a toy cash register. Around the age of twelve, inspired by *Better Homes and Gardens* magazine and the *Joy of Cooking,* I routinely prepared dinners for my parents' friends and served them wearing a dance costume. Other pieces of my history prepared me to write this book. For example, a bat bite caused me to be admitted into the hospital, where I rebelled against being "experimented" on and instead healed myself with food and dance. I home-birthed my children, and cared for them with only nature's medicine. I taught choreography for the Nancy Hauser Dance Company school in Minneapolis, and later, in 1982, choreographed a cooking school for the premier natural food store, Alfalfa's Market in Boulder, Colorado. When Alfalfa's withdrew their interest in a cooking school, the School of Natural Cookery was born. My choreography morphed into communicating the essence of all cooking. Today it thrives as "The Language of Cooking Without Recipes"— a lifework explaining the pattern of universal cooking so that everyone has access to a simple explanation of what happens to ingredients in the pot. Regardless of your reason for wanting to learn this approach (culinary art, health, curiosity,

or survival), you will come to understand how to stock a pantry with ingredients that heal, and devise a cuisine that utilizes simple, authentic food. You will be able to open a cupboard or the refrigerator, pick out the right size pot, and cook something that tastes great.

My intention is to raise the standard for cooking and eating food from the plant kingdom. I like to teach about plant-based ingredients because everyone eats them no matter which diet they choose. Plants are not complex. Their only movement is up toward the sun and down into the earth. They do not roam or need other plants to reproduce or comfort them while they grow; they stand on their own. Plants provide water, minerals, vitamins, protein, fiber, and fat—nutrients that keep our human machinery in good health. Most have little fat, unlike animal products, and therefore should not be cooked the way that animal-based ingredients are cooked. The secret to cooking food from the plant kingdom lies in understanding how to use fat/oil and salt.

The nutritional information in this book is intended to demonstrate the healing power of earth's products; it is not meant to be taken literally as a replacement for medicine. Healing with food relies on its energetic properties. In addition, using creativity to prepare food is healing, and maintaining variety is imperative for balanced nutrition. Incorporating an assortment of types and colors of plants contributes a diversity of nutrients and energetic qualities. Organic ingredients are the best choice, not only for their superior taste but because it just makes sense that plants grown in nutrient-rich soil would be more health-supporting. In the marketplace, there is a great deal of confusion about the meaning of the term "organic." I have no qualms about selecting produce from farmers who practice "clean" growing methods in healthy soil but who do not subscribe to the politics involved with getting food labeled organic. When food is used to maintain health, it is especially important that it is "whole." Even if food is organic, it is not healing if it has been refined. We eat plants at each stage of their life. They offer wholeness throughout their life cycle from seed, sprouts, leaves, roots, and fruits.

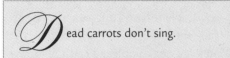

Dead carrots don't sing.

Today, genetically modified seeds do not reproduce. The energetic power of natural, whole food is evidenced by the ability of squash seeds to sprout and reproduce after lying dormant for thousands of years in Egyptian tombs. Standard nutritional information is based solely on laboratory research that analyzes various parts of a food rather than taking into account the food in its entirety. A detailed analysis, performed with chemicals and electronic instruments, puts food values on paper. Unfortunately, these laboratory values do not necessarily demonstrate how food is utilized in the human body. For example, I know that the starch in a potato affects my body differently than the starch in whole grain millet, yet according to the laboratory, the effect of these foods should be the same. This book's purpose is to illuminate the power of food and support your creativity so that you can maintain health through wholeness. Here is where culinary art meets healing whole food.

This book is designed for those who want to study cooking more deeply than what is typically offered in ordinary cookbooks. The information in this book is practical, and it will help you become an efficient cook. After I discovered the language of cooking, following a recipe felt tedious. Measuring utensils complicated my dance. My eyes had to move from cookbook to cupboard, from recipe to spoons, from food back to spoons, and finally to the pot. Now I just begin with the pot and select one ingredient from each of the required elements for the cooking method of the dish, and dinner is ready faster than getting in a car and going to a drive-through restaurant. When cooking feels boring but must be done, when fatigue from the day discourages creativity, the language of cooking will jump-start the process and dinner will be ready before boredom has a chance to set in. This language for cooking is to the culinary world what computers are to the workplace. It is the operating system used by grandmothers who "just know" how to cook or chefs who "just know" which ingredients go together. This book will bring to the surface the ageless knowledge deep inside every good cook.

There are three parts of cooking to study—ingredients, cooking methods, and consciousness. The first chapter outlines the basic theory of all cooking. The second details the cooking methods for the primary food groups. The third chapter depicts the primary food groups and their individual personality traits in cooking, along with several recipe sketches for each to spark ideas. Making dishes from this book is like a game of mix and match. Pick an ingredient from chapter 3 and a cooking method from chapter 2 or vice versa. Add the supporting elements of your choice, apply the basic theories from chapter 1, and voila . . . a dish!

TOOLS OF TRANSFORMATION

At its core, cooking is transformation. Transformation occurs under four conditions: fire, beating, salt, and time. These actions translate into cooking methods. Ingredients positioned in categories are transformed along with the person who cooks, without using the structure of a recipe.

Stages of Cooking

When I think about cooking, I envision preparing one primary ingredient (a grain, vegetable, or protein) at a time, in stages. I ask, "What happens first? Second? Third? When is it done? When do I need a sauce?" Pretreatments are cooking methods that manipulate the tone and texture of a dish. Dishes are not complete after going through a pretreatment. It's the first-stage cooking methods that completely transform the primary element. Second- and third-stage cooking methods add layers of flavor and texture, building complexity into the primary element. Each primary element responds a little differently to the same cooking method. Knowing these differences makes me very fast in the kitchen. I make more first-stage grain or beans than I need for one meal because first-stage methods take 30–60 minutes to cook and second-stage methods are ready in 5–10 minutes. Supporting elements, like tamari, pickle brine, miso, mirin, and vinegar, impart delicious flavor to food during the second-stage methods, much more so than if the food was simply reheated with water. Hot sauces embellish first-stage grain the way tomato sauce dresses pasta. Most vegetable dishes are prepared with first-stage methods and should be eaten freshly cooked. All bean dishes go to a second-stage preparation where salt finishes the dish. Salt defines a cooking method. When it is time for the salt to go into a dish, I know the cooking process will begin and my job is basically done.

> *S*econd-stage cooking methods reinvent first-stage dishes, like making a bedsheet into an evening gown.

My Kitchen, My Tools

Morning light blasts through my kitchen window, spraying a fine mist across the stainless steel range. Granite counters are polished, free of lingering sauce droppings and smudges from yesterday's cooking session. The thin film from oil in the air has been scrubbed off the blue and white tile wall. The tile colors remind me of Greece, but I purchased them in Mexico when I discovered my favorite cooking tool, a molcajete y tejolete (the Mexican term for mortar and pestle).

The molcajete (a hand-carved bowl made from volcanic rock) weighs about 10 pounds. I don't even think about picking it up with one hand. My hands are large, but together they don't reach around the bowl that stands precariously on three legs. The inside of the bowl was rough, before I made her ready. She reminded me of a gray-and-white-speckled woman. Then I put a little oil and rice in the center and began moving the hand piece (tejolete) clockwise, crushing the grain into the oil, into the pores of my stone bowl on legs. After 30 years, this bowl tells many stories. The most famous—guacamole. Each time garlic is crushed against her interior wall and blended with ripe avocados and lemon juice, the molcajete drinks it like a food facial. The rock's surface, now smooth as frozen water, will age gracefully for generations. I can just hear my great-granddaughter talking about it. "Cardamom crushed in her left her breath smelling like floral mouthwash, a welcome reprieve from the heat of ancho and chipotle chiles (smoked jalapeño chiles)." The molcajete sits on the top shelf, all by herself.

Glass jars of herbs and spices line the east wall of my kitchen. Forty sit on a custom rack that my father designed of copper tubes, allowing it to stand free. A mottled green patina dances on the bars. These dried plants have literally jumped out when they want to go into a dish. Like the time I cooked for Valerie. I opened her spice cabinet and a small, natural cloth bag full of mulling spices fell onto the counter. It was in my hand for only a few seconds before I realized that cloves, orange peel, and cinnamon wanted to go into the first-stage cooking liquid for the wild rice salad.

From the day the subzero refrigerator arrived, kale no longer was lost to freezer burn, or the ice cream to meltdown. We saved almost $80 a week, because most of the food that went into the refrigerator survived until we could eat it. And now it is snug in the schoolhouse—invisible, as if it were part of the wall. Its large door swings wide, and its shallow depth allows me to see everything at a glance, eliminating the frustration of digging for lost ingredients.

At the beginning of the day, each pot wears its lid. Glass bowls nest. The corner shelf holds pot holders and aluminum disks with holes, their wood handles happily missing. Shiny when new, these flame tamers now look rough and ready, like something from a salvage yard. They slow down the fire, prevent food from burning, and hold my dishes like a safety blanket. I use them on electric and gas ranges every time I know that the food will drink up all the liquid in the pot, or when I want the food to stay warm without cooking.

My arm easily reaches the crocks full of whisks, bamboo paddles, and long chopsticks used for cooking. A series of knives live in a custom-built holding block that my son Jake made in high school shop class. He designed it for my Japanese-style, square-end vegetable knives. I collect them. They are my swords. Each time I pick one up, I flick my thumb against the blade to check its edge.

It is easy to overload a kitchen with tools and equipment. I have hand tools like zesters, juice extractors, and garlic presses, but often I rely on a fork and a good knife to do the job. Hands and eyes are my tools for using salt, cooking liquid, oil, and herbs and spices.

My sensory system is in full use during a cooking session. I touch, hear, see, smell, and taste how fast the food is cooking, when it is time to stir, cover, turn off the fire, or add another ingredient. Pot lids bounce under an active boiling bath, and pressure cookers hiss in response to the heat.

The Heart and Nose of a Chef

By now you can see my attitude building. It's confidence. Each time I cook, I know if my nose and taste buds are working, if my eyes are balancing ratios properly, if my hand is heavy or light, and if I am paying attention or distracted. Thoughts about the leaky roof in the sunroom are moved to the back burner while my heart is focused on cooking. My whole body is engaged when I cook. Arguments stay out of the kitchen;

anger is not an ingredient I like in my food. Angst clouds a kitchen and fills the invisible space like a traffic jam in the airwaves. When this happens, I'm unable to hear the intuitive messages that tell me which ingredients or cooking methods to use. Sometimes these messages are imbedded deeply in my memory. Familiar smells and tastes emerge through my senses, and that's where my history lies. Through the language of cooking I find which ingredients and methods are needed to create a dish that calls to me, like braised Japanese eggplant. When the first baby in my belly craved Japanese food, I had never liked eggplant. The little pillars arrived on a very small white plate and looked like the color of meat, which I avoided then. Three pieces, one inch in diameter, one and one-half inches tall, glistened, spaced with just enough room for chopsticks to hug the sides. As the juice touched my tongue, I closed my eyes. I was swept away with the balance of flavor and unique creamy texture held neatly in a deep purple skin, melting in my mouth like black butter against tiny specs of chewy, pearlescent rice. I didn't know the language then. Fifteen years later, I saw shiny Japanese eggplant in the market. Memories flooded. The language quickly assembled the dish. Dark sesame as the oil, mirin and rice vinegar as the strong character liquids, ginger and garlic captured the herb/spice category, and tamari or shoyu was the salt seasoning. The cooking method? Had to be braising. It was the one method that would allow all the ingredients to function.

I ask my nose to choose ingredients for a dish. It's not a big nose, but it is a discerning nose. It knows the difference between good, bad, and neutral. It tells me if oil is still alive. A deep inhale of dead oil hurts my brow. Some people think the nose represents the heart organ. One year, while recovering from a broken heart, I took comfort in tobacco. It closed the capillaries in my blood flow so that I couldn't feel. And it shut down my taste buds. When I cooked, the nose worked—I could smell—but it was like looking through one-sided binoculars. There was no reference point for taste.

So, what is the love that everyone talks about in cooking? It comes from the senses provided by the nose and tongue; from that place in the skull near the tentorium located on the line where the throat and nose meet. Love is the ingredient that is missing from most standardized recipes and cooking instructions. Recipes leave out the smell-taste selection process. When I find pleasure in a combination of ingredients, my eyes roll up to the right, linger under my brow, and close on the way down the left side. I still jump when the smile hits my face. That's love. Love flows into the dish because my fingertips make the moves, not measuring spoons. Fingertips are an extension of my hand, which is an extension of my arm, which is a branch growing directly from my heart.

CHAPTER ONE

THE ALPHABET AND GRAMMAR OF COOKING

WHAT IS THE LANGUAGE OF COOKING?

The language of cooking is a natural system that gives definition to the invisible process of cooking without recipes. Dishes originate from inside a cook. Chefs and other people who cook with ingredients at hand (the way Grandma used to) use this system. People who browse through recipes to get ideas are accessing this language. This is how people who cook without recipes think. It is structured with an alphabet, grammatical theories, and colloquialisms. Attention during the transformation of food is the most important part of cooking without recipes. As Tita says in the book *Like Water for Chocolate,* "It's love." Love is the secret ingredient that makes her dishes noticeably delicious. Love equals attention.

HOW THE LANGUAGE OF COOKING WORKS

Cooking is simple. Recipes are an announcement and record of what ingredients move through which cooking methods. Each ingredient belongs to a category. I cook without recipes by knowing the function and purpose of the ingredient category along with the technical points of the cooking methods. Recipes also tell readers how much of an ingredient to use. With the language of cooking, ingredient amounts are determined by ratios and by the theories of "to fit" and substance, flavor, strength (SFS). You can read more about these theories on pages 15–18.

Composing a dish is like constructing a sentence. A sentence requires a subject and verb and punctuation that defines the end, completing the thought. Words are composed of letters, each having its own sound, shape, and purpose. Dishes are composed of ingredients, each with a taste, color, texture, and function. Grain, vegetables, and protein are defined as primary elements. Like subjects in a sentence, they are the main characters of a dish. In the language of cooking, cooking methods perform like verbs do in a sentence. They tell what the subject is doing. A simple sentence/dish in the language of cooking requires a subject (the primary element), a verb (the cooking method), and ending punctuation (salt). Take, for example, the following short sentence: Run, John! In the language of cooking, an equivalent simple sentence may be: Steeped carrots, or marinated quinoa. The art of cooking, like that of writing, would not survive with simple sentences alone. Complex dishes are successfully built on a solid framework where the function of each ingredient is known.

Complexity is built into dishes with the use of modifiers. Just as adverbs embellish verbs and adjectives enhance nouns, in the language of cooking it is the supporting elements that create interest. They are categorized by their function in the dish. The categories are oil, cooking liquid, and herb/spice. They are not always required to help the primary element express itself, but some cooking methods require oil and/or cooking liquid. Like adverbs, they modify the cooking method. Herbs and spices fit into one category, as they both function to embellish the primary element, acting like an adjective. An embellished dish might read like this: Carrots steeped with ginger water, glazed in orange clear sauce. Or: Job's tears, braised with tomato, Marsala wine, and herbes de Provence.

> Cooking with this language is as simple as walking. When I studied dance with Hanya Holm, we practiced walking for several hours every day for two weeks. She said, "All movement is based on the shift of weight. Until we master walking, there is no point in doing other movements."

Punctuation eliminates chaos and provides understanding. So does salt. A period or question mark at the end of a sentence is critical; it tells the reader when to stop and grasp the concept. In cooking, it's the category of salt/salt seasoning that is the final punctuation in the cooking method, because salt is the last element in the assembly of a dish.

In almost every cuisine, ingredients fit into a category. Sometimes ingredients bridge two categories; for example, olives are mostly oil

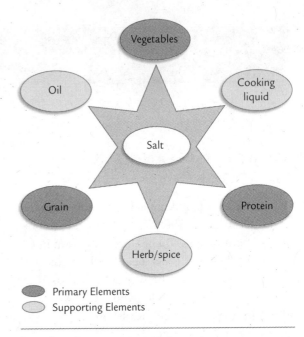

Primary Elements
Supporting Elements

Ingredient Star

but often include salt. Umeboshi vinegar is particularly confusing because vinegar falls into the cooking liquid category, but umeboshi, which is brewed with a major amount of salt, fits into the salt/salt seasoning category in the language of cooking.

NATURE AND ELEMENTS IN THE ART OF COOKING

As a natural cook, I play with nature's elements—fire, earth, air, and water. Nature provides nutrients energetically, as witnessed in the power of plants to heal, stimulate growth, and balance. I call this concept energetic nutrition. Nourishment begins at the hands of the farmer. The quality of earth, water, air, and sun influence our food. In my mind, all carrots are not created equal.

THE ALPHABET AND GRAMMAR OF COOKING

I remember walking across the Mississippi River in late February, garbed in thick cotton tights, knit bodysuit, and a skirt that brushed against the dirty snow. It was below-zero temperatures and over a mile from the east bank to Dinky Town. The windchill never reached my lungs because I dressed in layers. A Danskin beneath a silk T-shirt, smothered by a turtleneck, wool sweater, and down coat, left only my eyes peeking out to meet the frost. Heavy breathing steamed my face mask and it froze stiff as I hurried through the University of Minnesota campus to the Little Tokyo restaurant. The weekly pilgrimage rewarded me with tempura udon. Behind a cloth flap I could hear the metal pots against the stove, the sound of running water, and Japanese chatter all moving quickly, like the speed of my feet crossing the bridge. A combination of steam and hot oil filled the air. My finger played on the window pane leaving a clear streak for a moment until it filled in again.

I removed half the layers of clothing before dipping into fat white noodles swimming in a steaming pond of black broth. Lightly battered eggplant, daikon, sweet potato, and carrot crisply perched on top before they softened into the salty broth. The branch of tempura parsley reminded me of how the trees sparkle when ice freezes on them. Sitting for a moment, not wanting the bowl to end, I felt like I had been sealed in oil. I returned, crossing the bridge in half tempo. Each step firmly planted on the ice and snow, shoulders dropped from my ears, I lifted my chest to meet the cold. No face mask. The wind whipped and froze my breath, not my skin, which felt moist, soft, and cozy under the garments.

Fire

strength, comfort, danger

Fire equals sun. Once upon a time fire was the center of human activity, whether it revolved around the sun or a burning pile of wood. Fire is a nutrient with the power of life and death. In cold, moist climates, fire provides warmth and is nurturing. In hot, dry climates, the sun acts as the fire nutrient, reducing the need for cooked dishes. In cooking, I pay attention to how the earth relates to fire. The amount of time food spends on the stove is directly related to how much sun is available to the plant while it grows, which may relate to how much cooking liquid (water) is in the pot or in the plant and in what order vegetables go into a pot of mixed vegetables. Like an internal warmth generated by dancing, fire forces the cells of food to change. A carrot becomes bright under fire, and the taste of a sauce with multiple ingredients comes into focus. This won't happen in a microwave oven.

Earth

carbohydrates, vitamins, minerals

When a dancer's leg floats up into the air, the dancer isn't thinking about how high it will rise; thoughts are on the standing leg and how rooted below the floorboards it can go. Plants anchor us to the earth, teaching us how to reach for the sky. Primary elements—grain, protein, and vegetables—are the major food groups representing the earth element. They are seeds, big ideas waiting to happen under the care of a knowing cook. The energetic properties of the seeds in the primary element group contain heroic reproduction systems. Put one in good soil, with sun (fire) and water (cooking liquid), and it will multiply abundantly. One seed can produce a hundred offspring.

Air

protection, substance, vehicle for moving flavors

Oil reminds me of air because, like the wind, it moves freely, carrying flavors throughout a dish in much the same way the fragrance of roses, lavender, and lilacs are carried throughout the garden. In Colorado the midwinter winds might reach 85 miles per hour. I know when these winds are near because I feel edgy and my skin dries quickly. A creamy soup, grain croquettes, or tempura usually calms me, moistens my skin, and anchors my energy body, preventing my mind from "blowing away."

Oil

sensuality, satisfaction, safety

There are three reasons to use oil. One function of oil is to protect vegetables that are cut before they are cooked. Oil protects the vegetable's identity so that it won't "bleed" or be lost in major cooking liquid or a mixed-vegetable dish. It also holds in moisture, protecting the primary elements from drying out, especially if food is frozen. Another purpose for using oil is that it creates a smooth and weighty texture, adding substance to creamy soups and sauces. And third, oil is a vehicle to move flavor, carrying herbs and spices throughout a dish.

Oil should taste and smell like the food it comes from. For pastry, oils void of flavor are best. In savory cooking, oil should taste and smell like its name. Canola oil has no flavor because canola seeds have no flavor. Unlike a sesame seed or olive offering up its flavor, the canola seed goes poof in my mouth, leaving no taste. I don't use this energetically empty oil. Plants have very little fat, with the exception of olives, avocados, nuts, and seeds. Animal prod-

ucts have their own natural fat component. This is the main reason why classical cooking methods do not translate well to plant dishes. It has to do with the placement of fat, so vegetarian chefs need to master the use of this essential element. The amount of oil is optional. But if a cooking method asks me to use it, leaving it out is not an option. Sautéing in water doesn't make sense.

Storing Oil

Whole nuts and seeds are raw and energetically "asleep" when they arrive, so until the application of water or fire, they remain comfortably dormant in a dark, cool place, such as the freezer or fridge. Olive and coconut oils survive at room temperature for longer periods than other oils because they contain natural antioxidants that protect them from rancidity in average temperatures. Both of these oils are also partially saturated, so when they are cold, they stiffen up. Any oil that is subject to too much warmth for too long turns rancid; you can detect rancidity by the pain in your brow after you take a deep whiff. These oils are best stored in a cabinet away from the stove. All other oils should be refrigerated.

Herbs and Spices

embellish and deepen primary elements

This vast and mysterious supporting element also relates to air, because the aromas from herbs and spices find their way into the nasal passages like wind in a tunnel. As supporting elements, herbs and spices are not always necessary in a dish. Vegetables, a primary element, can easily stand alone, announcing their dynamic personalities without the help of herbs or spices. Grains and beans almost demand to be embellished. Like an adjective, however, herbs and spices are easily overused. Not in the quantity that goes into a grain or bean dish, as grain and beans require a heavy hand, but a confusion of flavors can occur when too many different herbs and spices are in a dish.

Dried herbs and spices need to bond with the oil at the beginning of a dish so that they don't float when the cooking liquid is added. They will also taste more like perfume than hay when anchored to oil, especially when crushed between the thumb and middle finger as they go into the pot. Fresh herbs need little fire. They go into a dish near the end of cooking. Fresh leafy herbs from a garden are more potent than fresh herbs boxed in plastic from the store. Spices are the seeds, bark, and/or roots of herb plants, and survive roasting, crushing, grinding, and boiling. They aren't delicate like herbs. Flavoring water with spice is easy because the whole seeds may be scooped out of the pot with an oil skimmer.

The herb/spice element creates the ethnic personality of a dish, changing its identity from Italian to Mexican to Indian in one sweep. Rules on using herbs and spices are about as secure as clothing styles. The amount and variety of herbs and spices that enter the pot depend on the personality of the main ingredient and the cook's preferences.

Respect for the power of spices rises when we consider the role they play in cooking animal-based food. Not only do garlic, ginger, pepper, and chiles kill toxins that reside in the muscle and fat of animal tissue, they distract the palate from meat's natural taste. In order to be digested, animal products require the strong acids found in our stomach, so the sooner they leave the taste bud area, the swifter their digestion. Flavor is instant. Step one, bite; two, chew; three, swallow. But grain dishes taste better the longer they are chewed. Herbs and spices help keep grain in the mouth where it mixes with the digestive enzymes in saliva. Chewing becomes the first step in digesting grains, beans, and vegetables.

My spice rack holds 40 varieties. Herbs and spices are visible so that I see an ingredient's color, but not labeled so my mind will not register its name. Then the choice rises from my physical body, not from an idea of what goes together. I like to explain how this works through one student's experience. She approached the herb/spice category during the composition of a baked grain dish and informed me that she didn't like anise and asked if I would steer her away from that spice. I encouraged her to close her eyes while she selected from the spice rack. Her hand picked a jar and her mind asked what it was. I asked her to smell it first, to see if her body said yes or no to using it. With her eyes closed, she smiled—her body approved. I made sure she put it in the dish before I told her it was anise.

Storing Herbs and Spices

Herbs are more sensitive to light and fire than spices and potentially die in the jar if not used within a few months. Dead herbs do not increase the fragrance of a dish. They kill it. And it is not a silent death. Dill weed is one of the most volatile. One day its elegant radiance and beauty are full, and only a few days later it tastes the way a barn full of hay smells. Dill weed kept in the freezer won't die as quickly as on the shelf. Cilantro and tarragon are also best used fresh rather than dried.

Water

creates substance and lightens
a heavy energy body

This supporting element, categorized as cooking liquid, represents all things wet. Water, the purest liquid, acts like a mirror reflecting the personality of ingredients in a dish. Anything other than water is called a character liquid. Some characters speak louder than others. Using flavored cooking liquids contributes background flavor and sometimes color to a dish; for example, I like using beer in first-stage beans or curry water for first-stage quinoa.

The quality of water makes a difference to the natural cook. Water takes on thoughts, feelings, and the nutrients of the earth from where it comes. These distinguishing characteristics are invisible to me when cooking. But chlorine is very much a part of my cooking experience if it is in the water. A water filter removes chlorine and general pollutants that are piped into the water supply. Water, in its simplicity, is the most significant cooking liquid.

Character liquids have a dominant flavor and taste. Water, vegetable stock, and nut milk are mild, water-based liquids, almost invisible compared to wine, beer, and vinegars, which have strong personalities.

The complexity of wine is confusing when preparing plant-based dishes, because although wine is a living food, the strength of its fermentation and alcohol content need to be balanced with the weight of the primary element. A good supply of oil/fat will help balance a dish where wine is used. The color of the wine influences the dish; reds turn dishes pink to mauve and whites keep the color light. Blended wines are recommended for cooking, but do not use wines that are labeled "cooking wine." I only cook with wine that is drinkable. Using the theory of taste/smell secures my choice so that I am not limited to which wine goes with which food.

Character liquids function as *major, minor,* or *accent liquids,* depending on the cooking method. Blended fruits and vegetables vary in their water content. Some, such as cucumbers, peppers, radishes, cacti, juicy fruits, and melons, can be used as major cooking liquids, as can juice extractions from vegetables such as carrots and beets. Rejuvelac is a major cooking liquid used in preparing living food (plant-based food that is alive, such as sprouts, and has been transformed without the use of added fire). Rejuvelac is made from sprouted whole grain that is soaked in water and exposed to air for two days, creating a fermented, effervescent liquid. This active, living liquid is used as a beverage on its own or in preparing blended dishes. It also initiates the fermentation action crucial to the process of making seed cheese.

When vegetables are the primary element in a dish, their strong identity makes using character liquids less important; the exception to this is when the vegetables are braised, marinated, or pickled in brine. Grain and bean cookery is enhanced by using character liquid in the first stage of cooking. Nut milks prevent grain from cooking completely because the oil in the nut milk coats the grain and keeps the liquid from penetrating it. If you want to cook grain with nut milk, keep the liquid very thin—use 1 part nuts to at least 20 parts water. No salt should be in the liquid used to cook beans until the beans have been fully cooked in the first stage. Sometimes canned tomato products are used as a cooking liquid for beans in the first stage. The sodium content in these products toughens the beans and interferes with their ability to become tender.

Cooking liquids have two functions. First, as a major ingredient, cooking liquids create substance during the transformation of food from raw to cooked. For example, in a pot of rice or vegetable soup, water is the major cooking liquid. The second function of cooking liquids is as an accent. An accent liquid is usually something sour, like lemon or lime juice and vinegars. It is used to lighten the energy body of a dish that feels heavy or dense, or in situations where flavors are strong enough but static, in which case an accent liquid rounds out flavors, making them move on the palate. Only one-quarter teaspoon of an accent liquid is required to lighten a five-quart pot of soup. The quantity is so small that its taste is not apparent. The same ingredient, perhaps vinegar or lemon juice, will be used as a major cooking liquid in a cold sauce where sour liquid is part of the substance and taste of the dish, as with a marinade. A major cooking liquid compromises 75–100 percent of the total amount of liquid needed. A minor cooking liquid makes up a smaller portion of the total volume. For example, a soup might use 75 percent water, 20 percent bean juice, and 5 percent wine. Water is the major cooking liquid; bean juice and wine are the minor cooking liquids. With braising and marinating, the character and strength of a cooking liquid needs to match the personality of the primary element (grain, protein, or vegetable). Whole-dish grain, beans, and some vegetables, like potatoes and eggplant, have dense energy bodies. They willingly absorb strong character liquids, unlike spinach or lettuce. If a strong character liquid is used to infuse these lighter vegetables, it should be limited to a small amount and balanced with a plain liquid, like stock or water.

Storing Cooking Liquid

Vinegar, mirin, and sherry are easily stored at room temperature. Nut milk, noodle water, bean juice, and vegetable stock are best kept cold and used within a week. Freezing may be an option for high-protein liquid and liquids with a generous fat content.

Salt

brings harmony and balances oil

Yes, my name is Saltzman, and I am here to tell you that salt is the single most important ingredient in cooking. Sea salt encompasses all of nature's elements through the cycle of rainwater, which is filtered through the earth's minerals until it reaches the sea; then it is evaporated by the sun and stored in the atmosphere until it is ready to rain again. Learning how to use salt transforms the cook as much as the food it touches. A cook who takes responsibility for salting food during the cooking process improves the health of people who might otherwise add salt at the table.

Salt is a chemical compound. It transforms food by letting the liquid held in the cell walls pass through. The function of this element in cooking is not to make a dish salty but to harmonize flavors. When salt is applied directly to finished food, its chemical action affects the human body, not the food. When I eat potato chips or salted crackers, the salt crystals touch my tongue and fluids rise into the bowl of my mouth, making me feel as though I am being transformed. Salt is the divine director of a composition, like the conductor of a symphony or the way punctuation defines the boundaries and expression of a sentence. Salt

Italian folklore is filled with fairy tales about food. My favorite is about a king who has three daughters. He begs each one to tell him how much she likes him. The oldest responds that he is dearer to her than the best bread in all the land. The second prefers him to the finest wine. He beams, pleased with their choices of comparison. When the youngest and most beautiful daughter tells him that he is more important to her than salt itself, he instructs his kinsman to take her to the forest and cut out her heart. The queen takes her youngest daughter to safety by hiding her in a tall candlestick. Eventually the candlestick is delivered to the dining hall of the neighboring kingdom. The young prince of this castle often ate his dinner late upon returning from his outing. Every evening a plate of food was placed on the table, and it stayed there until his return. One evening, shortly after the candlestick was placed in the dining hall, he found his dinner plate licked clean. He could not restrain his curiosity, so he decided to keep watch. Soon he discovered the beautiful young princess. A romance ensued, and not long after they decided to marry. When the prince's mother heard about why the young girl escaped, she devised a plan to invite the girl's mother and father to the wedding. The celebration food would be delicious, but they would use no salt in her father's food. The young princess hid until the meal was served. When the other guests were raving about how delicious the meal was, the girl's father begged his hosts' pardon and inquired why his food was dull. The queen explained that she had heard that he didn't care for salt, and so they left it out of his meal. At that moment the king began to cry for his beloved daughter. And then, of course, she appeared to the joy of all.

completes a dish. Without salt, ingredients remain asleep. Vegetables cooked collectively will not relate to each other without salt. Knowing how to use salt is critical when plants are the only kingdom in the pot. Salt balances oil, making dishes that contain oil more digestible. When vegetables are cooked with meat, the sodium inherent in the animal's flesh assists in transforming the vegetables. The salt content in cheese functions similarly. Consider using feta cheese as a salt seasoning.

Active people require more salt because their bodily fluids are in flux more often, and salt gives them endurance during physical activity. Infants and the elderly require very little salt.

The quality of salt is as important as the quantity. Table salt is highly refined and padded with other ingredients. Among these are agents that allow the salt to flow freely from a shaker; dextrose (sugar), to encourage more use of the product; and fillers like cornstarch. These additives dilute the potency of salt and cause us to use more than we need. I have learned to trust coarse salt, because the sensation of it (when I pick it up with my fingertips during the cooking process) helps me judge how much to use and prevents me from using too much.

Pure sea salt, the strongest chemically, is sun-dried sea water. Vegetable salt is a combination of sea salt crystals, dried vegetables, herbs, and spices. Some varieties include nutritional yeast or sea vegetables. Vegetable salt must be worked into the cooking method like plain salt crystals. While sea salt reflects, magnifies, and unifies the personalities of the ingredients in a dish, vegetable salt adds complex flavors.

In the language of cooking, the term "salt seasoning" is used when at least 70 percent of the seasoning is comprised of ingredients other than salt crystals. Sometimes I call them finishing salts, because they are often used at the end of the cooking process, and because they don't have the same potency as plain salt crystals to transform food during first-stage cooking. The term "character salt" is also appropriate, because these seasonings have diverse and complex flavors.

Salt seasonings are wet and salty. I have used olive and caper brine as salt seasonings, but the most common in my kitchen are shoyu and tamari, umeboshi, and a wide selection of miso. Shoyu and tamari are cousins. Both are a naturally brewed soy sauce, fermented with rice, soybeans, and water. Wheat is used in making shoyu but not in tamari. I select these like I would a fine wine. Many students ask about Bragg Liquid Aminos as an alternative to soy sauce. This is a good example of how the language of cooking defines the function of ingredients. According to the language of cooking, Bragg Liquid Aminos is a cooking liquid. This is because it does not contain any salt; therefore, it doesn't have the power to transform ingredients and harmonize flavors. Instead, as a cooking liquid, it adds flavor. Its strong mineral content gives the impression of saltiness, but Bragg Liquid Aminos does not awaken flavors or bring harmony to a dish.

Umeboshi products—vinegar, paste, and whole plums (also called pickled plums)—are traditional Japanese seasonings. Their character is equally salty and sour. The liquid version of this ingredient is marketed as "vinegar" because of its sour taste. In the language of cooking, vinegar is a cooking liquid that is unrelated to salt. However, because umeboshi vinegar is very salty, when it is used as a cooking liquid instead of a salt seasoning, a dish will become too intensely sour and salty, and it will be extremely difficult to correct a dish where this category has been misused. I caution against adding a sour cooking liquid with this salt seasoning. Umeboshi paste, the meat of the Japanese apricot, or plum, is less salty than the vinegar. At the School of Natural Cookery, students have carefully combined citrus juices or small doses of raspberry vinegar as the cooking liquid with this sour salt seasoning, as long as another light cooking liquid, like water or mirin, is also used.

Miso paste comes in a variety of shades from cream to almost black. The darker the miso, the saltier it is; the lighter the miso, the sweeter its taste. Miso is made from sea salt, beans, water, sometimes a grain, and a cultured rice called *koji*, which initiates the fermentation process. The color of miso depends on the kind of grain and bean used and the amount of time it ferments. I select miso to match the color of my dish. A light miso may require a little sea salt in the dish to do the heavy transforming. Mixing light with dark miso creates interesting flavors. Natural miso production uses whole, unrefined ingredients and time for the miso to mature, instead of flour, meal, and forced temperature controls to hasten fermentation. White miso is made from white rice and has a short fermentation time, whereas darker miso uses barley or brown rice and ferments for about two years. I keep a sample of miso that is more than 30 years old. When I store it out of the refrigerator it grows white fuzz. Now that it is refrigerated, it looks like dark chocolate. I bring it out to show how salt acts as a preservative and how delicious naturally fermented foods can be.

Rules for Using Salt

- Salt crystals and vegetable salt must be diluted by mixing them with a liquid, or they must be used with fire (heat).

- Salt crystals help to transform dishes that include salt seasonings like tamari or shoyu, umeboshi, or miso, but combining these salt seasonings will ruin a dish.

- Salt crystals do the heavy work in first-stage grain and vegetables dishes.

- Salt seasonings should be used primarily as finishing salts and in second-stage dishes and cold sauces.
- Do not use any form of salt in preparing first-stage beans.

Storing Salt and Salt Seasonings

Store dry, crystalline sea salt and vegetable salt in a sealed glass or ceramic container with a large mouth that allows fingers to easily find their way into the jar. *Fingers are my tool for staying connected to the dish. Staying connected to the dish eliminates over- and undersalting.* Liquid salt seasonings (such as tamari, shoyu, and umeboshi vinegar) are best stored in glass bottles with an easy-pour opening. Miso and umeboshi paste should be stored in the refrigerator (refrigeration stops the fermentation process). Tamari, shoyu, and umeboshi vinegar do not have to be refrigerated due to their high salt content.

THEORIES OF THE LANGUAGE OF COOKING

The foundation of cooking relies on five theories. They guide improvisation and the repeated preparation of a dish.

The Five Theories	
THEORY	FUNCTION
Wholeness	guides ingredient selection
Taste/Smell	guides ingredient selection
To Fit	guides ingredient quantities
Substance, Flavor, Strength (SFS)	repairs and balances
Five Tastes	repairs and balances

Theory of Wholeness

Confusion about what to eat is resolved by looking at an ingredient's state of wholeness. This applies to both the primary and supporting elements. If a food is whole, its edible parts are intact. Whole grain looks like a seed, not flour. Whole oil (from olives or avocados, for example) is chewed, not poured. Cooks process whole food to make it more appealing and digestible. For instance, whole nuts may be blended into nut milk and olives or avocado may be blended to be used in salad dressing. I consider peanut butter a whole food, although it is heated and blended.

Refining food separates parts from the whole. For example, olive oil is the fat that remains after the olive pit and fiber are removed. In order to make apple juice, the fiber of apples is removed. To make white flour, the bran and germ of the wheat berry are removed. Many people develop health problems from eating refined foods, whether they are concentrated fats (such as those in free oils), sugars (such as those in fruit juices), or stripped grain (such as the white flour used in most pasta, bread, and crackers). These refined foods are best in my body only for special occasions, such as holidays.

Theory of Taste/Smell

The theory of taste/smell engages our olfactory and taste centers simultaneously. Using taste/smell my body has an immediate experience of which ingredients work together. This lightening-fast transmission helps me cook quickly. Learning to trust it takes longer.

There are two steps. First, ingredients that have been selected are chewed, reaching all the corners of my mouth. In step two, I smell the ingredients one at a time from the element category needed to take the next step in the cooking method. Flavors meet in the middle, and my senses respond in one of three ways: "Yes, this will be a fabulous combination," or "No, not good." But more often than not, my senses say nothing, in which case using the ingredient in question will be fine, or at least it won't ruin the dish. It may not end up being a dish I write about, but I can eat dinner sooner than if I continue looking for the perfect match. As long as my senses don't say no, I will cook with any ingredient in the category I need.

This method of ingredient selection allows little chance for error. Every ingredient that goes into a dish is a definite choice. There is no way to pull lemon juice out of a soup. It is important to taste what is in the pot and smell a questionable ingredient at the same time. Just smelling both will not provide an accurate reading. When the brain picks an ingredient combination, it is usually based on a previous experience with it. There may be days when a traditional combination does not feel right to you, and taste/smell will be the avenue you need to create a comforting, inspired dish.

Theory of To Fit

To fit is the concept of knowing how to salt and season a dish to perfection without measuring spoons. It is the tangible connection between an ingredient and the heart's attention. To fit answers the question *how much*. In this language I say "to fit," not "to taste." Seasoning to taste is time consuming because whenever more seasoning goes into a dish, the dish has to be tasted. Repeated tastings tire the taste buds. Seasoning to fit simplifies the process. Corrections might need only one more adjustment (rather than several).

I cook to fit by selecting the size of the container (such as a pot or bowl) that will hold the amount of food needed. This method works for two servings or several hundred. Once the vessel has been selected, the amount of food in the container is divided conceptually into layers. What does one layer look like? A layer is equal to the amount of food that covers the bottom of the container. Molecules of liquid (such as soup) are closer together and denser than those of grain or vegetables (such as roasted potatoes), so there will be more layers. To effectively season liquids and other thin substances, I must pass my hand more times over the top of the container (each time releasing salt and herbs) than if the substance were solid.

When I use a deep vessel, I measure how many layers of food it contains by placing my knife on the outside of the pot, at the top of the food line, and sliding it down the side of the vessel, counting a layer each time it moves. Then, using my fingers, I zigzag the seasonings over the food, matching the number of times my hands make a pass with the number of layers I estimated. If my hand goes around in circles, the "measurement" won't be accurate. How much salt or herb/spice falls from my hand, or liquid from the bottle, in one layer depends on how close together I make the zigzags.

*N*erve endings in my fingertips send messages directly to my heart, letting me know if today is a heavy-handed day or not. A heavy hand lets larger amounts of ingredients fall into the pot. When I use a light hand, I press my fingers together more tightly. This is especially important when I am being careful with salt and cayenne.

All cooks must adapt their zigzag technique based on what they determine is one layer of food. I have seen what one person considers to be four layers turn out to be two layers to another.

But when they both lay out their zigzags, the first one makes wide spaces and the other makes narrow spaces.

Theory of Five Tastes

The theory of five tastes corrects a dish that is too strong in one direction: salty, sour, pungent, bitter, or sweet. The five tastes work to satisfy the senses. When all five are present in a main dish, dessert becomes unnecessary. If a dish is off balance (for example, too pungent, salty, or sour), an ingredient from any one of the other five taste categories will bring the dish into balance. Instead of automatically adding a touch of sweetener to a marinade that is too sour, soften and balance it with a salt seasoning or a bitter or pungent herb/spice. Freshly ground pepper is often added just before a dish is served because its pungent qualities balance one or more of the other flavors.

> *I* use my trained palate to balance a dish, even when I dine in a restaurant. When a South American–style soup is too pungent, I easily fix the flavors by adding lime juice and salted chips. If a salad dressing is too sweet or sour, I accept the attentive waiter's offer of freshly ground pepper.

Our language contains many phrases that incorporate our feelings about the five tastes. When we are very pleased with something, we may exclaim, "Sweet!" When we see someone unpleasant, we might say, "She's bitter" (an unfortunate expression for an important taste). When we are disappointed, we often say, "That experience left a sour taste in my mouth." When someone is a little rough around the edges, we might say, "He's a salty dog!"

Trying to define the five tastes, or distinguish them in the mouth, especially in combination, may be confusing, particularly for the untrained palate. Receptors for each of the five critical tastes are located on our tongue and in the walls of the cavity of our mouth. Sweet is focused at the tip-top center of the tongue. Salty rides the ridge on the top side of the tongue near the front. Receptors for sour lie beneath the salt receptors under the tongue's ridge. Sweet, salty, and sour are easily confused in the taste of a dish. To get an accurate reading, I consciously place the food at one of the receptor locations and observe my body's response. A sour taste is contractive, causing my face to pucker. A sweet taste is expanding; it relaxes and opens my heart. Bitter, a taste essential for balancing other flavors and valued for its contractive qualities, is found in some of the most powerful foods in the plant kingdom, dark leafy greens and herbs. The bitter buds are located in the center back of the tongue. Bitter makes me feel strong and centered. Coffee and chocolate, both predominantly bitter, are good examples of the search for this taste in our culture. Pungent, a term often used to express something dynamic and sharp, is a confusing culinary term. Even the thesaurus is confused, as it includes the word "salty" as a synonym for "pungent." In my language of cooking, a pungent taste is specific to the expanding qualities of hot ingredients, such as ginger, garlic, and spicy chiles. These flavors burst with great spectacle in all areas of my mouth, and when used excessively, pungent food creates an extreme reaction in my body, like stepping barefoot on a hot pavement.

Most ingredients clearly represent one of the five tastes, though sometimes they express more than one, like arugula, which is both bitter and pungent. Leafy greens (such as kale, collards, and spinach) are notoriously bitter, as are fresh herbs, chocolate, and coffee. The juice of lemons and limes represents the sour taste, while the oil in their skin (also known as zest) falls into the herb/spice category and is sweet.

Cooking helps to define certain flavors more distinctly. Carrots, onions, winter squash, beets, and parsnips carry sweetness into a dish without the use of added sugar. Their sweetness intensifies when they are cooked. Onions are both pungent and sweet. When they are raw, they are more pungent than sweet. After a long, slow cooking, their sweetness emerges. This is also true of carrots and parsnips. Cabbages, rutabagas, and turnips have a pungent quality when raw, plus a sweet capacity when cooked.

Quinoa carries a bitter background taste, sweet brown rice belies its name with bitter tones, and brown rice is sweet in character. The sour taste imparted from vinegar, lemon, and lime juice is also available in brine from pickles, sauerkraut, and other fermented ingredients such as umeboshi plum products or rejuvelac. Salt belongs in almost every cooking method, yet a finished dish should not taste salty. While the other four tastes should be noticeable, salt should not. The taste best described as "odd" feels dull, a bit rough, like the tongue up against a cement wall. It doesn't play an important role, like the basic five, which work together, but it does exist in my mouth. Sometimes it tastes like earthy clay; other times it is simply flat.

Theory of Substance, Flavor, Strength (SFS)

The theory of balancing substance, flavor, and strength arises when designing a dish or fixing flavors that have gone awry. Substance is body weight, the thickness or thinness of a dish. It is easily determined by the amount of cooking liquid in a soup, sauce, bean pâté, or a grain dish. Flavor is what the ingredients have to offer, which should not be confused with the tastes in the five-taste theory. For example, chocolate is a flavor, but bitter is its taste. In raspberry vinegar, raspberry is the flavor, sour the taste.

Strength refers to how much of an ingredient is used. A recipe tells the cook how much of each ingredient to use. The theory of to fit works in situations where a ratio isn't required. The strength of flavor is determined by the personality of the cook. When I taste a dish, I don't want my focus pulled away from a unified experience, like the leg of a dancer just slightly off from the synchronized chorus line, which is what happens when a dish is out of balance. Even worse, if a cook adds too many seasonings when just one or two could do the job, the taste buds become distracted, usually because none of the seasonings is strong enough. The character of a dish is neutralized with "a little of this" or "a pinch of that." In the language of cooking, there is no such thing as using just a touch of an ingredient unless it has a function. Flavor should be composed consciously or the dish will lack focus. If the flavor of a dish is weak, strength will come by increasing the amounts of the original ingredients, not by adding new ones. If a dish is boring, selecting an additional ingredient or two from the herb/spice category will increase the flavor. Substance, flavor, and strength are all interrelated.

DESIGNING A DISH AND COMPOSING A MEAL

I use the same principles of art and design whether composing a sentence, choreographing a dance, or cooking a meal. The theories are simple and founded in common sense. They apply to both creating a dish and to creating a meal.

Theory of Numbers

I don't know if this theory comes from my father's dinner table discussions on fundamental design principles in art or my experience of watching dancers on stage, but the numbers theory of design saves me from creating what I remember as "hippie food." In the 1970s, a meal often consisted of grain, beans, and vegetables piled together in a combination slurry, topped with soy sauce.

The numbers theory is about how many primary elements are in one dish. Mixing more than one whole-dish grain in a dish works best if the grains share the same lineage, like red and tan quinoa, wehani and basmati rice, or short-grain sweet brown rice and short-grain brown rice. Combining quinoa with buckwheat is a disaster. If you want to combine two grains, you will have the most success if you put them together in the second stage of cooking, because their first-stage methods may require different amounts of liquid or cooking times. Alternatively, you can use one as a major ingredient and the other as a decorative element so they don't have to fight for first position. I do not mix beans in the first or second stages of cooking because such combinations can be more difficult to digest. Fifteen bean soup is frightening.

The theory of numbers guides both vegetable dish composition and meal composition. Numbers refers to how many ingredients are in a dish as well as how many dishes are in the meal.

When preparing to make a dish, I first determine if it will have a single focus or a mixed focus. A single-focus dish has one major ingredient—for example, just rice, just carrots, or just tofu. A dish with a mixed focus is composed with more than one primary element, and all of them are in equal proportion. The numbers only count for primary elements used as major ingredients, not for decorative elements. Carrots with a green onion garnish is considered a one-item dish.

Odd numbers create balance in motion. An even-numbered vegetable dish has an equal number of parts (such as two, four, or six different kinds of vegetables), and the eye moves from one to the other and back again. It feels both tiring and static. Fortunately, any member of the onion family (also known as "the joker" or the "wild card") might turn even-numbered dishes into odd-numbered ones while adding flavor and moisture. For example, in a dish with equal parts carrot and kale, the eye has no place to rest. Add onion to the mix and notice that three equal vegetables keep the eye moving and feel restful. More than seven or nine items together easily looks chaotic.

Theory of Color, Texture, and Balance

The primary elements in natural food vary in color from black to white. Spices like turmeric, saffron, and paprika bring shades of yellow and orange to grain, soups, and sauces. Grains contribute black, purple, off-white, white, and brown. Steeped green vegetables maintain their brilliant color. Natural colors mix like the primary colors of an artist's palette: red and yellow make orange, green and red make brown. Blending paprika into a creamy broccoli soup will be ugly. If you are making a red pepper sauce, adding green bell peppers would destroy the color.

Texture—a crisp crunch, a velvet cream, a jaw worker, or an easy broth—gives my mouth something to play with and satisfies the emotional component of eating. Cooking methods create texture. Sauces and creamy soups, chewy whole-dish grain, crunchy roasted nuts and stir-fried vegetables, and soothing slow-cooked vegetables routinely provide variety in texture. Selecting a cooking method is just as important as choosing the right ingredients when it comes to creating texture.

Balancing a meal energetically means using a variety of cooking methods with primary elements, including nuts or seeds. Vegetable dishes draw on different vegetable families. The composition will include both a raw and cooked vegetable dish, such as a mixed dish with multiple numbers in equal parts, and the other a single-focus dish. A main plate composition includes the three primary elements (grain, vegetable, and protein) in a single-focus meal or one that is more complex. An example of a single-focus meal is a stew or casserole that includes all three primary elements and maybe a soup broth or sauce. Dishes in complex meals have distinct cooking methods for each primary element, including a separate soup, at least one sauce, and a minimum of two vegetable dishes. This meal design is good for serving many people.

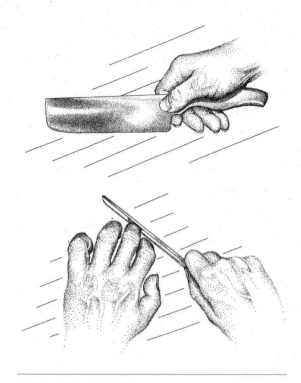

Knife and Hand Position

CUTTING VEGETABLES

To me, the knife is a sword. Japanese vegetable knives are designed to slide through plant ingredients. All motion slides the knife forward or backward. It's graceful and stress-free to use the entire length of the knife blade to slice through vegetables because the steel does the cutting, unlike the physical force of up and down chopping, which demands a break in the wrist with each action.

Vegetable cutting technique is about the relationship of the knife hand (the hand that holds the knife), the claw hand (the hand that holds the vegetable), and the motion they make. I focus on an imaginary line between the tip of my elbow and a point under my shoulder blade, rotating it down and back. This draws tension away from my shoulders and gives strength to the knife hand, which, after locking elbow and wrist into one line with the full length of the knife, gives strength for cutting through stubborn vegetables like winter squash. Linking the elbow to the hip increases the power as the hip thrusts forward.

Cutting provides visual rhythm. Visual rhythm is the experience of structure that satisfies visually like the auditory pulse of a musical signature in 3/4 or 4/4 time. It's comforting to the eye and gives dishes a sense of order. I use 13 different cuts for daily cooking. To invent a new cut, observe how the vegetable grows. Which part of it has a "tail" that digs into the earth? Which part reaches for the sky? Instead of cutting it through the middle, separating the two energetic forces, plan to have some of the head and tail in each piece (this doesn't always work for every vegetable, though).

How To Peel an Onion

Cut into an onion only if you will be using the entire onion in your dish. If small onions aren't available for a small job, use a shallot or green onion instead. Because both shallots and onions (white, purple, and yellow) have a top, a root end, and skin, you can approach them in the same fashion. The goal of peeling an onion with awareness is to reduce the amount of onion juice on the cutting board, because otherwise it will end up in the cook's eyes. I keep the sulfur in onion juice at bay by placing several matchsticks, heads facing out, in my mouth as I cut. This mitigates the intensity of the onion juice, making eyes tear less. Keeping the root end of an onion intact during slicing and dicing also helps to prevent watery eyes.

If you are right-handed, feel the weight of the onion sink into your left palm, keeping the top side of the onion up. In your right hand, hold the knife loosely between your thumb and index fin-

ger at the joint between the blade and handle. Using only your left hand, nudge the neck of the onion into position (it should be a fraction of an inch away from the bottom edge of the knife). Place the thumb of your right hand gently on the onion; it will guide the cut. Hold the knife still; its tip should be vertical. Hug your elbows to your waist and keep your hip connected to a counter for grounding. Slowly rotate the onion clockwise into the still knife. The blade of the knife should not move. Rotate the onion into the knife until all but half an inch of onion skin is sliced off. Reposition the onion and place the knife blade at the opening of the onion skin, entering only as deep as one thin layer of onion plus the outer skin. Hold the peeling onion skin up against the knife with your right thumb, while your left hand pulls the onion away from the knife, down and out, stopping at the root end. I rotate the onion and repeat the peeling action until a smooth, dry surface blooms. The only onion juice exposed is at the small insertion in the neck. With onion skin draping like flower petals at the root end, I put my knife down, gather the outer layers of onion skin, and twist them off, leaving the root end looking gnarly and intact. Carefully clean the root end, either by scrubbing it with a vegetable brush or by removing a very thin portion of it, taking care not to cut into the body of the onion.

Shapes and Cuts

Round

Round vegetables are reshaped into wedges, cubes, slivers, and sticks. Some have both a core and a root end, like onions, tomatoes, cabbages, and Brussels sprouts. Rutabagas, turnips, and potatoes don't have a highly visible core, so simply imagine where the core would be.

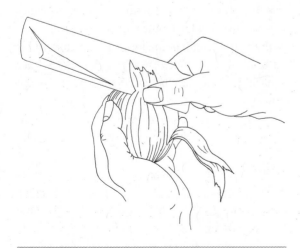

How to Peel an Onion

THE ALPHABET AND GRAMMAR OF COOKING

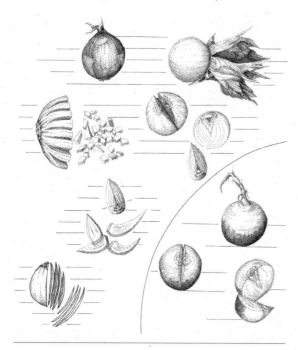

Round Cuts

Wedges, Fans, Boats

To make a wedge cut, place vegetable on the cutting board with the root end facing up. Move the knife forward through the middle of the small, round indication of where the plant connected to earth. Balancing one half with your claw hand, look down at the root end to see the core, a plumb line down the middle. Mark the center of the root end and slide the knife forward at an angle; this will determine the width of the wedge. The knife will land on the cutting board in the center of the top of the vegetable, which is touching the board. The root end will hold the layers of the vegetable together, making a fan cut. Removing the root end of the vegetable will turn the fat fans into boats.

Sticks, Cubes, Dice

Creating a square from a round shape is not possible without some waste. It is more important to me to eat a whole food than make perfectly symmetrical cubes. If you prefer a dish with movie star looks, slice through the round vegetable near the edge, squaring any hint of a curve into a rectangle. Slice the knife through the entire round, making slabs. If you stack the slabs, your first cut will create sticks (fat sticks will look like french fries; thin sticks will look like matchsticks). How wide the sticks are determines the size of the cubes, large or small. To make cubes, turn the stack of sticks 90 degrees, and move the knife forward, matching the width of the sticks.

Dicing onions does not have to be messy; it is not the same as chopping. Chopping is chaotic and not a good technique for maintaining the potency of an onion. Onion juice is for the dish, not for the cutting board. To avoid excessive bleeding of an onion, lay half of the peeled onion on the cutting board, with the cut edge down and the root end facing away from you. The knife should be perpendicular to the board, and the blade parallel to the third knuckle of the claw hand. A forward motion across the onion scores the skin, marking the width of the cubes. There is no need to follow the natural lines of the onion. Reverse for the second stroke by pressing the knife into the body of the onion but leaving the root end edge uncut (this will hold all the layers together). The next stroke mimics the first until there are fingerlike branches coming out of the root end of the onion. Finish the dicing by rotating the onion half a quarter turn and sliding the knife through the entire group of fingers, matching the size of the first cut.

Long Shapes

Oblong and tapered vegetables like carrots, daikon, parsnips, burdock root, and zucchini may be cut into diagonal, moon, and owl shapes, as well as into logs, which are then cut into boards and sticks. Other vegetables that do not grow in a long

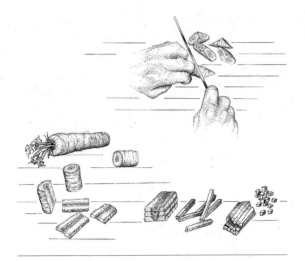

Long Cut

shape (such as broccoli, eggplant, and turnips) may be manipulated into a long shape with a knife, and these cuts may then be applied to them.

Diagonal, Julienne

If a vegetable has a tapered end, that is where I begin. With the knife right up against your claw hand, decide how thick the slices will be. Keep the knife perpendicular, at a right angle to the vegetable; the angle placement of the knife determines how long the cut will be. Short angles on a narrow vegetable will yield small pieces. Long, deep angles will make graceful ovals. Press the claw hand and knife against each other with equal pressure. The tighter the pressure the more delicate and thin the cut. Reposition the diagonal cuts, stacking them before moving the knife forward, brushing against the claw hand, to create elegant long, thin strips called julienne.

Moons (full, half, and quarter)

I rarely use a full-moon cut. Cutting a vegetable in rounds is boring to me. A vegetable sliced in half lengthwise initiates the half- and quarter-moon cut.

A half moon rises when you turn the cut vegetable parallel with the cutting board and slice through it crosswise. To make quarter moons, cut the vegetable lengthwise three times (to make four equal pieces), then slice through them crosswise. I especially like this cut for vegetable soup because the quarter moons fit into a soup spoon. My favorite moon cut is a half moon sliced on the diagonal.

Owls

The owl cut creates two eyes and a nose with every piece. Its bulky and broad exposure makes it a good cut for roasting, skewering, and stewing vegetables. As with the diagonal cut, the angle of the slice determines the size of the pieces. Rotate the vegetable 180 degrees so that the apex faces in. Mark this point, match the angle from the first cut, and slide your knife forward again through the apex. Vegetables that have concentric circles, like carrots, parsnips, and burdock, make more distinct owl eyes.

Pencil Shavings

When a long vegetable is very firm, it touches the cutting board on its point at about a 45-degree angle. Slide your knife from back to front, shaving the tip of the vegetable, while your claw hand rotates the vegetable about an eighth of a full turn

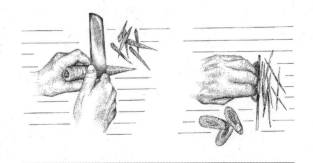

Pencil Shavings

THE ALPHABET AND GRAMMAR OF COOKING

in both directions, bringing the edge from the previous stroke to the top. Move the blade of the knife quickly, as if wielding a sword in midair, and pencil-like shavings will fall to the board.

Concave Vegetables

Celery and bell peppers are the most common vegetables that have a concave shape. To dice them, cut them into strips, then slice the strips crosswise. A more interesting cut includes the natural arch of the vegetable, highlighting the curve. Celery is beautiful cut on the diagonal. The hollow of a bell pepper cut into triangles becomes a miniplatter for spreads. My favorite cut for celery, once the strings are removed, is the slash-back. To make this cut, place the celery stalk on your cutting board with the round side up. The knife is parallel to the cutting board (as much as possible), and it slides from

the back of the celery to the front. The steeper the angle of the knife, the more truncated the pieces.

Leaves

Kale, collards, lettuce, and other big broad leaves have a rhythm that will guide you in cutting them. To remove stems, stack the leaves and use the tip of your knife to strip out their core. To use the stems in a dish, stack the leaves and just trim off the far end of the stems collectively. Stems may also be removed at the neck where the leaf begins. Mostly I use every part of the leaf, but I like to have options.

Squares

Flat leaves, stacked neatly, are ready to cut into squares. Leaves shrink considerably regardless of how they are cooked, so I make the first cut from the edge of the leaf a little larger than what will

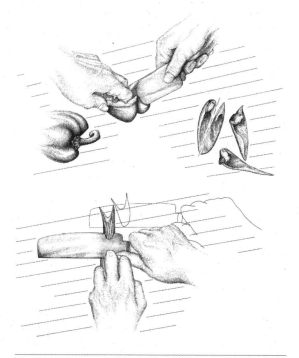

Concave Cut

Leaf Cut

comfortably fit in my mouth. I particularly like this cut for stir-frying. Move your knife forward, crosswise, across the stack of leaves, keeping the width of the strips equal. Gather the strips, rotate them 90 degrees, and slide the knife forward through the entire stack, sizing each stroke to match the first cut.

Shredding

Make a stack of leaves; then roll them tightly (like a cigar) into a log. With the claw hand holding the roll so that it doesn't come undone, slice the log crosswise on a slight diagonal. The resulting strips will look like strands of wavy hair.

Flower Cut

> The day I learned how to close my eyes while cutting, I shredded 50 pounds of cabbage to make sauerkraut. For several hours my knife pressed against the first knuckle of the middle finger of my left (claw) hand, and my right arm moved like a locomotive from the joint in my shoulder blade. Shreds of cabbage fell onto the board, all without using my eyes. This skill is useful when preparing mounds of onion slivers.

Vegetable Flowers

To cut the delicate heads of vegetable flowers (such as broccoli and cauliflower) so that they don't fall apart on the cutting board, I stand them on their head and operate from the bottom. The base of a vegetable flower holds the branches together. The stalk is delicious and contains valuable nutrients, so don't throw it away. Slide your knife into the base so that it stops short of reaching the flower head and doesn't hit the board. This will be more like scoring than a full cut. Then break the flowers apart with your hands.

This will maintain the natural ragged shape and you won't lose a single flower bud.

The skin of the broccoli stalk is tough and needs to be removed. As with removing onion skin and celery strings, slide your knife underneath the outer layer and hold it perfectly still; then pull the vegetable away from the knife. The stalk can be cut off at the base of the flower head to make two shapes, long (the stem) and flowers.

FORMS

In the language of cooking, forms define the placement of dishes in a meal. Dishes are created by cooking methods. If I cook with a particular method in mind, my technique will be focused on making the dish taste good. Then the dish goes into a form. Forms comprise the basic components of a meal—soup, salad, main plate, side dish, condiment, and sauce. They may also be used as hors d'oeuvres, snacks, sandwiches, decorative ele-

THE ALPHABET AND GRAMMAR OF COOKING

ments, or garnishes. Forms come in a variety of shapes—casseroles, stuffed vegetables, filled rolls or pastries, patties or croquettes, and molds.

A soup form can be a complete meal or an appetizer that begins the meal and prepares the appetite to receive the main plate. A salad form is not always made from raw ingredients. Marinated grain, protein, and vegetables are not always used as salads. The placement of salad in a meal may be as a main plate, or as a side dish served before, during, or after the main dish. Sweet salads are often served following the main plate; a savory salad before. A main plate includes all three primary elements—grain, vegetables, and protein—and often a sauce or nut and seed garnish. Main plates may take the form of soup or a salad or primary elements gathered into a sandwich, roll, or casserole. Main plate construction in miniature becomes an hors d'oeuvre, making good finger food for parties. Side dishes are placed in main plate compositions in rolled forms or as stuffing for containers made from primary elements. For example, pastry such as phyllo or pie dough can hold slow-cooked vegetables; bell peppers hold second-stage grain or beans. Deep-fried tofu, also called *age* (pronounced ah-gay), is a form stuffed with cooked sushi rice, and gluten, before it is cooked, may be stretched to hold a filling of any primary element. Sometimes side dishes may be used as snacks—an afternoon treat of roasted turnips is delightful. Sauces tie the primary elements in a main plate together and make good adjuncts to side dishes. Condiments, such as chutney and pickles, are intensified vegetable side dishes and are usually used to accompany protein and grain. Condiments may also play a role as garnishes.

Using dishes decoratively means that a completely cooked primary element is added to another primary element to bring more interest than a garnish, but only a small amount is used. Since beauty is created with the intrinsic color, texture, number of ingredients, and visual rhythm in vegetable cuts, garnishing in my style of plating is about texture and accenting taste. Most ingredients included in a dish may also be used as a garnish, but nuts and seeds, pickles, chutneys, and other condiments round out the meal composition and are not merely garnishes.

CHAPTER TWO

COOKING METHODS

Cooking methods are the action of a dish. Just as verbs define what the subject in a sentence is doing, cooking methods define the activity of primary elements. Animals eat food just as they find it, but humans wield fire, metal, earth, air, water, and time to make food compatible with our bodies. Even living food (a type of fresh, raw food preparation) requires elements of transformation. These transformations give cooks something to do. In the details of cooking, I watch nature's dance of fire, metal, salt, and time.

I ask my students to master the subtle differences among the primary elements and the respective methods used to transform them. Sometimes the only difference is the moment when the salt is added.

The first time a primary element goes through a transformation to make it digestible is called a first stage. First-stage cooking methods for grain and vegetables result in complete dishes because they use salt. But first-stage methods for beans do not render them ready to eat because salt needs to be worked into the second stage. Grains have five first-stage opportunities: boiling, baking, pressure cooking, steeping, and sprouting. Of the 18 cooking methods for vegetables, 16 are first-stage methods. They include the following: boiling (soup), braising, steeping, steaming, pressure cooking, pressure steaming, roasting, baking, grilling, broiling, deep-frying, teriyaki, pickling, pressing, sprouting, blending, and dehydrating. Vegetable protein—such as tofu, tempeh, and seitan (cooked gluten)—requires no linear order. Any of the 14 methods may be first, second, third, or fourth. Beans are sprouted, pressure cooked, steeped, or cooked in a crockpot during the first stage to break down secondary compounds. All of these methods are performed without adding salt. Once grain and vegetables are cooked in the first stage, you can opt to take them into a second stage. Deep-frying is a complete first-stage method for beans; if this method is not used, beans must go through a second stage where salt or salt seasonings are added and the beans are further cooked for at least 10 minutes to finish the dish. Second-stage methods for grain are marinating, refrying, braising, and deep-frying. Second-stage methods for vegetables are refrying and marinating. Second-stage methods for beans are braising, baking, blending, dehydrating, refrying, and marinating. Methods for sauces are defined by the binder that creates the sauce. Methods for living food include soaking, sprouting, blending, dehydrating, and fermenting.

Living food is more complex than simple raw food because it utilizes the element of time to

27

change the taste and awaken sleeping nutrients in grain, beans, vegetables, nuts, and seeds. The language of cooking shows how living food is brought into finished dishes through stages. Combining more than one living food method encourages invention. Salt is used differently in living methods than with fire methods. The layers of to fit are reduced by almost half those of cooked food. Sea vegetables are mineral intense, so when they are in a living food dish, I don't use sea salt. Cooking liquids range from the simplicity of water to the complexity of mixed vegetable juices that are extracted in a juicer. To me, rejuvelac is the signature cooking liquid for living food, because the liquid itself is enzymatic and very alive. The same theories as for fire cooking apply when using herb/spice in living dishes, including the theories of to fit and substance, flavor, strength (SFS). Some raw food chefs consider pungent spices like cayenne, garlic, and ginger to be a replacement for the fire used in cooking because these pungent ingredients produce internal heat.

Each cooking method creates a texture and personality of its own. There is calm in baking, intense centering in pressure cooking. Grilling leaves marks. Braising imposes flavors outside of the primary element. Stir-frying for vegetables is crisp yet fully cooked, while slow-cooked vegetables are melt-in-your-mouth soft. Steeped grains are ordinary. Steeped vegetables are more radiant and full flavored than steamed. When all three primary elements are combined in a single dish, they will each go through a separate, complete, initial cooking method. Unlike animal-based ingredients, where fat is naturally embedded, most plants have little to no fat. The key to successful natural cookery is in identifying where oil is inherent and where it needs to be placed. Table 2.1, Chart of Cooking Methods, shows which methods require

oil and which ones do not. It also outlines which cooking methods fall into which stages.

PRETREATMENTS

Pretreatments manipulate ingredients and help cooks break away from repetitive dishes. They are done before the first-stage method to improve the taste and texture of a dish. Pretreatments begin the transformation process for each primary ingredient. Students often ask me if washing is considered a pretreatment. No, it is a ritual. It honors the primary ingredient with a rub and a splash. Most grains, beans, and vegetables need to be washed before beginning any first-stage cooking method. Nuts and seeds don't require washing because their protective coverings are removed before packaging. Scrubbing whole grains is a pleasure. Covered with cold water, my hands give them a firm massage until the water becomes heavy with dust. Pouring off the top layer of water without a strainer allows foreign matter to float away. I refill the bowl and scrub again, repeating the process until the water runs clear. It usually takes only one or two cycles. Like hands digging into cool sand on a cold beach, the skin of my palms becomes mottled pink and feels gratitude. Once the grain is clean, I fill the bowl with water and swirl the grain into a strainer; water moves it gracefully, without my fingers or a spoon touching it. Do not wash rolled or cut grains (such as steel cut or rolled oats, cracked wheat, or buckwheat), as they absorb the washing water, and then your hands would be playing in clay rather than sand. White rice is simply placed in a strainer and rinsed under running water. Most vegetables require something between a rinse and a scrub. If the skins aren't marred, a vegetable brush made with natural plant fibers easily removes embedded stones and dirt, and you can then cook the vegetables without having to peel them. Before you wash beans, pick out any small stones, dirt clumps, or foreign objects (such as small twigs). The adzuki beans I use are clean as pearls, but I rinse them anyway.

DRY ROASTING

Dry roasting changes the oil inside seeds. No other oil needs to be added during this method, which is different from roasting (in roasting, the oil is applied externally to the food). Nuts and seeds and the germ of grains contain oil. The fruit family of vegetables (such as tomatoes) has many seeds that keep the vegetables moist while dry roasting.

Grain

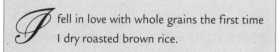

fell in love with whole grains the first time I dry roasted brown rice.

The point of dry roasting grain is to create a nutty taste and an open, dry, fluffy texture.

Dry Roasting Grain

TECHNIQUE

Step 1. *Wash grain, preheat pan or oven*

Wash grain, as necessary. Warm a skillet for stovetop roasting of two cups or less. For three cups or more, use a shallow baking pan in a preheated oven (350°F/177°C).

Step 2. *Lay out the grain in the pan*

Wet grain hisses on a hot skillet. Lay the grain evenly across the bottom. If using a baking pan, make sure the grain is thickly spread into the corners.

Step 3. *Stir*

If using a skillet, move the grain slowly at first, allowing the water to evaporate as the grains dry out. Holding a bamboo rice paddle straight up, perpendicular to the skillet, with thumb and middle finger held lightly around the neck of the tool, permits stirring as quickly as the fire demands, without flipping a single grain out of the rim of the pot. Move the paddle back and forth, from edge to edge, making it touch the bottom of the pan. If the grain doesn't keep moving, the seeds will pop open and scorch. Oven roasting larger quantities takes less attention; stir the grain briefly at the start, then just occasionally as it roasts. Be sure to check the corners of the pan, as the grain will roast more quickly there. The grain is done roasting when the color deepens and its aroma rises. Roasted grain can be stored in a glass jar for up to a month if it has to wait for a first-stage cooking method.

Nuts and Seeds

I roast only one kind of nut at a time for the same reason I take one lover at a time. The oil in nuts and seeds heats at different rates; therefore I combine them after they are roasted and salted. Then they are dressed and ready to party with other nuts, grains, or vegetables.

Dry Roasting Nuts and Seeds

TECHNIQUE

Step 1. *Preheat the pan or oven*

Nuts are best roasted in the oven because heat surrounds the bulky food evenly. Because seeds are flat, small amounts (less than 2 cups) can be roasted easily in a skillet; the oven works best for larger amounts. A pan made from ovenproof glass is my first choice. Preheat the oven to a low temperature (300°F/149°C), and warm a skillet before adding the seeds.

Step 2. *Stir*

When roasting nuts and seeds, you will need to monitor two factors: (1) the frequency and speed at which you stir and turn the nuts; and (2) the overall length of time the nuts spend in the heat (whether on the stove top or in the oven). I gauge these according to the requirements of the nut's personality. There are four types: the high-maintenance group, the tough guys, the respectable, and the shallow. High-maintenance nuts are petite to robust, naked, usually blond, and very creamy. Cashews, macadamia nuts, and pine nuts fall into this category. They require much attention. Turn them frequently, especially toward the end of their roasting time, even if they don't look like they need it. Almonds, Brazil nuts, and filberts (hazelnuts), classified as tough guys by their brown, stubborn skins, abundant fiber, and low fat content, are happy with being stirred at regular intervals, between two and four turns. Pecans and walnuts, the respectable personality couple, need only to be warmed through. One turn is usually enough. They roast quickly because their fiber content is less than their oil content. If you purchase these nuts in pieces rather than halves, you may find sharp-edged bits of shell in with them. For this reason, I prefer to pay extra for the halves. The shallow characters, pumpkin and sunflower seeds, are quickies—perfect for a craving that can't wait more than three minutes. Stir them as though you were dry roasting grain on the stove top, with your hand positioned on the tool in a way that can move quickly.

Step 3. *Salt*

It is easy to see when stove-top-roasted seeds are ready for the salt seasoning. They change color, sometimes pop, and smell heavenly. When nuts are hot from the oven, use a liquid salt, such as tamari/shoyu, umeboshi, or sea salt diluted in water, to finish them. These character salts dry in the hot pan and cling to the skin of the nuts or seeds as you stir them. Salt seasonings add flavor and assist in the digestion of the natural oils. Roasted nuts and seeds taste best at room temperature.

Vegetables

Eggplant, tomatoes, and peppers can be dry roasted on the stove top or under the broiler. Their natural oils keep their flesh moist during this blistering process. After the skin is blistered (often parched and blackened), place the vegetable in a paper or plastic bag, where it will steam in the residual heat. No salt is used during this method, which is why it is called a pretreatment.

Dry Roasting Vegetables

Step 1. *Wash vegetables whole*

Keep the vegetable from being punctured during washing.

Step 2. *Cook*

Place on a high, open flame using a stove-top roasting grate, if possible. Alternatively, the vegetables may be placed under a broiler for a similar effect.

Step 3. *Turn the vegetables*

At regular intervals, turn the vegetables so they cook evenly. A pair of tongs is the best tool to use. Don't let the tongs puncture the vegetable, though, or its juice will run free.

Step 4. *Remove and steam*

Once the vegetable's skin is black or fully blistered, place it in a paper bag or food-grade plastic bag. Seal the bag lightly. Let the vegetable sit until it is cool enough to handle.

Step 5. *Peel*

Peel off the blistered skin using your fingers. If the entire vegetable blistered, this will be easy. If there are spots that aren't cooked enough, they will resist.

SEALING/SAUTÉING

I remember the day I began my first book *Amazing Grains.* I was sitting at a desk in a boathouse overlooking the ocean in Kennebunkport, Maine. I waited for words to come onto the paper. My mind was scrambling to define what I knew about cooking and why I was bothering to write yet another cookbook. I was impregnated with the idea of the language of cooking when I realized that the definition of *sauté,* a term borrowed from French cuisine, means "to leap." I think of sauté as a quick, half in the air, half in the skillet method that uses oil. In the classical method, sauté sounds like a complete cooking method. I am not convinced this is true for plant cuisine; thus I reserve the word "sauté" to mean sealing the edges of vegetables. Sealing is a pretreatment, not a complete cooking method that is finished with salt.

Grain

There is no need to use oil in a grain dish unless it includes decorative vegetables and/or herb/spice seasonings. Sealed decorative vegetables and herbs will turn a normally boring primary element, such as grain, into one that is seductive and full of flavor.

Vegetables

Sealing protects and deepens the flavor of vegetables, which otherwise is often lost in the cooking liquid. The juices of vegetables merge with the oil to create a bouillon-like flavor at the bottom of the pot. This flavored oil is pulled into the dish with a cooking liquid, or by adding salt and covering the dish, as with slow cooking.

Protein

All forms of vegetable protein benefit from this pretreatment because they contain very little oil, if any. Beans feel sensuous without using oil. But vegetables and herbs and spices that are sealed with oil will infuse a bean dish with flavor faster than without them.

Sealing/Sautéing

TECHNIQUE

Step 1. *Heat the pan*

To seal/sauté, heat the pan before putting the oil into it. Warm it like an iron. Oil becomes thinner on a warm surface; food cools the oil. To prevent the oil from smoking, have the first vegetable ready to place into the pan. If oil is put into a cold pan, twice as much as needed will be used. Warming the pan before adding oil prevents excessive use of oil. I say, "Heat the pan, not the oil."

Step 2. *Oil and elements*

Add the oil and one primary or decorative element at a time, and cook until the ingredient is somewhere between shiny and limp. Plant food doesn't have to hiss. Vegetables don't mind warming up with the pan. Animal-based foods, however, should hiss when they hit the oil; this is essential, because if the pan isn't hot enough when the animal pieces are added, they will stick and be finished cooking before they brown. Rotating the pan in the air to coat it with oil heats the oil unnecessarily.

Step 3. *Seal*

The sealing process involves oil, metal, and fire. Together they work to put walls around cut pieces of vegetables. Lay the cut vegetables across the bottom of a pot or skillet so there is no metal exposed. I call this "floor space," and I recommend that you use it all whenever possible. If vegetables are on top of each other instead of on the metal, they will steam instead of seal. Floor space that isn't used is wasteful, like letting water run in the desert.

SOAKING

Soaking relaxes the protective layers of a seed, whether it is a grain, nut, or bean. Brown rice suggests a buttery feeling when it is soaked before cooking. Less soaking time is needed on a warm day. Seeds are saturated with water when they look puffy. Soaking brings just the right amount of cooking liquid into a grain, vegetable, nut/seed, or bean. As a pretreatment for blending and fermenting, this method awakens dormant seeds and is critical for easier digestion.

> *S*oaking reminds me of quietly bathing in a tub or floating in a pool. I relax and my feelings expand. When I'm out of the water, I feel softer, hydrated, not so brittle.

Grain

Soaking grain before using a first-stage cooking method makes for a softer cooked dish; it also prepares the grain for sprouting, if you are using it for a living food method. The texture of soaked grain is heavy and moist like a pudding. This pretreatment helps make it easier to digest whole grains, and is especially recommended for children, elders, and anyone who is ill.

Soaking Grain

Step 1. *Measure and wash*

Measure the grain. Wash whole grain in a bowl of water, scrubbing it with your hands. Rinse white rice or pearl barley in a mesh colander or strainer.

Step 2. *Cover with cooking liquid*

Measure the amount of liquid for the kind of grain and first-stage method you will be using. Place the grain and liquid into the same pot that will be used to cook it. Cover it and let it sit for 2–12 hours. Then cook the grain without transferring it to a different pot or changing the liquid. Grain used for sprouting always needs to be physically and energetically whole. Place it in a sprouting jar that has a screen secured to the top. Cover the grain with water and let it soak in a dark place for 8 hours. If grain soaks longer than 12 hours, it will start to naturally ferment. Slight fermentation is attractive in plant dishes, but care should be taken to distinguish serving foods that taste sour from dishes that are rotting. This occurs when bacteria grow from contact with a cook who has poor personal hygiene or when food is in the temperature danger zone of 41°F–135°F (5°C–57.2°C) for more than four hours.

Protein

I soak beans for one of four reasons: (1) I am preparing a living food dish with bean sprouts; (2) I haven't eaten beans for a while and my digestion is sensitive to this concentrated protein; (3) the beans are medium-cooking beans and the first-stage method is not pressure cooking; or (4) the beans are long cooking, such as chickpeas or soybeans.

Beans are notorious for being difficult to digest. Science points to a group of carbohydrate molecules called oligosaccharides as the culprits. I prefer Harold McGee's explanation in his book *On Food and Cooking*. He believes the secondary compounds in beans are the source of digestion problems. The function of these secondary compounds is to protect the beans' reproductive system. This powerful defense mechanism is conquered by fire, and the beans are completely transformed through proper cooking. When the beans puff up with water during soaking, they become easier to transform in the first-stage method.

> *N*uts, seeds, and beans are the protein sources in a living food diet. Nuts and seeds play a complex role by providing fat, protein, and some fiber. These food groups need to be soaked before any other method is effectively applied; otherwise, they will fight the body during digestion.

Soaking is not mandatory unless you haven't eaten beans for a while. The more frequently you eat beans, the more easily you can digest them, because your system will build up a tolerance for them. Soaking beans saturates them with water, usually within 8–12 hours. However, if at eight in the morning I decide to make hummus for lunch but the beans aren't soaked, I will quick-soak them in boiling water.

Soaking Beans

TECHNIQUE

Step 1. *Sort and wash*

Beans look like stones, and stones look like beans. Taking time to sort out foreign items from a pile of beans is as valuable as having teeth. Beans are not an expensive protein, but the dental work that could be necessary after eating cooked beans that were not carefully picked over is. Wash the beans as if they were a whole grain—in a bowl with water and a massage.

Step 2. *Quick and long soaking methods*

For the quick method, place the beans in a soup pot, and cover them with cold water by 3 inches. Bring to a boil on high heat and continue to boil for 10 minutes (do not cover the pot). Remove from the heat, cover, and set aside for one hour. Drain and repeat, if necessary (a second short soak is helpful for people with extra-sensitive digestion). The long method of soaking takes 8–12 hours. Place the beans in a bowl and cover them with water by 3 inches or more. Short-term beans will soak in 8 hours, medium-term beans in 10 hours, and long-term beans should go for 12 hours. Soak the beans in the refrigerator when the room temperature exceeds 80°F (27°C).

Vegetables/Fruits

Soaking this primary element is reserved for dried fruit, dried vegetables, and vegetable seeds. Dehydrated fruit and vegetables expand in cool water within 10–15 minutes, and then they go into a cooking method. Living food relies on many varieties of vegetable sprouts. The steps for soaking vegetable seeds for sprouting, like broccoli, fenugreek, and alfalfa, are the same as for grain and beans. Vegetable seeds are very small, however, so they need less water to cover them than grains and beans. Consider using the soaking liquid in soup, especially the soaking liquid of sea vegetables. Soaking is a way of cleaning a dried fruit or vegetable from the inside out. Hard-to-see soil and other matter relax in the soaking water and let go. Fruit and vegetables should soak for 15–60 minutes.

BLANCHING

The primary purpose of blanching is to loosen the skin on nuts and vegetables. Because the skin makes the food whole, it is rarely eliminated. But sometimes, for aesthetic effect, I remove almond, bell pepper, or tomato skins, and blanching facilitates this. Blanching is also used to heighten a food's color, although it feels wasteful to use it for that purpose. Steeping improves a vegetable's color without diluting its flavor.

Blanching

TECHNIQUE

Step 1. *Select pot, boil water*

Use any pot with enough water to allow the ingredients room to float. Bring the water to a rapid boil.

Step 2. *Boil the ingredient*

Place the ingredient in the boiling water for 30 seconds to 2 minutes. The longer the ingredient is in the boiling water, the more it will cook. Blanching should not cook a food. Take care not to let this be the first-stage cooking method.

Step 3. *Transfer the ingredient to icy cold water*

Cold water stops the cooking; it must be cold enough to shock the food. Tepid or mildly cold water will not be as effective.

Step 4. *Remove the ingredient from the cold water*

When blanching vegetables to gain a brighter color, it is important not to leave them in the cold water too long or the nutrients will be leached into the water. I take them out before I can say "one one thousand."

SMOKING

Smoking was developed for cooking and preserving animal-based food. It is the main flavor of barbecued food. I use a box made for indoor stove-top smoking, but it goes on my outdoor grill. Plant-based primary elements do not need the preservation qualities of smoking, but smoking is a great way to infuse another layer of flavor into a plant-based dish. Smoking will also affect texture. Pecan, apple, oak, cherry, hickory, and maple smoking chips, as well as corncobs and mesquite smoking dust, are a few of the flavors available. The amount of chips in the smoker helps determine how long the food will be smoking. The more food, the more chips, and the longer the food will cook. Smoking is not the only treatment the food will go through; plant-based elements will be cooked by another method as well. Because their energy bodies are lighter than animal ingredients, they require relatively little time in the smoker—only about 10 minutes.

Grain

Grains absorb the smoke flavor and at the same time take on a shade of color. This background flavor in grain is subtle and even. These grain dishes will benefit from oil; the oil may be in the sauté pretreatment after smoking or in a sauce that is served with the dish.

Vegetables

As a pretreatment, smoking dries vegetables out slightly and gives them a tinge of color. My favorite way to use this method with vegetables is as a pretreatment for soups and sauces.

Protein

All forms of vegetable protein respond to smoking as a pretreatment. Beans can be smoked after soaking or after the first-stage method. Tofu, tempeh, and gluten may be smoked at any stage method. One of my favorite uses for smoked beans is in developing a pâté with layers of flavor.

Smoking

TECHNIQUE

Step 1. *Select smoking chips, place in smoker*

The stove-top smoker is a high-sided metal pan with a cover that slides. Inside are two surfaces—one is a grate that is perfect for slabs of tofu or tempeh; the other is a flat sheet that can hold vegetables, nuts, or other small foods that would fall through the open slats of the grate. The smoking chips are placed beneath these surfaces, right on the bottom of the pan. Form a small pile to keep the miniature chips from turning to ash too quickly.

Step 2. *Position primary element*

Cut vegetables need to go on the flat sheet, or, if using a small amount, they can be placed in a mini pie pan on the grate (as can small amounts of grain, beans, or nuts/seeds).

Step 3. *Add fire*

The stove-top smoker is designed to go on top of one or two burners in the kitchen. I prefer to put it outside on the grill. A high flame smokes the dishes quickly. It would smoke at any temperature once the chips have burned, which is what creates the smoke.

FIRST- AND SECOND-STAGE METHODS

BOILING

Boiling is a turbulent, active method. Think of pasta rolling around in a pot of oceanic quantities of water. Energetically, boiling is an aggressively vigorous cooking method that uses an abundant amount of cooking liquid. This method is also time sensitive. Put a major ingredient into a boiling bath for too long and it will drink in as much liquid as possible, eventually becoming mush. This cooking liquid holds nutrition. Discarding it is only an option for grain cookery. Most boiling applications are used to create soups, stocks, or stews, so the nutrients in the cooking liquid are retained.

Grain

When I ask people how they cook their grain, the answer is usually, "I boil it." But their boiling is my steeping. Boiling is energetically turbulent because the cooking liquid needs to boil forcefully on a high flame the entire cooking time; with boiling, grain moves freely and does not absorb all the cooking liquid. Barley vegetable soup and wild rice in broth paint an image of boiled grain. If boiling is used for other than a soup method, the cooking liquid is discarded (just like when we cook pasta). The texture of boiled grain is delightfully uneven, individual, and particularly good for receiving a marinade in a second stage.

Boiling Whole Grains
and Whole Grain Pasta

Step 1. *Bring cooking liquid to rapid boil*

The minimum water-to-grain ratio is 8:1, but it is better to eyeball the amount of liquid for boiling whole grain, just as for pasta. Fill the pot, allowing about 3 inches of head room at the top. When boiling whole grain pasta, fill the pot only halfway, because more water will be added to the pot as the pasta cooks.

Step 2. *Herb/spice*

Spices are optional. Make sure they are big enough to remove with a skimmer tool (tempura strainer) before the grain goes into the pot. Whole cinnamon and cloves, large slices of fresh ginger, or mulling spices, for example, readily infuse boiling water and may be scooped out. Dried herbs do not work well. Boiling dried herbs that are not bonded to oil makes them taste like a hay field smells, and they are difficult to remove. Use fresh, on-the-stem herbs to make an infusion liquid.

Step 3. *Sea salt*

A token of sea salt is added to assist the transformation, but it is measured to fit when making soups. If the liquid will be discarded, I think of salting as just a polite gesture, and it's my choice of how much to use. Salt seasonings are only for finishing when the liquid will be included with the dish, as with a soup. With grain and pasta, the liquid is discarded.

Step 4. *Oil, if necessary*

I use a touch of oil when boiling millet and whole grain pasta. It keeps moisture in grain that is naturally brittle. Oil is an option with other kinds of grain.

Step 5. *Add grain or pasta and cook*

The water is boiling as fast as it can the entire time. Whole grains open according to their own timing, so from time to time select a few with the skimmer to see if they are open and soft. They become firmer when cool. If the pot is covered and the flame reduced, the grain will steep, and with that much liquid, the result will be porridge. Once whole grain noodles go into the boiling bath, the liquid activity slows down. While it is returning to the boiling point, the pasta cooks gently. When it regains a rolling boil, splash in some cold water to stop the action; then return it to a rapid boil. Repeat this process several times until the pasta is cooked through the center.

Step 6. *Strain*

Use a colander to catch the grain while the cooking liquid passes through. I save the liquid for clear soup if the herb/spice in the liquid is favorable. Pasta and grain may be rinsed with cool liquid to wash off the starch. If I don't use oil in the boiling bath, a touch of oil around the cooling grain/noodles keeps them from sticking.

Vegetables

Boiling a vegetable in the language of cooking means that this dish is on its way to being soup. During the boiling method more than 50 percent of the energy of the vegetable shifts into the cooking liquid, leaving the vegetable with partial potency. The classic term "blanching" is an offshoot of boiling, only it is more gentle and usually requires less water and less time. The purpose of blanching is to brighten the color of a vegetable (and in some instances, remove the skin of certain vegetables, fruits, and nuts). In the language of cooking, both boiling and blanching are replaced by the steeping method, which retains all the nutrients and heightens the flavor of the vegetable beyond what either boiling or blanching offer. I only boil vegetables if they will be served with the cooking liquid. That means soup. Or vegetables are boiled to bleed their flavor into a liquid and then discarded; that cooking liquid becomes stock.

I classify soup into six styles. Each style has its own set of cooking methods that defines the style of soup. The styles are creamy, clear, loose vegetable, bean, cold blend, and stew. Almost every famous soup fits into one of these styles. For example, miso, egg drop, thom kha, and hot-and-sour are "clear" soups. Minestrone and French onion use the "loose vegetable" soup method. The "creamy" style soups, both dairy and nondairy, are single-focus vegetable dishes such as cream of broccoli, cream of tomato, and cream of celery. "Bean" soup is a blend of beans, unlike a "loose vegetable" soup that has beans floating in it loosely. A "stew" incorporates all three primary elements and often has a binder. A "cold blend" soup uses fresh fruit or vegetables; examples include melon soup, gazpacho, or energy soup from living cuisine.

STOCK

A stock must have purpose or its life has no future. I make stock from vibrant, energetically valuable vegetable pieces; otherwise, the cooking liquid created has little power. It's analogous to picking a wine for cooking. If the wine is undeveloped, it affects the dish adversely. Conversely, a wine that is good enough to drink adds value to the dish. Just making a stock for stock's sake and landing it in the freezer misuses the food and takes up valuable space, because unless oil protects it, freezing will destroy the energetic qualities of the vegetables.

If you want the flavor of a vegetable stock to align with the flavor of your soup or stew, use pieces from the same vegetables that will be going into the soup or stew. Bringing in "outsiders" can be distracting. For example, even if carrots are in the refrigerator, they shouldn't go into a stock for broccoli soup. Carrots are a major ingredient in commercial stocks, but broccoli will fight with these sweet-natured vegetables because both are strong enough to vie for first place. The onion family, being the wild card, deepens, shapes, and merges with the background of a stock for any kind of soup, even broccoli. A general vegetable stock can be made from neutral vegetables (such as mushrooms, cauliflower stalks and leaves, cabbage, and celery), and they will enhance a mixed-vegetable soup or stew. Be cautious with rutabagas, turnips, and parsnips; although these vegetables make wonderful stock, they might also need to be in the soup. The point of using a stock is to add depth to the soup or stew, not to distract from the design. Select components as if you were making a mixed-vegetable dish.

Stock is optional when following the technique for each style of soup, except with clear soup, which depends on the cooking liquid for flavor. I use two kinds of stock—kombu/spice and boiled vegetable. They have no oil.

Kombu Stock

Kombu/spice stock lasts a couple weeks in the refrigerator. This is the best style of stock for clear soups and clear sauces. It is more about spices than vegetables. Once the spices have been chosen, vegetables may accompany this stock, but the stock doesn't rely on them.

Kombu Stock

Step 1. *Fill a pot with cold water*

Pick a pot to fit the quantity of stock you want to make. Begin with cold water, because as the water heats up, it will draw out the flavors from the vegetables and spices.

Step 2. *Add kombu and spices*

Estimate one inch of kombu per cup of liquid. For the spices, fresh ginger slices, lemongrass (sliced or crushed), kaffir lime leaves, cardamom, coriander, fenugreek, bay leaves, and fresh or dried herbs on the branch are some of the choices. Water is dense. It requires large amounts of seasonings to infuse it.

Step 3. *Bring to a boil*

The action of boiling pulls the flavors into the water. This stock may be covered while boiling to retain the essence within and avoid excess reduction. It takes about 20 minutes to infuse the water. Using a tempura strainer (oil skimmer) makes it easy to remove large pieces of herb/spice. Alternatively, strain the liquid upon completion.

Step 4. *Do not salt*

Do not put salt in a stock because the stock may reduce as it boils (making the salt portion too concentrated), and because stock is used with other cooking liquids, making the total layers of salt for the dish guesswork.

Vegetable Stock

I only use vegetable stock as cooking liquid to accompany a soup or stew when the vegetables used in the stock reflect the vegetables used in the soup or stew, and I have an extra pot or burner to make some.

Vegetable Stock

Step 1. *Place vegetables in an empty pot*

Putting the vegetables in the pot at the outset guarantees the stock will be as strong as possible. Fill the pot to the brim with vegetable pieces. Big pieces will take longer to cook, but other than that, the size doesn't matter.

Step 2. *Cover the vegetables with cold water*

The colder the water, the longer the vegetables will bathe in warm water, which opens their cells to release their essence. Add cold water until it comes just to the top of the vegetables. If this style of stock is started with a pot of cold water, and only a few vegetables are tossed into it, the result is a wimpy stock.

Step 3. *Boil*

Keep the stock at a rolling boil until the fibers of the vegetables are translucent and their character has been transferred to the water—spent. Then strain it. With or without a cover, the stock will reduce, intensifying the flavor. It is better to make a small amount of rich stock than have a large amount of diluted (wimpy) stock. Other cooking liquids easily join vegetable stock in a soup. Do not salt this stock; it is a cooking liquid. Salting is more accurate when looking at the total number of layers in a soup after all ingredients are in the pot.

Clear Soup

Step 1. *Create a major cooking liquid*

Kombu/spice or vegetable stock make good cooking liquids for a clear soup. Clear soup doesn't use oil except in a cooking liquid form, such as in nut milk.

Step 2. *Salt to fit with sea salt*

This is often a partial salting when I plan to use tamari, miso, or umeboshi. Sea salt transforms stock into soup.

Step 3. *Add decorative vegetables*

These may be cooked into the nature of the soup, as with hot-and-sour soup, or added at the end as a garnish, like a scallion sliver on top of miso broth.

Cream-Style Soup

I begin this style of soup as if I will not be using dairy cream. Then I have the option of adding a touch of heavy cream at the end, although the soup is not dependent on it.

The base of this dairy-free, creamy soup is puréed vegetables. When designing this style of soup, it is important to keep a clear single focus by using only one major vegetable, which creates the soup's identity. As such, it is considered a single-vegetable dish. For example, with cream of tomato soup, cream of mushroom soup, or cream of broccoli soup there is only one signature vegetable. Some vegetables are creamy in nature and have enough bulk to provide their own base binder, like carrots and squash. Others, like mushrooms, celery, corn, and onions, benefit from an additional base binder to stretch the body of the soup. A small amount of potato or cauliflower provides substance to support these lighter-weight vegetables. In addition, a neutral base binder gives body to a soup whose identity is an herb/spice, like cream of garlic soup.

Oil is an important element in this dish and can be worked in during step one, sealing the vegetables, or for a weightier body, use a thin nut milk as the cooking liquid. The amount of oil needed in the sealing step is less when cooking with nut milk or dairy cream. If no nut milk or dairy cream is used, it is important to be generous with the oil when sealing the vegetables.

Another critical component to creamy soups is the onion family. The presence of a large yellow or white onion distinguishes the soup from puréed vegetables, which resemble baby food. The onion family (including leeks, shallots, and others) helps create a depth of flavor and an appropriate substance without weakening the character of the dish. I use an abundant combination of the entire onion family.

My first choice is to use a pressure cooker, because the added intensity of pressure softens the vegetables and maintains their flavors. This procedure is almost foolproof. If you are not using a pressure cooker, begin with a heavy soup pot with a secure lid. The amount of liquid required for boiling is more than twice that for pressure cooking. In a pressure cooker, it is better to use large cuts, because they take up less floor space on the bottom of the pot and require less oil, which keeps the soup from feeling dull and heavy. When using a soup pot, cut the vegetables into small pieces. They will take up several layers of the floor of the pot.

Cream-Style Soup

Step 1. *Sealing*

Warm a heavy-bottom soup pot or pressure cooker. Add oil and immediately add the onion and any other onion family ingredients. If there is room in the pot, don't wait to add the signature vegetable. Tossing large vegetables in a pot to move oil around the edges is more effective than using a spoon or paddle. Swivel the pot, keeping its bottom parallel to the stove. Then flick it quickly one time to move the vegetables on the bottom of the pot to the top. Vegetables in a light-colored soup need to be intensified without over-browning. In contrast, a deep-colored vegetable becomes more delicious as its edges are sealed. This step strengthens the flavor of the soup. Allow plenty of time to seal the vegetables or the soup will be weak.

Step 2. *Herb/spices*

If herbs and spices are part of this dish, add them to the oil toward the end of sealing the vegetables. When judging the amount of herb/spice to put in the pot, consider where all the vegetables plus the cooking liquid will fill the pot. Then, after determining how thick each layer will be, imagine it all blended and count the number of layers of soup. Rub the dried herbs tightly between your fingers and move them over the pot, making one pass for each layer of soup and letting the seasonings fall into the pot as you go. Fresh herbs will go in after the cooking but before blending, unless the soup is orange or red in color. Green herbs will turn orange or red vegetables brown when blended. Fresh green herbs should be used decoratively in a red-toned soup after it has been blended.

Step 3. *Cooking liquid*

Add just enough cooking liquid to cover the vegetables by 2 inches for pressure cooking and 3–4 inches when boiling. It is important to take into account how the signature vegetable grows and its water content to determine the amount of liquid.

For example, if it is a wet vegetable by nature, like zucchini, use less liquid. If the vegetable grows below the earth line, like carrots, or is starchy, like winter squash, use the full amount. Cream-style soups benefit from some wine in the cooking liquid when nut milk or dairy cream is present.

Step 4. *Salt to fit*

Imagine all the vegetables and liquid blended together to get a sense of how thick this soup will be. Count the number of layers of soup. Then, with a light grip, hold some sea salt between your thumb and first three fingers and let it flow into the pot, moving across one time for each layer.

Step 5. *Pressure cook or boil*

The pressure cooking method saves time and ensures that the vegetables, even the most hardy roots, become soft. Pressure rises on high heat. Turn the flame down to medium-low. No flame tamer is needed. Table 2.2 (page 209) gives time guidelines for pressure cooking; add an extra 2–5 minutes to ensure that the vegetables are extremely soft.

Step 6. *Blend*

Do not judge the taste and substance of this soup until all the vegetable pieces and all the liquid are blended together. The first blended batch may be too thick or too thin, too weak or too strong. The depth of substance and flavor has been measured to fit, so the entire soup has to be blended before the taste is accurate. A hand blender is the easiest tool to use, although blending batches of soup in a traditional upright blender or food processor are other options.

Step 7. *Adjust with accent liquid (optional)*

Accent liquid rounds out the mouthfeel of a cream-style soup. It lightens the energy body when the soup feels dull or heavy from oil or dense vegetables and activates the flavors of multiple ingredients when there is enough salt in the dish. Only $1/8$ teaspoon of an accent liquid is needed to transform a three-quart pot of soup.

Loose Vegetable Soup

This style of soup is named from observing the freedom of vegetables floating in a broth. Loose vegetable soups are either a single focus vegetable, as with French onion soup, or mixed, as with minestrone. Loose vegetable soup may contain beans, but a true bean soup features blended beans. Lentil soup is usually a loose vegetable style with beans. Another distinction is that bean soups do not require the use of oil; loose vegetables definitely need oil as their protector.

Select vegetables for a loose vegetable soup the same as you would for any vegetable dish. First decide if the soup will feature a single vegetable or a variety. Loose vegetable soup has the reputation of being "refrigerator soup," the kind where all the tired vegetables end up in soup at the end of the week. It is critical to employ the theory of numbers and the energetic quality of how vegetables grow so that refrigerator soup doesn't end up without a composition.

Loose Vegetable Soup

Step 1. *Cut vegetables*

In general, vegetables are cut small. A loose vegetable fits in the soup spoon with other vegetables and some broth. Usually a dice or quarter-moon cut is used. Leafy greens shrink more than roots, so they may be cut larger.

Step 2. *Warm soup pot*

A heavy-bottom soup pot allows for the necessary long sealing time. Once the pot has been warmed, oil will glide easily across the bottom of the pot and will provide a true reading of how much oil is being used.

Step 3. *Seal*

Add the oil and the first vegetable together. Spread them out evenly across the bottom of the pot. Cook one vegetable at a time, adding the second, third, fourth, etc. after the previous one has had its time with the oil and hot metal. This is the single most critical step in making a good vegetable soup. There is no need for stock because this step brings flavor into the broth while protecting the vegetables. Members of the onion family go into the pot first, because oil slides off this wet vegetable making it available to the drier ones that will follow. Root family vegetables are second. Then the vegetables enter in order of how they grow: vine family, stalks, and finally leafy greens when the soup is nearly finished cooking. The exceptions are burdock and mushrooms, which precede any of the onion family.

Step 4. *Herb/spice*

Imagine how many layers of soup will be in the pot once the cooking liquid has been added. For each layer, which is thinner than a cream-style or bean soup, I am heavy-handed with dried herbs and spices, especially when water is the cooking liquid. Fresh herbs enter the pot with other leafy greens at the end of the session, when the soup is fully cooked.

Step 5. *Add cooking liquid*

How much? Vegetables need room to float, and extra broth is a signature of this style of soup. Major cooking liquids, such as stock, water, and vegetable juice, create most of the substance of this soup. On occasion, thin nut milk, wine, or beer is appropriate as a minor cooking liquid.

Step 6. *Salt to fit*

Judge the layers of a loose vegetable soup by the densest matter. These dense layers are thin, so a pot of loose vegetable soup will have many more layers than other styles. Sea salt or vegetable salt will bring all the flavors of this dish together; finishing salts are optional.

Stew

Vegetable stew is a complex dish. It should include a representative of all three primary elements. In addition, there is a saucy binder to unify the substance and flavors. Vegetable stews feature large chunky cuts of vegetables and a weighty substance. I like to use the owl cut for stew. Stew feels more satisfying as a mixed-vegetable dish instead of a single, but anything is possible as long as the grain and protein are also bound in a sauce.

Stew

TECHNIQUE

Step 1. *Seal the vegetables*

Warm a stew pot. Add oil and the first vegetable. Take time to seal each vegetable by adding the second one only after sealing the first, and so on, until all the vegetables have been protected.

Step 2. *Sprinkle in the grain and beans*

Wash and pretreat a grain whose color will be compatible with the vegetables in the stew. Quinoa and millet are my favorite grains for this style of dish because they have a neutral color and cook quickly. The amount to use is decorative; grain speckles the vegetables. The amount of beans to include depends on whether other protein will be added or if beans will be the only protein in the meal. First-stage beans may finish cooking in the stew. Tofu, tempeh, and gluten will already have been taken through a second stage and will not need to simmer in the stew at this step.

Step 3. *Herb/spice*

Herbs and spices bond to the vegetables through the oil. Vegetables offer much of their own taste, unlike grain and beans, so a smaller quantity of herb/spice is required in this style of soup than in others. Also, because the layers are thicker, there will be fewer of them in the pot.

Step 4. *Add cooking liquid*

The first pass of cooking liquid will steam the flavored oil deposits on the bottom of the pan. Release these deposits with a wooden or bamboo utensil. Add the remaining cooking liquid, using enough to cover the grain, vegetables, and beans by about $1/2$ inch.

Step 5. *Salt to fit*

Use sea salt to simmer with the mix and a salt seasoning at the end of cooking. I particularly like to work miso into this dish in step 7.

Step 6. *Cover and boil*

Cover the pot and maintain a slow boil on medium-low heat with a flame tamer to keep everything stewing. When the vegetables are fully cooked and the grains have opened, the mixture will look like boiled vegetables speckled with grain; there will be little liquid left.

Step 7. *Sauce*

My favorite way to create a sauce is by blending a small portion of the entire mixture, approximately one-quarter of the dish, and then returning it to the pot. A moment with a hand blender in the pot is the most efficient way to make a sauce. Alternatively, process a portion of the stew in a blender or food processor.

Step 8. *Finishing touches*

If you choose to add other protein, this is the time to do it—after blending, before serving.

Protein

Vegetable protein prepared with the boiling method also belongs in soups and stews. Tofu and tempeh in soups and stews are usually decorative, and they are often either roasted or deep-fried before playing a role in soup. Beans are the binder for bean soup. Tofu can work in this position, but tempeh and seitan cannot.

Bean Soup

I love that I can make this soup with no oil. The flavors of the decorative vegetables and herbs and spices bleed into the beans. Beer, wine, or nut milk as minor cooking liquids embellish this easy and inexpensive soup. Frozen and canned beans are at the first stage and ready to use.

Bean Soup

TECHNIQUE

Step 1. *Choose the pot*

Place first-stage cooked beans in a pot and cover them with cooking liquid (all or mostly water) by $1^1/_2$–2 inches above the cooked beans, depending on how thick you want the soup to be.

Step 2. *Add herbs, spices, and decorative vegetables*

In this style of soup, herbs and spices don't need to bond with oil because they will be blended into

the beans at the end of the cooking process. Decorative vegetables that are minced need no protection from oil, because their individual identity is boiled out of them (like a stock) and goes into the soup with their fiber included.

Step 3. *Salt*

Salt to fit with sea salt or vegetable salt. When using a finishing salt, adjust the amount of salt crystals accordingly.

Step 4. *Boil*

Boil for at least 10 minutes or until the vegetables are limp, onions are clear, and salt has had a chance to do its job.

Step 5. *Blend*

Blend a majority of the soup, all of it, or leave a few beans whole for identification.

PRESSURE COOKING AND PRESSURE STEAMING

The pressure cooking method requires a pressure cooker. The pressure cooker should be stainless steel or enamel. Pressure cookers with a heavy bottom support the pretreatment sauté and offer protection against burning. Even more important than a heavy bottom is smooth construction with no ridges. Modern pressure cookers have safety release valves to protect against an excessive buildup of pressure. If you listen to the action of your equipment and adjust the heat accordingly, your pressure cooker will be as safe as any other kitchen appliance.

The difference between pressure cooking and pressure steaming is that with pressure steaming the food sits above the cooking liquid in a steaming basket, and with pressure cooking the food sits directly in the cooking liquid. The texture of dishes prepared by pressure cooking is always wet and soft. Pressure steaming yields a firmer texture. The value of this method is that it ensures a predictable texture for all the primary elements. Energetically, it is centering. Primary ingredients are transformed with a feeling of core strength, like centering a wedge of clay on a potter's wheel. From a health standpoint, 15 minutes in a pressure cooker will destroy unfriendly bacteria in most food.

Grain

Pressure cooking is more about texture and centering than saving time. The longer grain stays in the pressure cooker, the more fire (nutrient) it holds. The cooking time will range from 10–60 minutes, depending on the kind of grain being cooked. A good texture is guaranteed when the pressure cooker is properly sealed, there is an accurate cooking liquid to grain ratio, and a flame tamer is interfaced between the stove and the pot. Pressure steaming grain is not applicable.

Vegetables

Pressure cooking vegetables makes them buttery soft, perfect for spreading or mashing. The amount of cooking liquid needed is determined the same way as steeping. There should be little extra liquid to be drained. A flame tamer will help to prevent burning.

The goal of pressure steaming is to preserve the texture of the vegetable as much as possible. Vegetables that are pressure steamed whole and cut into shapes after they are cooked will resemble steeped vegetables, just a little softer. Table 2.2, Pressure Cooking/Pressure Steaming Times for Vegetables (page 209), provides estimated times once the pressure has been established and the fire turned down. There are two variables to take into consideration when following the times listed in this table. First, you must account for the size of the vegetable. Larger vegetables need a longer cooking time. Second, take into account the age of the vegetable. The older the vegetable, the longer it will take to cook. By "older" I am referring to how long it has been away from the garden. No flame tamer is needed in this method because the liquid stays abundant and separate from the vegetable. The key to this method is time. The longer a vegetable is under pressure in the cooker, the softer it becomes, so it is important that the pressure be released quickly; this is usually done by running the top of the cooker under cold water. However, some pressure cookers respond to this cold liquid process by reversing the pressure so that a strong suction holds the lid in place, making it impossible to open the cooker without reheating it. By that time the vegetables could be overcooked. Check the manual that came with your cooker to find out the quick release method recommended by the manufacturer for your specific appliance. Vegetable families with lighter energy bodies, such as sea vegetables, leafy greens, and mushrooms, do not need the intensity of pressure cookers.

Protein

Beans respond best to pressure cooking when they are whole beans, not split like yellow and red lentils or split peas. A well-cooked split bean is mushy and has no clear shape. I do not recommend cooking split beans in a pressure cooker, because they have a tendency to clog the cooker's valves. It is better to steep split beans.

To pressure cook whole beans, begin by parboiling them to remove any foam that wants to escape from the bean. Include a one-inch piece of kombu (a sea vegetable) per cup of dry beans in this first stage. Kombu helps make the beans more digestible; its properties tenderize beans naturally. Because beans are a concentrated protein, it is important to break down their secondary compounds in order for them to be digestible. This occurs only in the first stage of cooking. The texture of pressure-cooked beans is predictable—velvety smooth on the inside, with tight skin on the outside. The more fire beans take, the more digestible and full-flavored they will be.

> *V*icki verified my theory that beans can't be overcooked if the right technique is applied and there is plenty of water in the pot. Vicki lives 45 minutes from Denver, in the mountains. A trip to the city is rarely less than a half a day's excursion. In the morning, Vicki put on a pot of black beans to cook using the pressure cooking method. After bringing the cooker up to pressure, she diligently put the flame tamer between the pot and the fire and reduced the flame to medium-low. When she was called at the last minute to go to Denver, she had forgotten about the beans. She returned five hours later to the smell of black beans that had permeated her home. Using the fast-release method to quickly bring down the pressure, she opened the cooker. Instead of seeing the burnt beans she expected, she saw beans that were plump, moist, buttery soft, and richer in flavor than the one-hour version.

The theory is that grains and beans cannot be overcooked like animal products, which might become tough. Follow the method impeccably and use just enough cooking liquid to help the bean through the transformation, but not so much that the seed expands into excessive liquid. The right amount of cooking liquid will help the meat of the bean stay in its skin. A bean with this kind of integrity can then be used in all of the second-stage methods where herbs and spices,

oil, interesting cooking liquids, and vegetables can complete the dish.

Pressure steaming is effective for preparing tofu and tempeh that will be used in a cold dish, like a spread or dip. The most enjoyable part of this method is selecting an herb/spice to go into the water. Kaffir lime leaves beautifully infuse tofu, and bay leaves are a good match with tempeh. Pressure steaming is not used for dry beans. Green beans are considered a vegetable, however, and they like to be pressure steamed.

Pressure Cooking

Step 1. *Pretreatment option for grain and vegetables*
Sautéing is optional with the pressure cooking method. Warm the pan before adding oil, and watch the oil move and become thinner. Add the first vegetable right away to prevent cooking the oil. One of the primary reasons to choose to sauté is to add herbs or spices. They go into the oil before or after grain and vegetables, but always before the cooking liquid.

Step 2. *Add the primary element and cooking liquid*
Grain uses a ratio of cooking liquid to control its texture. This is usually less than the amount needed for steeping (see Table 2.3, Grain Chart: First-Stage Cooking Methods, page 210). The amount of cooking liquid needed for beans depends on whether or not they have been soaked. During soaking, beans absorb most of the liquid that is required to cook them, so they only need enough cooking liquid to barely cover them when pressure cooking. Interesting cooking liquids infuse these simple primary elements with complex flavors, although it is critical to avoid using any liquids that contain salt. To pressure cook vegetables, figure the amount of liquid needed

in the same way it is chosen for steeping, unless you are preparing a soup or sauce, in which case the dish will need more.

Step 3. *Salt to fit*

Grain and vegetables require sea salt. Salt seasonings are too weak to be effective. The amount measured would be about $1/2$ teaspoon per cup of grain, but for vegetables, simply salt to fit by layers, taking into account the substance of the primary element.

Step 4. *The lid*

The lid provides a seal. Make sure there are no pieces of food in the rubber gasket, and if accessible, look through the air hole when the weight is removed. Not all pressure cookers have a removable weight system, so check the inside of the lid where the steam valves might get clogged with food particles and make sure they are clear and clean. Blow on it if necessary. Secure the seal, lid, and weight in place.

Step 5. *Increase pressure*

Bring the pressure up on a high flame. The pressure release valve will rise as pressure builds in the pot. For grains and beans, when the weight begins to dance, let the valve jiggle for about 30 seconds to secure the pressure inside the pot.

Step 6. *Reduce the fire and count*

Reduce the fire to medium-low and always use a flame tamer for grain and beans. The pressure will remain active but the weight does not need to rock. A quiet hissing sound is good company. If the weight is rocking actively, there is too much fire. When you are cooking grain, if the weight stops moving and the pressure release valve is down, it will be difficult to restore pressure because the grain may have already absorbed all the cooking liquid. Adding fire at that point may cause the food to burn.

The 30-second jiggle is insurance that the pressure will be maintained throughout the cooking time for grain and beans. Pressure cooking vegetables is easier because you can open the pot, check the contents, seal it back up, and put the flame on high.

Cooking times are relative to each vegetable. The closer the vegetable grows to the sun, the less cooking time it requires. For example, carrots, which grow underground, take longer to cook than broccoli, which grows above ground. (See table 2.2, page 209, table 2.3, page 210, and table 2.5, page 211.)

Step 7. *Decrease pressure*

It is possible to bring the pressure down quickly, but with pressure cooking grain and beans, a soft texture is preferred, so there is no hurry. Just turning off the fire will allow the pressure to come down naturally, making the pot safe to open. Set the cooker on a stone counter to decrease the pressure more quickly. When the safety release valve drops, jiggle the weight (if your cooker has one). Lift the weight slowly, letting the steam escape. When steam stops escaping from the valve under the weight, it will be quiet, and you can open the cooker safely. Most modern pressure cookers have safety features that prevent them from being opened until the pressure has been completely released.

Pressure Steaming

TECHNIQUE

Step 1. *Cooking liquid and basket*

Place approximately 1 inch of liquid in the bottom of the pot. A small piece of kombu in the water will help draw out the flavors in the vegetable. For bland elements, also put an herb/spice in the liquid. When a steaming basket isn't available, invert a bowl inside the cooker and balance the food around the sides.

Step 2. *Place primary elements*

Primary elements are laid in the basket. These are usually large, uncut pieces.

Step 3. *Salt to fit*

Sprinkle sea salt directly onto the ingredient. This is lightly layered, like a tickle.

Step 4. *The lid*

The lid provides a seal. Secure the lid and weight in place.

Step 5. *Increase pressure*

Bring the pressure up on a high flame. The pressure release valve will rise as pressure builds in the pot. As the pressure comes up, the weight will begin to dance. Reduce the fire to low, where the pressure is still active but the weight does not need to rock. If the weight is rocking actively, there is too much fire. If the weight is not moving and the pressure release valve is down, restore pressure by adding fire, turning it up to high again.

Step 6. *Turn down the flame and begin timing*

A high flame is too much for the full duration; turn the flame to medium-low. With pressure steaming there is an abundant amount of cooking liquid, so a flame tamer is not required. The cooking time is relative to each vegetable. The closer the vegetable grows to the sun, the less cooking time it requires. Carrots take longer than broccoli. For estimated cooking times, see table 2.2, page 209.

Step 7. *Decrease pressure*

Take the pressure down quickly if you are concerned about the texture of the vegetables. When pressure steaming vegetables, I usually use the quick-release method to bring the pressure down fast, placing the whole pot in the sink and running cold water over the nose of the pot, positioning it so the water doesn't creep into any valves.

When the safety release valve drops, jiggle the weight. If the pressure cooker has a weight, lift it slowly, letting any lingering puff of steam escape. When steam stops escaping from the valve under the weight, it will be quiet, and you can safely open the pot. Most pressure cookers have safety features that prevent them from being opened until the pressure has been completely released.

STEAMING

Steam is the vapor produced when water is heated. It is intensely hot. Food does not touch the water that rapidly boils; instead, ingredients transform in the vapor. It is a superficial method to me. It brings color to vegetables, but it has little power to transform them unless they are cut ever so small and touched with sea salt. It has been deemed the "healthy" cooking method only because it doesn't require oil.

> *S*teaming is a highly overrated cooking method, in my opinion. Almost every restaurant offers steamed vegetables as the "healthy" choice. It doesn't make sense to me that a boring vegetable would be healthful, because tasteless and boring are sure ways to keep people away from vegetables. It is best to steep vegetables to access the most flavor.

Grain

As a first-stage method, steamed whole-dish grain is not an accurate use of the language. Such a method doesn't exist. There is a special pot called a rice cooker that manufacturers say steams the grain. But in fact the grain absorbs all the cooking liquid first, which is actually steeping.

Vegetables

Steaming is appropriate for vegetables when they need to be cut prior to cooking to attain a decorative or very fine look. Such a look cannot be achieved when vegetables are cut after cooking.

Protein

Steaming tofu and tempeh prepares them for use in a cold dish, like a salad, spread, or dip. Flavoring the water beneath the basket is fun to do, and flavored water adds variety and depth to a bland ingredient. However, I don't consider this a complete method for these vegetable proteins. They will need a salt seasoning to give them interest. Fresh tofu has a pleasant, subtle taste after steaming, but tempeh needs oil and salt seasonings, at the least, to make it palatable.

Steaming

TECHNIQUE

Step 1. *Place water beneath basket insert*

Steaming baskets are made of stainless steel or bamboo. I prefer bamboo because it is easy to work with and imparts a comforting aroma. Both are equal from a technical aspect. Your pot will need a cover. Assemble a steaming pot so the steaming basket sits above the water. An inverted bowl may replace a steaming basket. It might rattle, so use something stronger than china. The water should be below the bottom of the basket.

Step 2. *Primary element and salt*

Toss sea salt among the vegetables when steaming is a first-stage method. For protein items, like tofu and tempeh, steaming is more of a pretreatment and won't need salt.

Step 3. *Cover and cook*

Bring the water to boil on high, and maintain the temperature until the color of the vegetables becomes bright. Quickly remove the vegetables from the heat and stop the cooking by plunging them into icy cold water for less than one second. Tofu and tempeh will take about 15 minutes to steam. Tamales are done when the corn husk peels away from the masa.

STEEPING

The name of this cooking method was invented to describe how primary ingredients soak up cooking liquid and end up cooked. Like tea, which is infused water, steeping is where the cooking liquid and food become one in such a way that there is no liquid left when the food is cooked.

Grain

Steeping is one of the most common cooking methods for grain, but most people call it boiling. That's because the first step is to bring the cooking liquid to a boil. The rest of the method has nothing to do with boiling. The majority of time the grain is in the pot it gently drinks in the hot liquid until it is swollen and the liquid is no longer visible. Energetically, this method is even-tempered, balanced between active and passive transformation. As in most languages, there are simple sentences with a noun, verb, and ending punctuation mark, and there are complex sentences with adverbs, adjectives, dialects, colloquialisms, and multiple punctuation marks. The technique described below is for whole-dish grains. It is a simple method for an uncomplicated ingredient. Variations of this technique apply for "dish" grains and "bread" grains that are not whole—famous dishes with an established technique appropriate for their refined character. Polenta, for example, a dish made from milled corn (bread grain), uses all the cooking liquid, but the grains are stirred as they cook. Risotto, a soft rice dish (made with short white Arborio rice), also uses more cooking liquid than the basic steeping ratio, yet all the cooking liquid is steeped into the grain. The Persian technique for long-grain white basmati rice is another variation of the steeping method. Rice is covered by $1^1/_2$ inches of water with oil and salt. In an open pot on a high flame the liquid is boiled away quickly. A rice paddle shapes the grain into a cone. Then a clean hand towel placed between the lid and the grain absorbs extra moisture as it continues to cook on a very low flame with a flame tamer. The rice is cooked when the grains are fluffy and have doubled in length. The cloth keeps extra moisture out of the grain, making this a very fluffy dish. In paella, short paella rice is boiled and then dried in the oven or under the sun, without a lid, which creates three distinct textures—soft, medium, and al dente. The key to this method is the shallow, open skilletlike pan. Paella demonstrates a variation of steeping, with roasting, but it is its own method, a colloquialism of cooking.

Steeped grain becomes more interesting with pretreatments. Both dry roasting and sautéing before steeping creates a pilaf texture and allows for many flavors to enter through the oil. The amount of cooking liquid controls the texture. See table 2.3, page 210, to determine the amount of cooking liquid and yields for different grains. Steeping whole-dish grain in a larger amount of liquid will create a porridge.

Steeping Grain

Step 1. *Pick a pot*

A pot for steeping grain needs a good lid and should fit the size of the burner. If the pot is too big, the grain will not cook evenly; if it is too small, the fire will be wasted. Choose a vertical pan, not horizontal. Heavy bottoms are preferred for even cooking and doing pretreatments, but a flame tamer will help any kind of pot used for this method.

Step 2. *Pretreatments (optional)*

Sauté decorative vegetables and herb/spice before adding grain. Sautéing grain is more about mixing grain with the oil that has herb/spice and decorative vegetables in it than about sealing the grain. Oil imparts a creamier mouthfeel, but it shouldn't be used without the supporting elements, which make this first-stage method feel complete.

Step 3. *Cooking liquid, grain, sea salt*

If the cooking liquid and grain begin together, cold to cold, the dish will be heavy and stickier than if it is started with hot cooking liquid or hot (sautéed or dry roasted) grain. A respectful pinch of sea salt goes into the pot to be dissolved in the cooking liquid. Only salt crystals are recommended in this first-stage method.

Step 4. *Cover and cook*

The cover should be in place when the cooking liquid meets the fire. This is an important measure that controls the texture of the dish. Letting steam escape compromises the technique. Once the cooking liquid is boiling with the grain, reduce the flame to medium-low and place a flame tamer between the pot and fire. Begin timing. Do not stir. The grain is finished cooking when all the liquid has been absorbed. To look for this, insert a table knife vertically and move it sideways slightly. This will reveal any remaining cooking liquid.

Vegetables

No other cooking method heightens the taste of a vegetable as well as steeping. In my mind it is the Zen art of vegetable cookery. It honors a vegetable by intensifying the character, bringing out its true flavor in the simplest, least manipulative way. Steeping reflects a vegetable's personality better than any other method—it draws out 110 percent of a vegetable's potency versus about 75 percent of its flavor with steaming. Steeping means that all the carefully measured cooking liquid disappears into the vegetable when the vegetable is perfectly done. Vegetables are best steeped alone because sea salt brings out the vegetable's own character liquid, which merges with the beginning cooking liquid. Two or more vegetables in the same steeping pot would loose their individual identity. Steeping keeps the vegetable firm so that it can be cut into most shapes after cooking. More than with any other cooking method, there is a noticeable difference between organically grown vegetables and vegetables grown conventionally with chemical supports.

This method demands careful judgment, full awareness of what is happening in the pot, and knowing how vegetables grow. Steeping is challenging because it is uncomplicated. Any and all vegetables can be steeped, but the sea vegetable family is the least recommended for this method. Choose steeping when vegetables don't need to be cut before cooking. If they require a very fine julienne cut or a thin decorative shape, they should be cut first and steamed instead of steeped. Cooking a vegetable whole may seem cumbersome, but doing so truly retains the energetic quality and flavor of vegetables. There are two approaches—one for vegetables that grow above the ground, close to the sun, and another for vegetables that grow below the ground. When steeping root vegetables, begin with cold liquid. Above-the-ground vegetables should be started in boiling, salted liquid.

Steeping Vegetables

Step 1. *Select a pot*

The first step with steeping is choosing the correct pot—one that has a tight-fitting lid with a good seal will work best. The size and shape of the pot needs to fit vegetables that will be cooked whole; the vegetables should cover as much of the bottom of the pot (floor space) as possible. Practice this technique with one layer first before adding multiple layers of the same vegetable. For example, long, tapered vegetables like carrots, parsnips, asparagus, and celery will lie down in a skillet. I even use a skillet for leafy greens because the whole leaf can spread open and fill the pan. When cooking only a small amount, use a small pan. Deep saucepans and Dutch ovens work well when steeping round shapes, such as beets, potatoes, rutabagas, or onions.

Step 2. *Cooking liquid*

Measure the cooking liquid by eye. It should just be water. The more water that nature puts in a vegetable, the less is needed to cook it. A bunch of leafy greens, for example, requires only a half layer in which to dissolve the salt; this is because they go into the pot after they are washed and still wet. Cauliflower, broccoli, and zucchini take less time to cook than root vegetables and consequently require less cooking liquid. Because the cooking liquid should disappear completely, using too much will overwhelm the vegetable and make it soggy while deflating its character. Judge cooking liquid amounts for all vegetables from a measurement for root vegetables. A skillet with one full layer of carrots across the bottom will have water halfway up the big end of the carrot. If carrots do not cover the bottom of the skillet in one complete layer, reduce the amount of water accordingly. Above-the-ground vegetables use less water according to how close they are to the sun. The closer vegetables grow to the sun, the less water they need for steeping.

Step 3. *Salt to fit*

Sea salt is required in this method in order to change the cell structure of vegetables from raw to cooked. Salt opens the cells, allowing the vegetable's liquid to merge with the cooking liquid. The amount of salt is modest to fit the vegetable. For above-the-ground vegetables, dissolve the sea salt into the cooking liquid after it is measured to fit the liquid and vegetables; then remove the vegetables from the pot. Bring the water to a boil, preheating the water and pot. Below-the-ground vegetables are tickled with salt, which is then moved into the liquid to dissolve.

Step 4. *Cover and cook*

Cover the pot with a tight-fitting lid that lets no steam escape. Maintain a high temperature the entire time. A steady stream of steam or condensation on the outside of the pot during cooking might indicate that the liquid inside the pot needs to be replaced. But too much liquid in this method makes the vegetables soggy, so replace missing liquid only when the liquid is totally gone and the tenderness of the vegetables has been checked with a toothpick. Should the vegetables need more cooking time, add a little more water and keep the flame on high. The lid is a critical part of this method. It should be squarely on during the entire cooking time and taken off only for a quick peek inside the pot. Sometimes the lid will rattle and steam will escape because the flame is high. The flame may be lowered slightly so that it is as high as it can be without forcing the lid to release steam. It is imperative that the vegetables cook as fast as possible. Turning the fire to medium or low will produce a soggy texture, overcooked vegetables, and a dull color.

Step 5. *Quick peeking*

Quick peeking into the pot on occasion is important to avoid burning the pot. The majority of the cooking happens in the beginning, while the cooking liquid reaches the boiling point and mingles with the vegetable's juices that are extracted by the salt. More liquid will accumulate, then, fairly quickly, the liquid will disappear back into the vegetable. The vegetable is done when all the liquid is gone and a toothpick easily enters the largest part of the vegetable. It should cling to the toothpick as it is lifted out of the pot. Leafy greens are done when the core is translucent and the greens are brighter than bright.

Step 6. *Cold water dunk (optional for green vegetables only)*

Stop the cooking quickly by removing the vegetables from the pot immediately and plunging them into icy cold water for less than one second (drain, and squeeze out the liquid in the leaves). This way, green vegetables will retain their intense color and flavor for hours.

Protein

Bean protein uses a similar technique as grain steeping. It is a first stage for dried beans and gluten, but a second stage for tofu and tempeh. The stage tells me when to use salt. Salt cannot be used while steeping beans in the first stage, but it may go into the pot once the beans have integrity and continue to steep for about 10 minutes. Living in an altitude over 5,000 feet, I only steep short-term and split beans. Long-term beans (such as soybeans and chickpeas) do not become soft enough in this method at any altitude. The problem with steeping beans is that the amount of cooking liquid is variable, which is the controlling factor in the texture of a cooked bean. Too much and the beans turn to mush; too little and they aren't digestible. On the other hand, the integrity of a completely cooked split bean is supposed to be mushy, with no identification of its original shape. Water, wine, and beer are my favorite cooking liquids for beans, because nut milks and vegetable juices are too thick to penetrate for proper cooking.

Steeping tofu and tempeh is a second-stage method, because these products have already been cooked without salt. Using sea salt in a steeped dish with these bland ingredients is not productive unless there is also oil and/or an item from the herb/spice category added. Alternatively, using a more complicated cooking liquid will enhance the end result. If tempeh contains grain or vegetables, it will fall apart more easily than pure soy tempeh.

Gluten made from wheat or spelt can be steeped as a first, second, or even third stage of cooking. Gluten, a refined bread grain product, requires much infusion of flavor. I accomplish this by steeping it in wine/water and bringing in a variety of herb/spice.

Steeping Protein

Step 1. *Create a cooking liquid*

Put enough cooking liquid into a pot so that the primary element will be covered. Beans will be covered by 2–4 inches of liquid depending on whether they are soaked or unsoaked. Unsoaked beans use more liquid. Cover tofu, tempeh, and gluten by 2–3 inches of liquid. A heavy-handed herb/spice infusion makes these dishes more interesting.

Step 2. *Bring to a boil*

Beans are parboiled without a cover if they have been soaked, because sometimes foam is released during the boiling action. Before the first-stage method, foam is easily removed by skimming it off with a flat spoon. Gluten, tofu, and tempeh go into seasoned, boiling cooking liquid.

Step 3. *Cooking*

Cover and reduce the flame/heat for protein steeping, unlike vegetable steeping, which remains on a high flame. Use a flame tamer at this point as a safety measure. I prefer most of the liquid to be gone by the time the primary ingredient is cooked. For tofu, tempeh, and gluten, being cooked means that the flavors in the liquid have infused the food. Whole beans are done in this first stage when they are soft on the inside while the skin of the bean is still intact. Split beans, like red or yellow lentils or split peas, are cooked when they have no individual identity left and are nothing but a smooth paste.

Salt is the key transformer in this cooking method, which is used only for vegetables. Grain and protein do not respond to this method. Pressing produces a dish with an energetically fresh feeling that is short lived and best when prepared close to serving time.

Vegetables

Vegetables that offer up their liquid in the process respond best to pressing. Lettuce, cabbage, and other leafy greens are first choices, but even carrots, celery root, turnips, and beets have enough liquid to be receptive to this process. Pressing/wilting is the only method that utilizes a cut vegetable and doesn't protect it with oil. The primary transformation in this cooking method occurs from the chemical effect of sea salt opening the cell walls to let the vegetable's liquid out combined with the act of applying pressure. In the quick method, for above-the-ground vegetables, I hold the salted cut vegetables as I would hug a loved one, firmly without gripping. Below-the-ground vegetables need to be held for a longer time. My favorite tool for this is a Japanese vegetable press, which is a modern version of the primitive crock, plate, and rock method of pressing. It is a plastic container with a perforated pressure plate on a spring attached to the lid. Mixed-vegetable dishes made with this method are best when the vegetables have a similar water content, such as radishes, cucumbers, and lettuce, or carrots, beets, and celery root.

I like to work the fresh herb/spice category into this dish and finish it with a touch of character liquid. Since this is usually the last dish made in a meal, it is easy to choose a cooking liquid that balances the five tastes (see page 16). If the meal needs something sour, lemon or lime juice performs well; if something sweet is needed, mirin or orange juice completes the dish.

Pressing/Wilting

TECHNIQUE

Step 1. *Wash and cut*

These vegetables will shrink, so I cut them slightly larger than what fits comfortably onto a fork or into a mouth. The wetter the vegetable, the more it will shrink.

Step 2. *Determine the layers*

I can hold enough pressed vegetables in my hands to serve six medium portions. Begin by spreading the first vegetable out on the cutting board. If creating a mixed-vegetable dish, place the vegetables on top of each other. Herb/spice joins the group until all the ingredients are on the board. Determine how many layers there are. A layer in a vegetable press is bulky and thick, so maybe one or two will be enough.

Step 3. *Salt to fit*

Sea salt is the most powerful way to press/wilt, but occasionally it leaves the dish too salty. This is why it is a good idea to add a cooking liquid at the end; it washes off some of the salt. The salt seasoning umeboshi vinegar brings the sour taste, adding flavor.

Step 4. *Pressing*

Tossing the vegetables mixes them and combines them with the salt. The dish is ready to press when liquid begins to emerge from the cut vegetables. I gather the vegetables in the palms of both hands and hold them, bringing my fingers together lightly; avoid closing your fingers and crushing the vegetables. Toss, regather, and hold the vegetables until the liquid comes out, their colors brighten, and they become limp. It is easy to overwork this dish, making the vegetables look tired. When using the pickle press, salt each layer before tossing. Then screw the lid in place as tightly as possible, tucking any loose vegetables beneath the plate.

Step 5. *Finishing touch (optional)*

A character liquid splashed over the dish needs only to be tossed with the vegetables.

PICKLING

For the sake of simplicity and creativity, I categorize pickles as either a pressed, brine, or paste method. Pickling is a time-proven method for preserving an abundance of any kind of harvest. As with all other cooking methods, salt is the key; but here it also acts as a preservative. Pickles stimulate enzymatic activity that enhances digestion. Many grain-eating cultures design pickles for their cuisine. This is a highly inventive cooking method for the vegetable element, not for grain and vegetable protein. A finished pickle is crunchy, translucent, and tangy in a good way. Once it reaches that point, stop the transformation by putting the vegetables and liquid in a glass jar in the refrigerator. Whereas pickles made with the pressing method cook from the inside out, pickles prepared with the brine method cook from the outside in.

Vegetables

The pressed method for pickling requires a naturally wet vegetable and is characterized by the use of salt, which draws out the vegetable's natural juices so it ferments in its own liquid. With too little salt, vegetables will mold or rot. Too much salt inhibits transformation.

Cabbage responds well to this method. Napa (Chinese) cabbage is popular in the Korean dish kimchee, while green head cabbage is the essence of sauerkraut.

Pickles by Pressing

TECHNIQUE

Step 1. *Cut vegetables*

The vegetables are cut so they can take their time while they shrink. Cabbage for sauerkraut is finely shredded. Cabbage for kimchee is cut into squares.

Step 2. *Herb/spice and sea salt*

One layer of vegetables in a crock or pickle press at a time is sprinkled with a generous amount of potent spices or dominant herbs and sea salt. This is repeated with each layer.

Step 3. *Pressing*

Everything is tossed in the crock or pickle press before applying the weight. Place a plate or glass pie tin on top of the vegetables; it should fit neatly to the edge of the crock and will hold the weight. Place a clean muslin cloth on top of the plate before adding the weight; this will catch any future foam or floating brine that may become moldy. Place a heavy rock or gallon jar of beans on the plate. The larger the crock, the heavier the rock. (The rock might need to be protected with plastic.) The goal is to have the plate submerged. The food will only be protected from rotting if it is swimming in its own liquid and air doesn't penetrate the brine. Watch for the liquid to rise above the vegetables. If it doesn't within 24 hours, add more weight, more salt, or both. The larger the volume of food, the longer it will take. The warmer the temperature, the less time it will take. The ideal temperature range to produce lactic acid is 45°F–65°F (7°C–18°C). Usually within four to five days the bubbles are brewing. Change the muslin cloth as needed. I use another lightweight cloth to cover the whole apparatus so that dust, flies, and flying food don't land in the salt bath.

Pickles with Uncooked Brine

TECHNIQUE

Step 1. *Cut vegetables, pick jar to fit*

Choose a bulky cut for the process of pickling, and then cut the vegetables into smaller pieces prior to serving. Cut turnips into quarter-inch slabs, onions into quartered fans, and carrots into logs. The cut should fit tightly into a glass jar. Boiling the jar will sterilize it.

Step 2. *Salt*

Salt the vegetables heavily with sea salt. The salt to liquid ratio is about 1:7. If using a liquid salt seasoning, use sea salt with it in order for the major transformation to take place. Pack the vegetables into a sterilized jar.

Step 3. *Cooking liquid*

Anything wet will contribute to a brine pickle—vinegar, tequila, lemon juice, and water are only a few of the options. Bold combinations require taste/smell if you want to be secure in your improvisational choices. Brines should be too strong to enjoy straight. Fill the jar with cooking liquid, covering the vegetables by one-quarter inch.

Step 4. *Herb/spice*

Beet powder, turmeric, and curry powder work well for dying the pickle. Spices like dill seed, coriander, allspice, cloves, peppercorns, garlic, chiles, mustard seed, celery seed, fennel, horseradish, and cumin are easily infused into a brine.

Step 5. *Cover and wait*

A tight lid on the jar will seal it well. These pickles "cook" in the refrigerator. Because they are not canned with heat, they must be stored below 40°F (4°C); however, they will keep for a long time in the refrigerator.

Step 6. *Serving*

I like to sliver these pickles into very small, delicate pieces to accompany a meal as a raw dish condiment in the composition.

Pickles in a Paste

TECHNIQUE

Step 1. *Select a salty paste*

Miso, umeboshi paste, or rice bran soaked with salt water are good pastes to make a simple pickle. Herb/spice may be added, but when vegetables are mixed in a salt paste their liquids flavor each other.

Step 2. *Add vegetables*

Root family vegetables pickle well in this method. Their distinct tastes merge with each other and take on the flavor of the paste. The thicker the slices, the longer the vegetable takes to cook through. Liquid from wet vegetables thins out the paste in a good way.

Step 3. *Refrigerate*

Waiting for the pickles to ferment in a paste is quicker at room temperature; it may take only three days until the flavors have penetrated and the vegetable is limp. But unless stirring is a routine you don't mind adding to daily life, the refrigerator might be a more comfortable choice.

Step 4. *Serving*

Vegetables are pulled from the paste, rinsed well, and slivered for serving. They are served and eaten like a condiment.

Baking takes place in the middle of an oven, an environment where the pot is surrounded evenly by heat. The energetic quality of this method is gentle because fire approaches the food from a variety of heat sources and directions, the bottom, the top, and the sides. Convection ovens swirl the heat. Standard gas and electric ovens begin with heat from the bottom. By the time food is warmed through, heat is evenly supplied from all angles. A cover defines this technique because it is used for holding in moisture. Bake at 200°F–400°F (93°C–204°C), depending on how fast the primary element needs to cook by dinnertime. The average baking temperature is 350°F (177°C), but plant-based foods don't care how hot the oven is; their only concern is that they have enough liquid.

Grain (whole-dish)

Baked grain dishes are convenient. I use this method when my burners are busy, or when I have to leave the kitchen for a period of time. Grain opens into the amount of cooking liquid it is given, so measure the amount of grain to liquid (see table 2.3) and make sure the cover is in place. When a baked dish is finished cooking, all the liquid should be absorbed and a dark ring of crust will outline the dish. If the cover stays in place once the pot is removed from the oven, any bottom crust will steam away from the metal pan, making it easier to remove. When sautéing is used as a pretreatment, the added oil will help the edges of a baked dish release more easily. With a pretreatment on the stove top, the baking pan is preheated, which will save time in the oven. Dry roasting before baking is my favorite combination for opening grain; but if I don't sauté or dry roast, I preheat the pan by bringing the cooking liquid to a boil before adding the grain, sometimes infusing the liquid with an herb/spice. If the dish needs to have a finished appearance, I sauté decorative vegetables and herb/spice to add to it. When grains go to a second stage, then these pretreatments become less important.

Vegetables

Baked vegetables are moist. A covered pot keeps the natural liquid of vegetables in the pot, so flavors in mixed-vegetable dishes merge. Adding water dilutes the personality of the vegetable. I don't recommend adding any cooking liquid when baking vegetables. If the food is too dry, an onion family member, like leek or yellow onion, will contribute enough moisture without weakening the dish. It is only necessary to stir this dish once, after some caramelization has occurred. Too much stirring of soft vegetables breaks them apart. A baked potato, wrapped inside foil as the cover, creates a moist skin. But if the skin is leathery, the "baked" potato has been roasted, even if it is served whole.

Protein

Beans may be baked as a second-stage method. One way to do this is to combine them with vegetables and a sauce, making them into a casserole. Another way to bake beans is to blend them with decorative vegetables and nut butter (as oil) and shape the mixture into a pâté. Pâtés are complex and artistic. Beans provide the color and substance for multiple flavors that have hours to merge. The key for baking vegetable protein is oil. Oil protects beans from drying out and carries the many flavors of the supporting elements. Tofu and tempeh gain nothing from baking unless they are worked into a casserole or pâté. Gluten may be baked in a liquid as a first-stage method, turning it into seitan, or baked during a second or third stage in a sauce.

Baking Grain and Vegetables

Step 1. *Cut the vegetables into the desired shapes*

Cut the primary elements or decorative vegetables into shapes that fit the pot, the fork, or the platter. Allow for shrinkage.

Step 2. *Oil, herb/spice*

There are two ways to work oil into a baked grain or vegetable dish. One is the sauté method as a pretreatment for grain; the other is rubbing oil directly onto large vegetable pieces. If herb/spice is included in the dish, it should follow the oil in a sauté method or should be blended into a paste, beating the herb/spice category into the oil.

Step 3. *Salt*

Sea salt to fit is rubbed into vegetables or mixed into the paste. I use my hands to toss the ingredients, unless I use the sauté method of sealing where the food and pan are hot; then I use bamboo or wood. In a grain dish, sea salt dissolves into the cooking liquid.

Step 4. *Cover and bake*

A lid is important because in grain baking the liquid to grain measurement is precise, and in vegetable baking the liquid released from the vegetable is precious. If the cover is foil, I put the shiny side toward the food and make it tight. In some casserole forms, like lasagne, where an acidic ingredient such as tomato sauce will eat a hole in the foil, interface the foil with parchment paper.

Baking Beans, Casserole Form

Step 1. *Cut and seal decorative vegetables*

Decorative vegetables are cut to meet the size of the bean. The amount may be decorative or major. This depends on the meal's composition and the balance of protein and vegetables. Seal the vegetables in the baking pot to preheat it.

Step 2. *Add beans and herb/spice*

If herb/spice is not inherently part of the sauce, be generous and give seasonings time to bond with the oil.

Step 3. *The sauce*

A variety of binders work with this quick sauce method. Dissolve the binder in the cooking liquid in a container other than the baking pan. Here are just a few sauce possibilities: nut milk with flour, nut cream with wine, or tomato juice. Using a whisk, gently work the sauce into the vegetable bean mixture. It will thicken as the fire heats it. Adjust the amount of liquid until everything is smooth and you are confident that there is enough liquid to keep the dish moist and allow the ingredients to grow into it.

Step 4. *Salt to fit*

Sea salt will do most of the work to bring the many flavors of this complex dish together. Miso, tamari, umeboshi, and other salt seasonings work well in combination with salt crystals.

Step 5. *Cover and bake*

A cover that fits well is secured to the casserole. If using foil, place parchment paper between the food and the foil. The dish is done when the largest vegetable is fully cooked and there is a "glow" around the edge of the pot.

Bean Pâté

Step 1. *Blend decorative vegetables*

In a food processor, wet vegetables turn to liquid. Their color and flavor influence the pâté. An onion family member adds depth and substance.

Step 2. *Add cooked beans*

If liquefied decorative vegetables fill one-fourth of the food processor, beans should be double that amount.

Step 3. *Blend oil, herb/spice, and salt*

I use nut butter to obtain the creamy consistency needed for a pâté. One thick layer will do. It can be roasted or unroasted nut butter. Use roasted nut butter only if the flavor of the nut needs to show up. The herb/spice layers are heavy. These ingredients add multiplicity to the pâté. My favorite salt seasoning to use for a pâté is miso or umeboshi paste. These substances match the texture of the pâté. A liquid salt would make it too wet. Sea salt adds no flavor; it only reflects the ingredients from the other elements. The amount of salt paste should be one-third the amount of nut butter. Blend everything until smooth. Sea salt might be needed when using light-colored miso.

Step 4. *Bake in a pâté pan*

A pâté pan has two parts. One part is a container that holds the pâté. The other part fits on top, inside, and is strong enough to press the pâté from the top. Any shapes that can be pressed after the pâté is baked will work; I have used two mini bread pans, springform pans, and muffin tins. The pâté pan should be lined with parchment paper on the bottom and oiled on the sides. The mixture should fill the pan with at least 1/2 to 1 inch headspace (more for larger amounts) to allow the pâté to rise. Cover the pâté with parchment paper, smooth the top, and place a lightly secured piece of foil over it, shiny side down. Set the oven temperature between 250°F (121°C) and 350°F (177°C). I prefer the lowest temperature when I plan on baking the pâté for a longer time. The pâté is finished baking when the steam holes and surface color are even across the top.

Step 5. *Pressing*

Take the insert plate and put it directly on the pâté over the foil and parchment paper. Put a weight on the surface of the plate and leave it there until the pâté has reached room temperature. A weight can be a jar full of beans or a full and heavy teapot.

Step 6. *Serving and storing*

Pâtés develop flavor over time. If the pâté won't be eaten within two weeks, freezing is a good way to store it. A pâté may be served as a spread on bread or crackers, as a filling for scooped out peppers or tomatoes, or as a side dish as the protein in the meal.

ROASTING

Roasting, an energetically intense cooking method, is like baking without a cover. A shallow pan is used so that the heat reaches around the primary ingredients, which are only one layer thick. This way metal has a chance to burnish the food that touches it. This method requires oil as a protection. Unlike baking, roasting usually occurs at a high temperature (400°F/204°C). The texture of the roasted food is leathery to crisp on the outside and soft on the inside. Salt seasonings work best at the end of the cooking method so they don't burn. Roasting is a first-, second-, or third-stage method. It is different from dry roasting, which is a pretreatment, because, as a cooking method, roasting requires oil and salt.

Grain

The grain dishes that respond to roasting are second-stage polenta and mochi. These ethnic dishes are soft in the first stage, hard when cool, and then cut into shapes before roasting. Polenta is often prepared with cheese, giving it an inherent fat content. Mochi is soaked and mashed sweet rice, and it loves to be rubbed with a little oil before going on the roasting sheet.

Vegetables

Vegetables are a popular element to roast. Oil protects the surface, while salt pulls the natural moisture out of the vegetable, but only as far as the wall of oil. For a mixed-vegetable dish, roast different vegetable families on separate sheets; because they contain different amounts of moisture, they require different amounts of time with fire.

Protein

My favorite beans to roast are soybeans; roasting them is a first-stage method following soaking. You can add oil, herb/spice, and/or salt/seasonings, or dry roast the beans like nuts—both are delicious methods. Tempeh loves to be slathered with oil. Tofu, tempeh, and seitan/gluten all need a heavy-handed infusion of herb/spice. Roasting

is my favorite preparation for tofu when I want to add it to a pot pie or sauce or mix it with stir-fried vegetables.

Roasting

TECHNIQUE

Step 1. *Select size and shape of cut*

Vegetables will shrink during roasting. If they are small and thin, they will become leathery all around with little moisture on the inside, almost like a crouton or a chip. To prepare thick vegetables like winter squash, potatoes, or sweet potatoes that are roasted whole or in halves, I poke a fork into several areas of the body. With cut squash, the seeds are removed. Potatoes get poked halfway through roasting.

Step 2. *Oil, herb/spice, and salt*

Except for potatoes, vegetables need little herb/spice if at all, unlike tofu, tempeh, beans, and gluten that take a heavy hand. Oil goes directly onto the primary element unless making a paste with oil and herb/spice. Sea salt to fit touches the primary element after the oil is applied, or it is mixed into the paste, which completely surrounds the edges of the primary element.

Step 3. *Cook*

Roasting is best done in a preheated oven on a shallow baking sheet, but these are not critical. Plant-based foods will adjust to the heat at any temperature. Place the baking sheet near the bottom of the oven until the edges of the food "glow." Stir once the first side has a good seal; the first side usually takes the longest to cook. When roasting vegetables that will later be stuffed, like mushroom caps or squash, it is important to face the cavity up so that it collects the juices of the vegetables; these juices will disappear back into the cavity of the food as it continues to roast, heightening its flavor. Do not put these vegetables upside down, because then they will steam, especially if water is added to this method.

BROILING AND GRILLING

The energetic quality of broiling is like that of being inches away from the sun where even the strongest sun tanning lotion won't protect. This high-temperature cooking method (500°F/260°C) works best with ingredients that need little time in the fire and have some inherent moisture from fat or from being soaked or marinated. Stay in the room during this method, because food can go from perfectly done to scorched in a matter of seconds. Broiling coils are at the top of the oven, and the racks are placed in a position nearest them. Having only one layer of ingredients on the baking/broiling sheet will produce the best results. Grilling is similar to broiling, but the fire source is beneath the food and radiates up instead of radiating down from above. Grill marks are the signature of this method. In order to make marks, the steel grid has to be very hot, and there should be some oil to protect the food. For home cooks, the most common grill is the kind used out of doors. I think the origin of this method was a campfire, and animal-based protein was the most popular ingredient. Basting grilled and broiled primary elements helps keep them moist and instigates steam when the liquid hits the fire.

Grain

Broiling or grilling whole grain has no purpose. But I might butter or brush flat bread or slices of bread with an herb-flavored oil and broil it to create a quick toast.

Vegetables

Summer vegetables sliced thin respond well to a broiling method, like pattypan summer squash and tomatoes with basil. Grilling vegetables is popular, but I prefer this as a third-stage method if grill marks are the goal—steeped, marinated, and then marked on a grill.

Protein

Tofu, tempeh, and gluten require oil, herb/spice, and salt seasoning to make grilling/broiling a viable method. Marinating as a pretreatment brings moisture and basting liquid into this drying method. Then the marinade becomes a basting sauce. The best way to use this method for vegetable protein is as a second- or third-stage method.

Broiling and Grilling

TECHNIQUE

Step 1. *Preheat the broiler or grill*

Set the rack near the top of the broiler; scrape and oil the grill. Turn the fire to high or adjust the broiling indicator on the thermostat.

Step 2. *Prepare the ingredients and select the pan*

Cut the ingredients to size, knowing that vegetables will shrink. Large pieces will fit on a grill without falling through, but small pieces are best in a special grilling pan that allows the flame to touch parts of the vegetables. Skewers are good for presentation and an effective technique to keep small pieces from falling into the flames. Soak bamboo skewers before grilling/broiling to keep them from catching on fire.

Step 3. *Oil, herb/spice, and salt*

If oil, herb/spice, and salt are not in the primary ingredients or in their marinade, they need to be applied before the food touches the grill. A paste with oil, herb/spice, and salt or salt seasonings can be applied once before cooking and then used repeatedly to baste, stroking the primary ingredients with a brush as they cook.

Step 4. *Turning and finishing*

Cook on the first side for one-half to two-thirds of the entire cooking time. I turn the food only once, but this is a personal choice. Having grill marks is the signature of this method. The less turning, the deeper the marks.

SLOW COOKING

Slow cooking and stir-frying are as different as hip-hop dancing and a waltz. Slow cooking does not mean the dish is on the fire for a long time. It means that through the technique of this method, the vegetable will be romanced, coaxed, and warmed into giving up its flavor and essence. Some vegetables are quicker to do this than others. For example, root vegetables benefit from more heat. Leafy green vegetables require less time under fire. So spinach will be slow cooked in 2 minutes and carrots in 30 or more.

The energetic opposite of stir-frying, slow cooking creates a soft texture and is for vegetables only. This intimate cooking method merges flavors when using more than one ingredient. As a single-vegetable dish, this method emphasizes the flavor of the vegetable because it cooks in its own juices. No extra cooking liquid is added. This method is easy to do in a pan with a tight lid and a heavy bottom. It is not the same as sautéing, because even though the first step seals the vegetables, they do not have to "leap" over a high flame. And it is the placement and use of salt in this method that manages the transformation.

One day, more than 30 years ago, I was cooking with some friends. We thought we were doing a stir-fry. Oil went into the wok, vegetables into the oil, stir, stir, stir, stir, it was getting dry. "Shall we add more oil?" my friend asked. I was in deep observation. Good grief, I thought, we had already added oil twice. Then a message came through: Just use salt. I didn't understand, but I followed the voice and salted the two layers, continuing to stir. Within a few seconds small beads of moisture decorated the vegetables. As we moved them around, their color became brighter. Today I call that a half-assed stir-fry, but to make an authentic method out of that information, I call it slow cooking and deliberately don't stir, capturing the precious moisture with a cover.

Grain

Slow cooking is not appropriate for first-stage grain.

Vegetables

All vegetables benefit from this method. I explore new ingredients in the slow-cook method because it tells me how much moisture each plant has, and it reveals their personalities. An onion combined with drier vegetables like potatoes, burdock root, and winter squash will bring moisture. The longer a root vegetable slow cooks the sweeter it becomes. Rutabaga and turnips have many complex flavors and this method highlights all of them. Slow-cooked vegetables are often thought of as overcooked because they are soft. This is a great method to store fire. The longer the vegetables cook, the more fire power enters them. Often a dish cooked in this method becomes a step in a larger vision, such as vegetables prepared for a pot pie or spanakopita. If keeping vegetables crisp is important, press or stir-fry them; these methods honor the taste and texture of "crisp."

Protein

Slow cooking is not appropriate for vegetable protein. However, protein dishes prepared with other cooking methods are good added to slow-cooked vegetables.

Slow Cooking

Step 1. *Numbers and cuts*

A suitable cut for this vegetable method allows the surface area of a vegetable to touch the metal.

Step 2. *Heat pan*

Warm the pan or skillet to control the amount of oil. If the pan is too hot the oil will smoke, which is not optimal, but a hot pan can easily be remedied in the next step.

Step 3. *Add oil and first vegetable*

The amount of oil I use in this step is relative to the kind of vegetable being cooked and how much I can afford in my meal. Vegetables like eggplant, mushrooms, and potatoes drink oil, so I use more with them than with onions, celery, or cabbages, where the oil rolls off the vegetable easily. For taste, I like to use as much oil as my meal composition will allow because it moves the flavors in this dish, and the more oil there is to carry the flavors, the more luscious the taste. But it is not necessary to use more than one very thin layer for most vegetables. If the meal has any dishes that are heavy in oil like nut sauce or tempura, use little oil in the slow cook.

Determining the first vegetable to cook in this mixed-vegetable dish is subjective. These are my guidelines: Almost always use an onion first, because onions are very wet and the oil prevents their juices from running all over the place. Plus they leave oil for the next vegetable. Root vegetables usually follow onions, and vegetables that grow from the ground upward go into the pot in their growing order. There are two exceptions: mushrooms and burdock root. Mushrooms demand first place. They sponge up oil and release it only after they have used it. Burdock doesn't soak in the oil like mushrooms. Instead, it releases a sharp odor in the first moments of cooking, kind of like a skunk. So when burdock has a first chance at the oil, the other vegetables are protected because the burdock has been sealed.

Step 4. *Add other vegetables*

Give each vegetable a chance to shift from raw to sealed before adding another. It is time to add the second vegetable when the onions become clear, not caramelized (that is too late), when carrots are brighter orange by a shade, or when mushrooms are squeaking and colored from golden to dark brown.

Step 5. *Add salt and cover*

Once the vegetables appear half cooked and sealed, sprinkle salt crystals to fit across the top of the vegetables. Toss the vegetables to help them sweat, then cover the pan immediately to capture the natural moisture. The vegetables then cook in their own juices. If the vegetables don't begin to release moisture, add another layer of sea salt.

Step 6. *Reduce flame and cook*

Stir once or twice, taking care not to break the vegetables by overstirring them. Notice if there is liquid in the lid of the pot. If the taste is slightly short of exquisite, add a layer of finishing salt. I will minimize salt in step 5 to allow for the addition of a finishing salt. It brings in another dimension of taste. A flame tamer protects dry vegetables when slow cooking.

I teach this as a method, not as a dish. The difference is that a dish is defined by the choice of vegetables, oil, herb/spice, cooking liquid, and salt that go into it. A method opens up the opportunity to create a dish using any of the ingredients from the elemental categories. For example, most people associate this method with Asian vegetables, sesame oil, ginger, and garlic for herb/spice, and tamari/shoyu for salt seasoning. To change the ethnicity of the dish, change the elements using basil and garlic with olive oil for broccoli or kale (Italian), or curry with sunflower oil for cauliflower and snap peas (Indian). Stir-frying is one of the most intense cooking experiences the cook and the food can have. I learned to stir-fry from a Japanese chef. It was an awakening. Stir-frying is three separate steps. These steps have to be in sequence, the timing guided by a sequential brightening of color. Watch closely, as the vegetables darken and shine with each step. Unlike the soft texture of slow-cooked vegetables, stir-fried vegetables are famous for their crispness. Crunchy yet thoroughly cooked is their trademark. Stir-frying is not doing an incomplete job of slow cooking, removing vegetables before they are cooked so that they will be crunchy.

Grain

Grain is not an element that responds to stir-frying techniques. The closest method for grain is the second-stage braise or refry.

Vegetables

This cooking method is only for wet character vegetables. The only roots that work are watery ones like daikon radish. The best families for this method are onion, leaf, vine, fungus, fruit, and stalk. Vegetable flowers—cauliflower and broccoli—are best cooked alone through all three steps and then added to a mixed dish, because they require more flashes of ice water than the wet vegetables. Use small portions of each vegetable because there has to be room to move them quickly.

Protein

Protein in a vegetable stir-fry dish doesn't go through the technical steps of the stir-fry method. When vegetable protein is part of a stir-fried dish, it needs to be cooked separately and completely with oil, herb/spice, and salt first. Then it will be good company for a vegetable stir-fry.

Stir-Frying

TECHNIQUE

Step 1. *Prep*

Have all the ingredients ready before turning on the fire. Vegetables should be cut, and the order they will go in the pot (first, second, third, and so on) should be determined in advance. The tendency is to cut vegetables too small. Wet vegetables shrink under intense heat. Salt, oil, and ice water need to be kept at hand. Ice water should be in a container that pours small amounts easily; this is my favorite use for a measuring cup. Open the oil bottle.

Step 2. *Heat pan*

This method works in a wok or a skillet, on a gas or electric burner. Whichever you choose, watch the fire relationship to the pan. Remove the grate from the gas stove and set the wok directly on the burner so that the flames are driven up the sides. Imagine a small campfire. The bottom of the wok will remain cooler than the sides. Food cooks when it hits the sides of the wok, which are scorching hot. In a skillet, the heat is on the bottom of the pan and there isn't much room up the sides, unless the pot is a Dutch oven or casserole.

Step 3. *Seal*

Drop only a small amount of oil in the center of the wok. Sealing, the first part of stir-frying, seals the cut vegetables against the metal, protecting the individual character of each vegetable. This step is why onions still taste like onions, celery like celery, after being stir-fried. The first vegetable, usually onions, will be in the hot pot the longest. Don't wait to add the next vegetable. As soon as the first vegetable looks shiny, which means oil has glimmered its sides, add the next vegetable without missing a beat, stirring the entire time. In a mixed dish, small portions of each vegetable are added in this manner, one at a time. Use a long-handled wooden or bamboo paddle to stir the vegetables in the tempo of "Jingle Bells," with enthusiasm.

Step 4. *Salt to fit*

This step requires sea salt crystals, not salt seasonings. Soy sauce will burn and is not strong enough to transform the vegetable from the inside out. The amount to use is guided by the quickness with which the vegetable begins to release its juices. A clear sauce will balance oversalting. Vegetables won't change color unless there is enough salt. They should turn a shade brighter and shinier from salting.

Step 5. *Steam*

The pan is terrifically hot by this time, since the high heat has not been reduced, so when a small splash of ice water hits the side of the pan, it creates steam, which feels just as hot as the fire. Keep moving the vegetables, humming in the rhythm of "Jingle Bells." The wetter the character of the vegetables, as with snow peas, green beans, napa cabbage, and zucchini, the fewer splashes are required. Broccoli and cauliflower, and some cabbages, require more dousing. Let the water dry out completely between splashes. The color should be vibrant at this point. Remove the entire group of vegetables quickly and begin again. There is no need to wash the wok between batches unless something sticks, which won't happen if water is the splashing liquid.

BRAISING

Braising imposes flavor on primary elements. Whereas the objective of most other cooking methods is to bring out the personality and character of a vegetable, grain, or protein, braising is a chance to influence the dish by bringing in additional ingredients. The trick is to not overwhelm the delicate ingredients. This is a two-step dish. Sealing and steeping are the techniques required. After the primary element is sealed, a special braising liquid steeps into it. This liquid is created by combining a liquid salt seasoning, character cooking liquids, and herbs and spices.

Grain

This method reinvents grain that has been refrigerated or left on the counter for a couple days. The ratio of salt seasoning to liquid is equal parts of each. I rarely use water as the braising liquid for grain because water dilutes the flavors and adds nothing new. If water is the choice, then I call this method a reheat, not a redo.

Vegetables

Braising liquids need to match the strength of the vegetable. Strength is measured in two dimensions—flavor and substance. For example, potatoes are a bland flavor and sturdy substance, so they benefit from an intensely flavored braising liquid. Lettuce is also a mild flavor, but it has a lightweight substance, so the braising liquid will be mild. Mild is controlled by the character of salt seasoning and cooking liquids, and by the amount that is steeped into the food. The element that controls this strength is the salt category, because creating a braising liquid always begins with salt. Too much salt to fit will yield too much braising liquid. If there is extra braising liquid at the end of steeping it will become a sauce. A sour salt seasoning plus a sour cooking liquid will need to be modified with water to reduce its intensity.

Protein

All forms of protein are good braised. An infused braising liquid turns bland beans, tofu, tempeh, and gluten into complete dishes that may then be combined with finished grain or vegetable dishes.

Braising

TECHNIQUE

You can either create a braising liquid from ingredients at hand or use a liquid that is salty, like pickle juice, sauerkraut juice, or caper brine.

Step 1. *Cut and seal*

Almost any kind of cut will do. Larger pieces hold up well to make a statement on the plate, whereas small ones are nice as a decorative element in a first-stage grain dish. Seal vegetables in a preheated skillet or, for large quantities, use the broiler. The amount of oil needed is only enough to surround the vegetables.

Step 2. *Making a braising liquid from scratch*

Braising liquids begin with pouring the correct amount of salt seasoning using the layering method. If using miso, estimate the amount by imagining the paste spread across the major ingredient for each layer. Estimate how many layers of salt the dish requires. Hold a separate bowl in one hand at the edge of the pan that contains the sealed food. A liquid salt seasoning is in the other hand. As if the salt seasoning would fall into the primary ingredient, catch it in the bowl instead of moving the bowl across the pan to fit. Looking at the amount of salt seasoning, double it with a character cooking liquid. This liquid is then ready for braising grain. For vegetables and beans, once this character liquid is on top of the salt seasoning, add a mild cooking liquid, like water or juice; the amount should be equal to the total amount of both salt and cooking liquid. Use bean juice in place of water for braising beans, if it is available.

Step 3. *Add braising liquid and steep*

Steeping can take place in the same pan as the sealing, or move the primary ingredient from the broiler to a suitable pot. Essentially the liquid will disappear when the vegetable is done. The braising liquid may appear to be more than is needed for steeping in water, but braised vegetables and protein dishes are designed to have a sauciness when finished. Grain absorbs all the liquid. The braising liquid should steep slowly, covered. Use a flame tamer when necessary to prevent burning. Braising also works in the oven. The dish is done when the primary element has absorbed enough liquid to be reheated.

TERIYAKI

Japanese friends revealed this method to me when we were discussing language. The cooking method came to mind when she defined the word "teriyaki": *teri* means glazed, and *yaki* means fried. Learning that the Japanese language is in reverse of English, I decided that I would fry (seal) first and then glaze to finish. I also thought teriyaki was a kind of sauce that used tamari, ginger, and garlic. But the key to this sauce is the sugar category, because sugar creates the glaze. Applying the ingredient variations available in the sugar category, I began exploring this delightful cooking method. Soon brussels sprouts were prepared teriyaki-style with umeboshi and rice syrup, and burdock root was done teriyaki-style with tamari and mirin. The technique is easy and pleases most palates because there is a balance of fat, sugar, and salt. My choice of sweeteners includes rice syrup, barely malt, mirin (a rice sherry), agave, and diluted unrefined cane sugar. Teriyaki is a first-stage method suitable for vegetables, tofu, tempeh, and seitan.

Vegetables

Dry vegetables, like burdock root, may have a crisp/candied edge to them when prepared teriyaki-style. Because I don't usually use a sweetener in savory cooking, teriyaki vegetables are used as a decorative contribution to a simple grain dish or as a garnish for a soup.

Protein

This is a favorite method for slabs of tofu, thin pieces of tempeh, and scant strips of gluten.

Teriyaki

TECHNIQUE

Step 1. *Heat the skillet*

Don't use too large or too small a skillet. If your skillet is too large, excess oil will bond to the pan, making it hard to clean (unless it is made of cast iron). If your skillet is too small, the primary element will be piled and won't be evenly exposed to the surface of the pan. The vegetables need to be in a single layer in order for all the edges to make contact with the metal of the skillet.

Step 2. *Seal in oil*

The amount of oil is slightly generous in this method, as most of the cooking happens during the sauté step. Take enough time to cook the vegetables or protein until almost tender before finishing off the dish. Don't salt during this step because it will pull moisture from the vegetables. This step takes the longest time.

Step 3. *Herb/spice*

Because the primary elements cook for such a long time in oil, add the herb/spice category toward the end of sealing. If the herb/spice category requires a liquid spice, such as ginger juice or lemon/lime oil, add this after the glazing process in step 4.

Step 4. *Glaze with a form of sweetener*

Add liquid sweetener to create a glaze. The amount is flexible. When malt sweeteners are heated, they thin out. The longer they cook, the harder they become when they cool. Move the vegetables around in the sweetener until they look shiny.

Step 5. *Salt to fit*

It is easy to burn the dish at this point. If your pots, like mine, are quite heavy and retain an intense heat for a long time, avoid burning by turning off the fire before adding the salt, especially when using a liquid salt seasoning. Toss the vegetables and then remove them from the pan.

MARINATING

One of the most popular methods suitable for all primary elements, marinating penetrates food, adding a broad range of intensity and flavors from mild to dynamic as easily as if sitting in a cool bath. Notice how salt and oil are used differently in the preparation of each element. Marinating is a second-stage method for grain, vegetables, and plant protein. Marinating requires a marinade-style cold sauce. Details for inventing this sauce are on page 86. It takes five minutes to prepare a marinated dish, and it will last a week in the refrigerator. Grain, vegetable, and plant protein marinades take the form of salad. Alternatively, these marinated primary elements may be used decoratively.

Grain

Tabouli is the most famous grain marinade. Traditionally, it must have bulgur as the primary element, olive oil as the oil, lemon juice as cooking liquid, fresh mint for herb/spice, sea salt, and parsley as a major amount of decorative veg-

etable. Variations to this simple dish can be exquisite, but I don't call them tabouli—they are a grain marinade. It's fun to play with the texture of first-stage grain for a marinade. Dry roasting gives it a nutty flavor and prepares the individual grains to soak up the cold sauce. I also like to give some background flavor to the grain, so I infuse the cooking liquid with a strong dose of spice and color, such as turmeric or curry. Use an equal amount of decorative vegetables as grain, because they soak up the sauce and distribute it evenly throughout the grain, adding beauty. The ratio of oil to cooking liquid for grain marinade is 1:5. This is a low dose because grain needs little protection. The function of oil in this dish is simply to carry the flavor. Using too much oil makes the grain heavy and seals it, making it difficult for the infusion to take place. The high ratio of cooking liquid makes this cold sauce very strong, too strong for a vegetable, but strong enough to penetrate the density of whole grain over time. Unlike vegetable and protein marinades, grain marinade completely absorbs the sauce. If sauce is showing at the bottom of the bowl after an hour of sitting, there is too much, and more grain should be added.

Vegetables

Marinating vegetables is my favorite way to keep a vegetable dish for days. Marinated vegetables are a worthy addition to salads and bean pâté sandwiches. Decorative vegetables aren't required in a vegetable marinade because the vegetables' color is enough, but speckles of grain or protein may be used as decorative ingredients. The ratio of oil to cooking liquid in a vegetable marinade is 1:1 or 1:2, depending on the density of the vegetable. Vegetable marinades contain more oil than grain marinades, because with vegetables the oil functions as protection. Above-the-ground vegetables need the higher ratio of oil to cooking liquid (1:1) than below-the-ground vegetables; and then any remaining marinade may be used as a light dressing for leafy greens, which are the most delicate. Beets and potatoes appreciate the higher oil to liquid ratio (2:1) because they are dense and can handle the stronger liquid input. Water dilutes the SFS in marinades, so the only time to use it is when nut butter is the oil.

Protein

Bean marinades make a popular salad, especially if the total amount of decorative vegetables is equal to the amount of beans, which prevents overloading on bean protein. The ratio of oil to cooking liquid in a bean marinade is 1:3. Only use first-stage beans that have integrity. That means the skin is intact and the inside is soft. When beans are cool, they firm up, but the inside "meat" of the bean will be evenly colored throughout, no white parts. The key technique in creating protein marinades lies in the salt category. Beans do not have salt in the first-stage method, so when determining the amount of salt needed in the cold sauce, take into consideration the quantity of beans when you count the layers. Tofu, tempeh, and gluten utilize the marinade method as a third stage. Adjust the salt in the cold sauce accordingly.

Marinating

TECHNIQUE

Step 1. *Create a cold sauce to fit the bowl*

This procedure requires picking the container that will hold all the elements—the cold sauce, the decorative vegetables, and the primary elements. There should be one-half to one inch of cold sauce in the bowl for a full bowl of decorative and primary elements. (For information on making cold sauces, see page 85.)

Step 2. *Decorative vegetables*

Decorative vegetables are important in grain and bean marinades. Lightweight vegetables break up the heavy concentration of grain and beans. They are usually raw and wet like cucumber, onion, bell pepper. Parsley, cilantro, and arugula may function as both decorative vegetables and herb/spice when used abundantly. These wet vegetables dilute the intensity of a cold sauce that is too strong. Decorative vegetables also define where the cold sauce is among the beans and grain, showing an even distribution. If decorative vegetables enter the marinade dish after the primary element, they have less opportunity to take on the flavor of the marinade and will taste separate and unincorporated into the dish as a whole. I don't like the texture of raw carrots in a grain or bean marinade, so I steep them first.

Step 3. *Soaking primary element*

Grain, vegetables, beans, tofu, tempeh, and seitan need to soak in the cold sauce for a minimum of an hour. If vinegar is used in the cooking liquid, refrigerate the protein dish, because the sour taste needs to be from the cooking liquid, not from a fermenting primary element. Fermentation of protein is undesirable, not only for taste but for health. Vinegar, lemon/lime juices, and other sour cooking liquids speed up the decomposition of protein, which is increased at room temperature or warmer.

REFRYING

Although this method can be used to reheat primary elements, I usually create a new dish and make this a second-stage method. By using oil with a new decorative or major vegetable, and/or some herb/spice category in the oil, a dish is recreated. Refrying is a very quick cooking method, similar to braising except it does not use any additional cooking liquid. I choose refrying when there is enough moisture in the first-stage grain, protein, or vegetable to be reheated. This method is my favorite for using salt seasoning, umeboshi, tamari, and miso. Salt seasoning here is used in place of sea salt to balance the amount of oil used in sealing. The primary ingredients have already been salted in their first-stage method, except for beans. So the power of salt only needs to be in the liquid form, which adds interest. Salt crystals need liquid to be dissolved, and in this method, there is no additional liquid.

Grain

The irony of saying "fried rice" is that I usually include mirin, which, because it is a cooking liquid, makes it a braising method. This is a good example of how the language of cooking is for the cook, not the diners. I tell my family the dish is fried rice, knowing that I braised it. I can't think of one grain that doesn't work in this method. It is more challenging with wet, sticky grain, like amaranth, teff, and Job's tears, but they respond to this method well enough. The amount of oil used in refrying is variable. The more oil used, the more opportunity of gaining a lovely crust. But the quantity of oil is not important. A true refried grain dish uses grain with moisture in it. If grain is dry, then I braise it.

Vegetables

Refrying vegetables is popular with potatoes. Other applications include creating spreads with soft vegetables; for example, pressure-steamed

cauliflower for dinner becomes refried for lunch the next day when it is mashed with oil and herb/spice, and umeboshi vinegar is used as a finishing salt. This spread goes on bread or crackers. When a whole carrot is steeped, cut, and refried, it shines on the plate.

Protein

Tofu, tempeh, and beans love this method. It is easy, tasty, and quick. They don't loose their identity; instead, it is enhanced. These bean proteins have no salt in the first stage, so working an interesting salt into this second stage is natural. As with fried rice, I use a cooking liquid with the classic dish "refried beans." Often this is the bean's cooking liquid, which doesn't impart additional flavors. First-stage beans that have integrity have just the right texture to shape into a patty. Very small, almost minced decorative vegetables and salt can be worked into this form before refrying.

Refrying

TECHNIQUE

Step 1. *Heat skillet*

My first choice is a cast iron skillet. I like the way it works with oil—some oil is for the food, some for the skillet—and it is easy to clean. Warming the skillet before adding oil allows the oil to move easily and enables you to see more precisely how much oil is in the pan.

Step 2. *Oil and first vegetable*

Oil and the first vegetable go into the pot together. Don't move the oil around a hot pot without a vegetable. Stir vegetables, one at a time, into the oil, and arrange them into a layer across the bottom of the skillet covering its floor. Decorative vegetables go into the skillet in order of how they grow—from beneath the earth upward—with the onion family going in first.

Step 3. *Herb/spice and primary element*

Dry herbs and spices enter after the vegetables have had a chance to seal, but before the primary element is added. They might dry out the vegetables as they bond to the oil, making a paste, but there is no need for more oil. Carrots or other below-the-ground vegetables should be approximately 70 percent cooked before adding the primary ingredient. Mixing the primary element with the oil, vegetables, and herb/spice until the decorative vegetables are speckled throughout assures me that oil has touched the grain, protein, or vegetable and now it can cook.

Step 4. *Cooking and salting*

Because salt is the final step, the primary element should be heated thoroughly first. To have a crust, be generous with oil and don't stir the dish until a crust forms on the bottom. This is one of the few times a metal spatula, acting like a shovel, peeks underneath to see if a crust if forming. When the crust is established, turn the mixture over once, draw a salt seasoning across the top to fit, and continue cooking slowly, if needed. This whole process takes 5–10 minutes.

DEEP-FRYING

Deep-frying is my special, cold-weather event. Notice the placement of salt in this method. Each food group handles salt differently. Most often it lies in a companion soup or cold dipping sauce.

Batters with sugar and salt attract excessive oil, giving this method a bad reputation (think of doughnuts and french fries). Good technique combined with good oil is not unhealthful. Proper deep-frying uses very little oil, less than pan frying. A fresh oil may be used about three times if it is kept clean during cooking and refrigerated as soon as it cools. After that I use it in bread or for making popcorn.

Grain

Deep-frying is a second-stage method for grain. In order to create a suitable texture in the first-stage method (so the grain will hold a croquette form), pressure cooking cold to cold is recommended. Decorative vegetables need to be minced for croquettes to prevent cracks in the form. Cracks allow oil to seep into the grain. Deep-frying is meant to cook just the outside of the croquette while it warms the inside. Croquettes need smooth edges and a solid center. Like a snowball pressed tightly so that it can travel through the air without falling apart, croquettes need to be pressed tightly to withstand hot oil. When free-form rice is dropped into hot oil, it puffs and crisps, making a crunchy garnish for a simple vegetable dish or just a snack.

Vegetables

There are two approaches to deep-frying vegetables. With the first approach, vegetables are dropped directly into hot oil without protection. With the second, vegetables are coated with a batter (tempura) that creates a crisp wall for the vegetables to steam inside. The challenge of direct deep-frying is with how salt is used. Starchy vegetables require pressing/wilting as a first stage. To avoid using salt crystals directly on cooked food, use a cold dipping sauce as the vehicle for salt. Salt is needed to make the oil in this dish digestible.

TEMPURA BATTER

A good tempura batter is crisp on the outside and transparent enough to see the vegetable on the inside. Keeping the vegetable cold is important before and during the cooking process to create contrast between the hot oil and the cold vegetable. This method of deep-frying uses the least amount of oil. Mix equal parts of the following flour mixture with sparkling water. The flour mixture is comprised of equal parts of brown rice flour, unbleached white flour, arrowroot flour, and either sweet rice flour, for a white batter, or corn flour (not cornmeal), for a golden batter.

Protein

Deep-frying vegetable protein is very easy and satisfying. For beans, it is a first-stage method. For tofu and tempeh, it is a second-stage method. Seitan can be deep-fried as a first-, second-, or third-stage method. Falafel is the most famous bean croquette. I like to deep-fry steeped gluten/seitan, but since any flavors from the steeping or cooking liquids (including salt) will migrate into the oil, this is the last time I will use it.

Deep-Frying

TECHNIQUE

Step 1. *Prepare primary element*

Grain

First stage, cold to cold, add decorative elements, and press into forms for croquette. Make the edges smooth and the body dense enough to withstand light pressure for 5 seconds before it falls apart. I place my hands under running water at the sink and shake off the excess water before I dip them into the bowl of grain that is waiting to become croquettes. A handful of grain, with little pieces of cilantro or lemon zest, is pressed between both hands, firmly. Because I am right-handed, the ball of grain is placed in my left hand. The fingers of my right hand cup the ball as it balances in my left palm between the heel of my hand and my tightly bound fingers. Gentle pressure is applied so the croquette takes shape. Equal force between the heel and fingers of the left hand against the pressure of the right hand's fingers smoothes the edges and forms triangles, logs, or ovals.

Vegetables

Clean and cut vegetables into various sizes according to their density. The pieces should be small enough to eat in one or two easy bites. Since the vegetables will be in the oil just a short time, root vegetables need to be cut thin ($1/4$ inch thick) and mushrooms may be whole, halved, or quartered, depending on their size. Trim the stem but leave the "stump" in the cap for better cooking. When using the tempura batter method, cut vegetables can wait to be cooked; store them separately in covered containers in the refrigerator so they stay chilled. If the vegetables will cook without a batter, keep them in salt water. To do this, heavily salt the vegetables to fit, and then cover them with cold water. When the oil is ready, remove the vegetables from the cold water and towel them dry before cooking.

Protein

Beans are soaked, drained, and blended with all the ingredient categories except oil. To make a falafel-style bean ball, one light-handed layer of baking powder to fit creates space inside the dense mixture, allowing complete cooking of this first-stage bean dish. Shape the mixture into small, flat balls. Seitan, tofu, and tempeh need no protection or preparation for direct deep-frying, but they should be patted dry before they go into the oil. If a batter is used for these vegetable proteins, they will turn into more interesting dishes if, prior to deep-frying, they go through an entire first- or second-stage method.

Step 2. *Heat oil*

Safflower oil may be mixed with a smaller portion of coconut or palm oil as an option. If I used a thermometer, it would read between 375°F (191°C) and 400°F (204°C). Instead of using a thermometer, however, I watch for the oil to move. When it shimmers at the surface like a still pond being attacked by a mosquito, I test the oil with a sample of free-form grain or a drop of tempura batter. Grain and bean croquettes will drop to the bottom of the pot of oil and resurface in a full one one-thousand second. Vegetable tempura takes one-eighth the time.

Step 3. *Cook primary element*

Lower the element close to the surface of the oil, separate the fingers holding it, letting it gently fall into the oil as the hand moves directly up and away. This way there is no reaction that could create the painful "hot oil in eye." For tempura, either cooking chopsticks or fingers move the vegetables around in the batter and lift it out of the batter without dragging the sides on the bowl, as is natural with a paintbrush. Dragging it would remove the batter, which is there to protect the vegetable. Excess batter that drips into the oil should be skimmed out quickly to prevent the oil from smoking. This also keeps the oil clean. It's very important not to let oil get into the batter, so the chopsticks must not touch the oil on delivery. If they do, wipe them dry and begin again.

Vegetables cook more quickly than grain and beans. In order to prevent the oil from getting too hot or too cold, put a continuous supply of new, cool primary elements into the oil as soon as the bubbles from the previous supply slow down. The slower the bubbles, the more cooked the food.

Step 4. *Remove from oil*

Grain, vegetables, and beans are done when the outer edge is hard. They do not have to brown. The newer the oil, the lighter the finished color. Use an oil skimmer to collect several items at a time, tipping the strainer against the side of the pot to let excess oil drain back into it, instead of draining onto paper towels or into the food.

BLENDING

The blending method uses many tools: the molcajete, a whisk, two forks back-to-back, a blender, a food processor, or an extruder. I select my tool in relation to the weight of what I am blending. A molcajete is used for soft, solid oil, like nut butter and avocado. It also mashes garlic more deliciously than a garlic press. Two forks back-to-back are my whisk, when I can't find the wire one. They blend lightweight sauces, like the emulsion of oil and cooking liquid in marinades. The shape of an electric blender determines its efficiency in blending liquids. I prefer blenders with a narrow base and wide opening. The food processor is designed to mix more solid substances, breaking them down into a spreadable consistency. An extruder is used for solid, crushed ingredients that maintain texture better than a food processor would, like sprouted bread dough.

Grain

Before blending, grain is soaked to soften and awaken the germ, which then sprouts. When sprout tails are as long as the body of the grain, blend the grain with supporting elements—cooking liquid, oil, herb/spice, and decorative vegetables—to prepare a "living" cracker, bread, or dessert form to be dehydrated. Cooked grain may be blended before it is shaped into patties, croquettes, or loaves.

Vegetables and Fruit

Take color and taste into account if you want to design a blended dish with fruit and vegetables. Determine whether the dish will be a soup, sauce, pâté, or beverage, where flavors and color merge. The theory of numbers will apply to keep the dish focused on a primary element, enhanced by decorative and supporting elements.

Protein

Nuts and seeds used for living food dishes require soaking before blending. But beans require the full transformation of a first-stage cooking method before they become part of a sauce, soup, or spread. Cooked protein forms that require blending are pâté, soup, sauce, and patty or loaf.

Blending

TECHNIQUE

Step 1. *Select equipment for blending*

Use a blender for liquid forms like soups, sauces, and dips. Thicker substances, like nut butters, spreads, fillings, and preparations for dehydrating, are best in a food processor. An extruder, which is most easily found on juicers that have long noses and blank inserts where the screens are placed, is best for substances that do not have cooking liquid added—frozen fruit, sprouted grains, uncooked nuts.

Step 2. *Follow directions for blending*

With a blender, begin on a low speed so you can see how far up the liquid rises. Once you see how much the food will expand, it is safe to turn up the speed. This is most important with hot liquids. For added safety with hot liquids, place a hand towel over the container and stand back, taking care not to hold the lid down. Holding the lid may seem like a natural move to help the blender do its job, but it is unnecessary and a waste of time.

SPROUTING

I know that a seed is powerful when I see the activity of sprouting. Seeds sprout in two directions. One end goes into the earth; the other rises above it. When a grain or bean does not sprout, I suspect genetically altered growing methods, which can produce sterile seeds that don't reproduce. Since the healing value of food lies in the power of the seed, sprouting is the ultimate view for potential life.

Grain

Sprouting whole grain requires air, water, and time in the dark. It is a slow method that takes approximately 30 hours. Small grain take less time to sprout. I use grain sprouts as a decorative ingredient in salads and as the body of bread, crackers, cookies, cakes, bars and rejuvelac in living cuisine.

Vegetables

Sprouted vegetable seeds, such as radish, fenugreek, fennel, broccoli, and alfalfa, embellish any living food dish. Their unusual and often potent taste is welcome in a soup, sauce, cracker, spread, or salad.

Protein

Beans, nuts, and seeds in sprouted form have many variations. I usually only eat a sprouted bean that has been fully transformed, which means the sprout tail is longer than the original body of the bean. Think of mung bean sprouts. This method uses up the entire reproductive capacity of the bean, thereby making it digestible. I shy away from eating sprouts of long-term beans that don't grow long tails, like chickpeas. When nuts sprout, they separate and split down the middle. But few nuts actually sprout because they need a house or skin from which to charge through. For example, almonds have a thick skin. When they sprout, the tail peeks through the skin. Cashews, on the other hand, have a shell that is removed before it comes to market. The shell contains a strong liquid toxin, so sprouting a cashew is not possible. Seeds that have shells sprout beautifully, like sunflower seeds. Once the sprout has grown past the shell, it is ready to eat; the shell is removed before serving.

Sprouting

TECHNIQUE

Step 1. *Soak*

Soaking begins the sprouting process; as seeds fill up with water, the swelling supports the sprout to grow. Place seeds in a wide-mouth glass jar. Cover the seeds with water by 2 inches. Secure the top with a screen cover. Place a dark-colored hand towel over the top. There are many styles of containers for sprouting. A lightweight colored cloth provides a dark place where sprouts can grow. A vertical jar, open on top with a screen secured around its neck, is another option. There are commercial sprouting jar covers available with screen-like openings; alternatively, you can use cheesecloth or window or door screens, custom cut into a shape to fit the top of the jar and secured with a fat rubber band.

Step 2. *Rinse, drain, and sprout*

Usually rinsing twice a day is enough to give moisture to the growing seed. Cover the seeds with water. Pour off any excess, and reposition the container so the sprouts will drain. This action should be repeated at least twice a day until the sprouts are ready. To encourage green tops, remove the dark cloth and expose the sprouts to light. Move the sprouts around in the jar while rinsing to prevent mold from growing.

Step 3. *Storing sprouts*

Sprouting can take three days to a week. Timing the sprouting process so that fresh sprouts are a daily food is as powerful a ritual as brushing teeth. Cut sprouts may last a couple days in the refrigerator, but it's best to eat them as they mature.

DEHYDRATING

Some of my favorite foods to store for the winter are fresh corn off the cob, tomatoes, onions, and Colorado peaches. Then, midwinter, I open the jar, smell the memory of summer, and drop them into soup. It took 10 pounds of onions dried into flakes to fill a half-gallon jar. Fifty ears of corn kernels cut from the cob filled the same size jar after dehydrating. With very little preparation on my part, they both were sweet as candy.

Dehydrating primary elements is an exceptional way to store their vitality and create texture in living cuisine, which relies on blending fresh ingredients. In hot and dry climates, drying racks are laced with cheese cloth and food dries in the open air. I use a dehydrator box constructed to create air flow and low heat. The trays slide in and out from the front. Long-term storage of dehydrated ingredients is best in glass, unless you have food-grade storage containers with secure lids. A dehydrated dish might look like camping food and can be rehydrated or chewed dry. Compose dishes using this method with the same principles as a cooked dish. Ask if it has a single focus or mixed. Major or decorative. Don't mix oils and protein. Think about color.

Grain

Dehydrating is a third-stage method for grain. After the grains are sprouted, blend them with supporting elements before they go into the dehydrator.

Vegetables and Fruit

Drying fruit and vegetables is an extremely easy first-stage method. When blended to a thick liquid, poured onto a flexible sheet or parchment paper, and dehydrated, the resulting leathery texture can be shaped and used for a roll form.

Protein

Beans must be soaked and either sprouted or blended before they are dehydrated. I can't think of any reason to isolate them from the other elements. Oil or nuts and seeds will help carry any flavors that might be dressing them up, and grain complements protein, both nutritionally and in substance. Nuts and seeds play the roles of protein, fat, and fiber, so blending them with a grain or fruit and vegetable combination enhances the

dish. Fruit blended with nuts or seeds makes a dehydrated living cookie, while nuts and seeds blended and dried with vegetables and grain make a living cracker.

Dehydrating

Step 1. *Prepare major element*

Wash vegetables and fruit well. All the flavors should be blended into the mixture before it goes into the dehydrator. Grain and protein will need a pretreatment and at least one first-stage method before they are dehydrated. Cut fruit and vegetables into medium-thin pieces, depending on whether you want the end result to be chewy (bigger pieces) or brittle (thinner pieces). The important thing is to cut them evenly so that they dry evenly.

Step 2. *Lay on drying sheet*

A solid sheet of either baking paper or food-drying plastic is placed on the tray first. Individual fruit and vegetable pieces will shrink at least by one-third their original size. Pack them as closely as possible without creating layers. Thin layers come from blended substances and thicker layers from processed mixes. Spread them evenly.

Step 3. *Time and temperature*

The higher the temperature, the shorter the dehydrating time. Temperatures for living food range from 110°F (43°C) to 145°F (63°C). The length of time will also depend on how thick or thin the substance is and the desired texture. Crackers may dehydrate for 15–24 hours.

All unrefined plant foods are made up of complex carbohydrates. When the carbohydrate molecules break down, their simplest denominator is sugar. When that sugar undergoes glycolysis, further fermentation produces either alcohol or lactic acid, or the food decomposes altogether and rots. This change is stimulated by a variety of friendly fungi, bacteria, or yeasts. My favorite fermented foods offer lactobacilli in the form of pickles and rejuvelac. These foods assist in breaking down large starch molecules. The tradition of pairing carbohydrates and fermented pickles is centuries old. In living cuisine, seed cheese and rejuvelac play the fermentation role. Fermentation also creates sourdough bread and beverages like wine, beer, root beer, and ginger ale. Breads that use yeast are also in this category, and they rely on the yeast and sugar of the carbohydrate to expand the dough, creating air bubbles (as also happens with carbonated soda). In her booklet *Rebuild Your Health*, Ann Wigmore says that this kind of fermentation is user friendly with diets that avoid yeast. Another kind of fermentation is one that I don't like. I feel it in cooked beans that have gone sour from decay, often originating from the saliva off a cook's finger or sitting in warm temperatures for too long. This sour taste reads as "rotting, decay." The stomach knows it soon after ingestion, but the mouth and mind should catch it in the taste buds before it gets to the stomach. Sometimes it's identified in the smell.

Grain

Fermented living food dishes with grain show up in two forms: rejuvelac, which is used as a cooking liquid, and sour sprouted grain crackers or bread. A natural-rise whole grain bread created from slow fermentation may be created with a base from soft first-stage grain.

Vegetables

Fermented vegetables are called pickles. I don't ferment vegetables without salt. Salt acts as a preservative with pickling, but it also draws out the moisture from the cells, allowing the vegetable to have its own brine to cook in.

*I*magine sitting in a glass jar, the lid is on, it's dark. Somewhere water or moisture comes into the jar, either from perspiration or maybe a puddle was there in the beginning. Without air, carbon dioxide begins to form. During this period of time the cells burn, creating heat while they burn, from the inside. That heat translates as "energy," simply from the lack of oxygen. When that energy is captured, harvested, it is a powerful form of transformation. According to scientists, fermentation is a naturally occurring event that predates oxygen in the earth's atmosphere. Fermenting has a varied reputation, but it is the key to a living food and grain-based diet. To those who enjoy sourdough bread, cheese, wine, miso, and sauerkraut, it is not a scary cooking method. Instead, it inspires creativity within a healthy environment for the transformation of raw ingredients, without adding fire.

Protein

I don't recommend fermented gluten or beans, including tofu or tempeh, but nuts and seeds respond well to a careful fermentation process.

Soy products, like miso and shoyu/tamari, are not a protein category; they function as salt seasoning even though they are made with soy and grain. Yogurt and buttermilk are often eaten alone, but in the language of cooking, they both are cooking liquids. Like nut milk, they are cooking liquids with fat in them, playing a dual role.

Making Rejuvelac

Step 1. *Wash and soak grain for 8–10 hours*

Ann Wigmore recommends using soft pastry wheat for rejuvelac. I have made it with hard wheat, quinoa, rye berries, and mixes of kamut and rye. As with beer, the lighter the grain, the lighter the taste of the rejuvelac. Place $1/2$ cup clean grain in a half-gallon wide-mouth jar and cover it with water 2 inches above the grain. A screen over the top of the jar secured with either a rubber band or the ring of a canning lid makes rinsing and sprouting easy.

Step 2. *Rinse and sprout*

Pour the soaking liquid out through the screen lid. Replace the water, swishing it around the seeds, and drain it again. Support the jar at an angle that allows the liquid to drain, but not so steep an angle that the grains cover the air flow in the screen. A dish rack works perfectly. Cover the jar with a dish towel to reduce light. Twice a day, repeat the rinsing until the grain has a sprout tail as long as its body. This takes about two days, depending on the warmth of the climate (warmer means the sprouts will grow faster).

Step 3. *Fermentation*

After rinsing the sprouts with fresh water, fill the jar with filtered or spring water. Set the jar upright.

This liquid works with the grain in the same way that sourdough starters become enzymatic. In two days, 48 hours, fine bubbles will rise from the grain. It will look like champagne.

Step 4. *Replenish*

Pour off the first batch of rejuvelac, keeping about one-quarter of the liquid in the jar with the sprouts. Then refill the jar. A second batch takes only one day, 24 hours. At that point the grain sprouts will be spent, although I notice that horses and birds eat them.

Sour Crackers

Step 1. *Sprout grain*

Sprout different types of grain separately.

Step 2. *Soak sprouted grain in rejuvelac*

Rejuvelac jump-starts the fermenting process the way baker's yeast prepares a bread dough. Use just enough rejuvelac to moisten the grain sprouts. I soak them until I like the sour taste; depending on the heat of the room temperature, it could be about 6 hours.

Step 3. *Blend*

Blend the sprouts with the soaking liquid in a food processor. Add grated onion, if the mixture is dry enough, or add some minced green onion, other herb/spice, or other decorative vegetables at this time. Often the supporting elements will be blended or chopped fine before adding the soaked grain sprouts. Oil in the form of soaked nuts/seeds smooth out the cracker, make it flaky, and carry the herb/spice flavors around my mouth. But salt finishes it. Blend the mixture as smooth as it can be, because large grains dehydrated are hard to chew.

Step 4. *Dehydrate*

Line the dehydrator's rack with parchment paper or a coated sheet that comes with the dehydrator. Spread the batter evenly on this sheet. The cracker is usually ready to eat when it snaps easily. The hours and temperature are relative. If it is too slow (that is, if the temperature is not hot enough), the crackers will continue to ferment.

Seed Cheese

TECHNIQUE

Step 1. *Soak nuts/seeds*

I have explored sunflower seeds, almonds with skins removed after soaking, pine nuts, and walnuts to make an interesting spread known as seed cheese. Soaking and fermenting take place in the same stage using rejuvelac as the cooking liquid. The amount of liquid used will determine the consistency of the spread.

Step 2. *Cover*

Using plastic wrap, I seal the bowl and place a towel over it to darken the environment. The mixture will ferment in 8-12 hours depending on the warmth of the room. The warmer the room, the faster fermentation will occur. You can gain more control over the process in warm weather by putting the bowl in the refrigerator.

Step 3. *Blend*

Using a food processor, blend the seeds with herb/spice or decorative vegetables; then repeat step 2 and let the mixture rest for 2–4 hours. The longer time is needed for heavier nuts/seeds like almonds, Brazil, or cashew.

Step 4. *Store*

Keep in an airtight container in the refrigerator. Should keep for two weeks.

SAUCES

> *I*f I'm eating a delicious sauce and can identify the binders, the cooking liquid, oil, and herb/spice, I'll know how to make it.

A good sauce boosts the edibility of the most boring foods, often covering up a fumbled technique. Sauce carries a mystique that can frighten a beginning cook, but the language of cooking's guidelines to sauce-making systematizes the thought process, making sauces simple. Even though the following information begins by studying the individual binders and how they compose a sauce, many sauces utilize more than one binder. An example of this is Trice and David's Wedding Sauce (page 167), which includes three binders: blended vegetables (mushrooms and onions), clear starch (arrowroot), and nut butter (cashews). Sauces are prepared either cold, by blending, or hot, with fire. Cooked sauces may be used in cold dishes and cold sauces may be used in hot dishes. Cold sauce techniques are classified into three styles: marinades, dollop, and dipping. Hot sauces are named by the binder that defines the technique.

HOT SAUCES

Flour Binder

The binder of flour sauce is flour. Avoid wheat flour, especially whole wheat flour, because this grain sucks flavor out and adds little. Rice flour is my favorite for a white sauce, but I have used quinoa, corn, chickpea, sweet rice, barley, and wild rice flours. Bean-flour sauces are constructed as a flour sauce because of the technique. Ground spices look and act like flour, becoming part of the binder of this style of sauce (for example, ground red chiles in an enchilada sauce). Roux is the mixture of fat and flour that also identifies this sauce. Because the flour is usually a ground grain, pretreatments such as dry roasting, sautéing, or both deepen the flavor and darken the color. This sauce has also been made by soaking bread, a "backwards" technique. The ratio of flour to oil determines how rich the sauce will be. Each flour binds differently, so I don't recommend measuring the liquid. I use two techniques for building a flour sauce. The long method is used when I am improvising with new grains and flavors, and the quick method is used for familiar ingredients or when the sauce is a binder for vegetables and beans in a casserole form. To learn about the different grain flours, use the long method technique.

Flour Sauce, Long Method

TECHNIQUE

Step 1. *Warm pot, add oil*

Warm a saucepan. Begin with a warm pan to judge the amount of oil.

Step 2. *Add oil*

Use a maximum of $1/4$ inch of oil in the bottom of a pot to fill the pot with sauce.

Step 3. *Flour*

If it were measured, the ratio might look like 1 part oil to 2 parts flour. Flour absorbs the oil, making a paste. Grains absorb oil differently, so don't measure. Look for moistened flour that will form a pasty ball. Sauté the flour to deepen the color and flavor. Theoretically, this would be the time to add herb/spice, but because the substance

of the sauce hasn't been established, the number of layers of herb/spice are unknown.

Step 4. *Establish substance*

Cooking liquid determines the sauce's substance once the sauce has been cooked to thicken. Whisk liquid into the paste, allowing the flour to swell and become smooth. Cook whole grain flour sauces for about 10 minutes on a medium flame to see if the cooking liquid will fill in and smooth out the grain. When it does, the sauce substance will not feel grainy on the tongue. If the sauce is too thick and has a grainy mouthfeel, add more cooking liquid, cover, and continue to cook it until it is both smooth and thin.

Step 5. *Herb/spice and salt to fit*

The left brain counts the number of layers and the hand crosses the pot with herb/spice and salt crystals as the major salt. Undersalt the entire dish when using finishing salts after the flavors have cooked for at least 15 minutes, covered, on low, with a flame tamer.

Flour Sauce, Quick Method

TECHNIQUE

Step 1. *Seal vegetables and herb/spice*

Warm the pan and add oil. Seal decorative vegetables before the herb/spice goes into the pot because they would make a paste, stealing the oil. Toasting the herb/spice by dry roasting first heightens their flavor, but I rarely take this extra step. To use only one pan, dry roast first, remove the herb/spice, sauté the vegetables, and then add the herb/spice into the vegetable mix. Herb/spice to fit by estimating how thick you think one layer will be according to how full the pot will be after step 3.

Step 2. *Mix cooking liquid and flour*

Select a bowl that will hold at least half of the entire amount of liquid needed. The liquid should be cold or room temperature, but not freshly hot. A whisk will ensure the flour does not clump in the cooking liquid. Hot liquid would clump the flour, but fierce whipping smoothes it. That's too risky an action for me.

Step 3. *Establish substance*

When grains in the flour sauce expand outside their boundary, the sauce becomes smooth. Heating the mixture allows the substance to thicken. Stirring occasionally as it heats keeps it smooth. Liquid is added and cooked, as needed, until the grains are no longer felt on the tongue.

Step 4. *Salt to fit and cook covered*

Most of the salt layers are sea salt because there is usually a lot going on with the herb/spice and cooking liquid category that needs to be pulled together. If I know that I'm using a finishing salt, I shorten the layers of sea salt. A cover keeps the substance from becoming too thick, and cooking for at least 15 minutes on low integrates the flavors. A flame tamer is preventative.

Clear Sauce

Clear sauce is one of the few styles of sauce where you have the option of using oil. The binder is a starch/flour, which, unlike grain/flour thickeners, becomes clear upon cooking. The starch may be derived from grain, vegetable, or bean sources; with a grain starch (such as wheat and corn starches), the fiber and protein are removed from the seed. Vegetable starches from roots are more whole, less refined. Kudzu, arrowroot, and tapioca are my first choices for this style of sauce. Arrowroot and kudzu are energetically opposite. Touching kudzu, I feel the rock hard dry powder. Rubbing arrowroot between my fingers feels like face powder. Kudzu yields a smooth, velvety substance. It is my first choice in most dishes. Arrowroot has a viscous nature like egg white. Although it is more economical than kudzu, the ratios have to be more precise to avoid an unappealing substance. Clear starches only reflect the flavor of the supporting elements, unless a major vegetable defines the sauce, in which case oil is used to intensify and protect that vegetable. The ratio of cooking liquid to starch is generally 1 cup cooking liquid to 1 tablespoon starch for a medium-weight sauce. Using less liquid turns the substance to almost a glaze; more cooking liquid makes the sauce too thin to hold up on a grain or vegetable, but it works for binding a clear soup. These starches have specific requirements.

- They must be dissolved in a cold or room-temperature liquid before heating.
- The sauce may break, rather than bind, with active stirring or a rolling boil.
- The sauce may not bind when cooked with ingredients such as miso, honey, and rice syrup that contain live enzymes.
- The sauce begins opaque and is finished heating when the starch becomes clear.

Clear Sauce, No Oil

TECHNIQUE

Step 1. *Create a cooking liquid*

The cooking liquid is the most important element to pay attention to. The entire taste of the sauce develops in the first step, before any starch or heat is added. Is the liquid worthy of becoming a sauce? Is there enough interest? Will it hold up next to whatever it is served with? If water is the liquid, something else must provide interest. That interest comes from flavoring the water through a vegetable stock technique or a flavored water technique (kombu or spice stock). For sweet sauces I like to use fruit juice. Wine helps create the sauce, and by using nut milk, oil sneaks into the composition. How the sauce will taste depends on salt harmonizing the flavors in the liquid. Here is an exception to the theory of salting to fit when the substance is established, although it is common to measure ratios of cooking liquid to binder in this style of sauce, which secures the substance.

Step 2. *Mix starch*

Dissolve the starch into a small portion of cold or room-temperature cooking liquid. If the cooking liquid is hot, transfer some to a small bowl to cool first. Kudzu rocks mash more easily in a small amount of liquid, whereas arrowroot dissolves with less effort. Liquefied starch can then be stirred into the major cooking liquid without lumping. Alternatively, use a blender.

Step 3. *Establish substance and add finishing salt*

When the starch and liquid cook, the sauce thickens. If the sauce is too thick, add more cooking liquid; if the sauce is too thin, step 2 must be repeated, only this time go for a paste substance. Bring to a slow boil and simmer until the sauce is clear. Do not overcook, and stir only occasionally.

Clear Sauce with Oil

Step 1. *Seal vegetables and herb/spice*

Heat the pan, and add the oil and the first vegetable. In a clear sauce where the identity of the sauce is in the vegetable, I use a single-vegetable composition. Oil is used to protect and deepen their flavors so that when the cooking liquid enters, the vegetables

don't look or taste boiled to death and the liquid becomes worthy of being a sauce.

Step 2. *Cooking liquid and salt*

A major cooking liquid simmers with the vegetables. Using salt crystals, salt to fit and cover the pot while the salt works on the flavor. Pull some out to cool before dissolving it with the starch at room temperature. If the liquid is too warm, little balls of starch will float in the sauce and will never dissolve, and the sauce will not thicken. It is a bust and the entire liquid/starch mixture must be redone.

Step 3. *Establish substance and add finishing salt*

Dissolve starch in a small amount of the sauce's liquid that has been cooled to room temperature. A few minutes in the freezer speeds this action. Add it to the simmering sauce, stirring gently with a whisk. Cook until the sauce thickens and becomes clear. This is a gentle boil. Frequent stirring is not necessary once the starch has been diluted. Taste to see about a finishing salt.

Nut Sauce

Cream-style sauces seduce most primary ingredients because the element, fat, derived from whole nuts, is top-of-the-line soothing. This sauce, composed of nuts/seeds, cooking liquid, and salt/salt seasoning, begins with nut butter (like tahini and peanut butter) or whole nuts (like almonds, cashews, walnuts, and pecans). Nuts provide the fat and sometimes the flavor. For example, peanuts and sesame tahini have dominant personalities that are difficult to hide. Macadamia, pine nuts, and cashews lose their identity more easily, giving way to the herb/spice or cooking liquid category for an identity. With roasted nuts, their identity shows up. I select ingredients for sauces by color. Blond nuts make a creamy, off-white sauce. Nuts with skin offer shades of tan. The color of a salt/salt seasoning also guides choices. Umeboshi and light-colored miso are used for blond sauces; dark miso and tamari/shoyu are permitted if the sauce will be dark in color. Salt is key to the binding action of this sauce. Just heating cooking liquid and oil together isn't enough to create the substance; it needs salt to thicken. Use only salt crystals when the cooking liquid has a dynamic personality, in combination with at least one herb/spice element that is the focus. The nut's flavor does not have to be the focus, but salt seasonings are often interesting enough when water is the cooking liquid. The substance of this sauce thickens when it cools. When made with a heavy ratio of nuts to liquid, this sauce becomes a rich spread.

If using nut butter, make the sauce directly in the pan. Nut butter is easily made in a food processor by turning it on and letting the nuts turn to meal, then to paste. It is also easily found in natural food markets. The entire sauce can be made in a blender with whole nuts. I prefer narrow-bottom, wide-top blenders because they don't waste any time making a nut milk smooth, and I don't need large quantities to fill in the space of a wider blender bottom.

Nut Sauce, Blender Method

TECHNIQUE

Step 1. *Nut cream*

Nuts and water blend into a beautiful creamlike liquid. Begin by chopping the nuts to a fine meal in the blender. Add cooking liquid and blend on high for a minimum of two minutes. No straining is necessary when the nuts become smooth. This is the goal. If making more than four cups of sauce, don't put all the cooking liquid in the blender at once—add just enough to make the nuts entirely smooth. Use the rest of the liquid to rinse the blender after the first batch was placed in the pot.

Step 2. *Salt/salt seasoning and herb/spice*

When using a salt seasoning in paste form, like umeboshi paste or miso, estimate about one-third of the nut's volume will be salt seasoning. If using a liquid form, like tamari, or crystals such as sea salt or herbal salt, imagine how thick the sauce will be to determine what one layer is, and then salt to fit the number of layers. Repeat the same number of layers with the herb/spice category before blending it all together.

Step 3. *Establish substance*

Heating the sauce makes it thick. Bring it to a slow boil and immediately reduce the flame. Place a flame tamer beneath the pot and gently stir once or twice. Each nut thickens differently. Additional liquid can thin the sauce more easily than blending more nuts. Cook for at least 10 minutes to bring the flavors together. A cover maintains the substance.

Cream Sauce from Nut Butter

TECHNIQUE

Step 1. *Nut butter in the pot*

The size of the pot tells you how much sauce can be made. One thick layer of nut butter will make about half a pot of sauce.

Step 2. *Salt seasoning*

With a whisk, mix a salt paste of miso or umeboshi, estimating the amount to be about one-third of the volume of the nut butter. Increase this amount when using a light-colored miso. If salt crystals are used in this sauce, they will go in after the cooking liquid so you will be able to measure layers.

Step 3. *Cooking liquid*

Water is my favorite liquid for this sauce. Whisk it as the sauce turns into a milky substance; keep it thinner than the end goal because it thickens with heating.

Step 4. *Heating*

Heat is visible when the sauce begins to move. Reduce the heat, cover, position a flame tamer, and finish cooking. It's done after 10 minutes when the separate tastes of all the character ingredients become one. The cover is optional.

Vegetable Sauce

Tomato sauce is the most well-known vegetable-style sauce. I have seen it thick, using a tomato purée, and thin, simply using sautéed fresh tomatoes, with their own juice as the cooking liquid and their delicate fiber a lightweight binder. The technique for vegetable-style sauce below is not about tomato sauce. It offers the chance to invent sauces with ingredients you have on hand, and to compose it with vegetables that may not be traditionally used. In natural cookery, a vegetable sauce is not merely the extracted and reduced juice of a vegetable. It means that the entire vegetable is blended and the fiber becomes a binder, which identifies the sauce. Because vegetables in this sauce are required to merge, consider this a single-vegetable dish. The onion family is always welcome and merges easily with any vegetable, but blending carrot and celery together dishonors both, leaving no focus. To avoid the "baby food" experience of blended vegetables, use a large onion or a mix of onion family members, except in tomato sauce. This not only adds depth of flavor, it stretches the blended vegetable substance into a sauce. To add the dayglow effect, a decorative amount of colorful bell pepper creates an iridescent glow. Red and orange bell peppers magnify winter squash; yellow pepper dramatizes yellow zucchini. Use only a small amount, because they are only for tinting and the flavor of pepper may not be desirable. The amount of oil used during the method varies. More oil in the first step of the method is used when nut milk will not be part of the cooking liquid.

Vegetable Sauce

TECHNIQUE

Step 1. *Cut vegetables for the pot*

Cutting vegetables for a sauce is specific to the kind of pot they will cook in. I prefer to make this sauce in a pressure cooker. No pressure cooker? Boil the vegetables in a soup pot. Because a pressure cooker softens the vegetables, large pieces are best in this pot; they take up less floor space. Onions are simply quartered, and carrots are cut into large owls. This allows the largest possible surface area of the vegetables to lie on the pot's metal floor. The boiling method needs spoon-size pieces so that they become soft quickly.

Step 2. *Seal, intensify*

This is the most important step in making a vegetable sauce. It develops depth of flavor and affects the color. Orange, red, and gold shades of vegetables are easier to seal because their flavors should be taken right to the edge with long, slow cooking. White, yellow, and green vegetables are trickier to seal, because although browning is attractive with the darker vegetables, it is not for these. They need to be moved more often than the dark vegetables to keep them from browning; at the same time, hot metal is needed to seal the vegetables so they reach their core flavor. I swirl the vegetables in the pot clockwise. When they have some speed, I flick the pot so the vegetables on the bottom move to the top. This is the most effective technique for large cuts. Stirring with a spoon is cumbersome and doesn't move all the vegetables in a balanced way; avoid using a spoon unless the vegetables are stuck to the pan.

The onion family is first in the pot, unless mushrooms are the personality of the sauce. For mushrooms, use an additional skillet that has more floor space than a pressure cooker. It ensures that the mushrooms have a chance at the metal and are fully browned and intensified. Then I seal them until they squeak. Once the vegetables are near their maximum sealing, add the herb/spice so that they bond with the oil. If bulky herbs or spices, like ginger slices or lemongrass, are selected, they go into the cooking liquid and are removed before blending. All the vegetables go into the pot at one time if there is enough floor space.

Step 3. *Cooking liquid*

Deglaze the pot with the first splash of cooking liquid. When wine is one of them, it goes in first, steaming the vegetables with its flavor and pulling the flavors on the bottom of the pot into the sauce. It's easy to overwhelm vegetables with this fermented fruit liquid. The more oil in the sauce, the easier it is to use wine. The color of wine needs to match the color of the sauce. The amount of cooking liquid for a vegetable sauce depends on the pot and how vegetables grow. In a pressure cooker, the cooking liquid volume rises to one-half or three-quarters of the body of veg-

etables. In a boiling pot, cooking liquid must cover the vegetables by one-half to one inch. The variation in amount is relative to how wet the vegetables are from the start. A summer squash binder contains much more liquid than a winter squash or root vegetable. Liquid determines the substance of this sauce. The more liquid in the body of the vegetables, the less is needed in the sauce (and vice versa).

Step 4. *Salt to fit*

Imagine the thickness of the sauce when it is blended and consider a layer of salt for each level. It takes the power of salt crystals to make the flavors come together. It is always possible to add salt after the blending step, but it is more efficient and the taste is better if salt is measured to fit right-on the first time. Then it does its magic with heat. Reduce the number of layers of sea salt to replace them with finishing salt.

Step 5. *Cook until soft, and blend*

Vegetables under pressure cook quickly. Use table 2.2 (page 209) to determine how much time is needed, and then add a few minutes for insurance. By the time the boiling method makes the vegetables soft, the liquid line has been reduced, even with the top of the vegetables. Evaluate the sauce only when everything is blended. A hand blender, a counter blender, or a food processor finishes the sauce.

Step 6. *Accent liquid (optional)*

Once the sauce is blended it should be perfect if everything was measured to fit. But in situations when there is more flavor in the sauce than is showing up, or when I slip with the oil bottle and the sauce feels heavy, flat, or dull, a few drops of sour liquid round out the energy body of the sauce and bring the flavors full throttle.

Bean Sauce

Bean sauces rely on the identity of blended beans. Although a touch of oil makes the flavors move around better, beans are smooth enough to satisfy the quality of a sauce without adding oil. The substance is guided by cooking liquid and the integrity of the beans. If the beans are wet to begin with, if they have burst through their skins in the first stage, then reduce the amount of cooking liquid from the ratio guide that is used for beans that have integrity. The color of a bean sauce will rarely be white; even so-called white beans are off-white to tan in color when they are cooked. Bean sauces are very fast to make when you begin with a can of first-stage beans or pull some from the freezer. Work in interesting herb/spice categories or a portion of beer or wine to deepen the flavor and color. Alternatively, build interest into first-stage beans with herb/spice or cooking liquids without salt.

Bean Sauce

TECHNIQUE

Step 1. *Establish substance*

In a blender, cover beans with cooking liquid by 2–4 inches, depending on the integrity of the bean and your objective for the substance of the final sauce. Blend well, knowing that when the sauce is cooked it will thicken slightly.

Step 2. *Decorative vegetables and herb/spice*

Add decorative vegetables and herb/spice to fit. Blending again is an option.

Step 3. *Salt to fit*

At least a small amount of sea salt makes the major transformation of this sauce. Finishing salt follows the heating step, because there will be a more accurate reading.

Step 4. *Heat*

It takes about 10 minutes on a medium flame once the sauce is warmed through to finish the cooking. The substance should thicken a little, but the flavors will continue to be enhanced by cooking.

Step 5. *Accent liquid*

Any sour liquid in very small amounts, like $1/8$ teaspoon for 2 quarts sauce, will move the flavors around and enliven the herb/spice category. It is almost always used in a bean sauce.

COLD SAUCE

Cold sauces do not require heating to make the flavors come together. They are usually blended by hand or machine. This doesn't mean that a hot sauce could not be served cold; rather, it means the cooking method does not use fire. There are three basic styles: dipping, dollop, and marinade. They are identified by the amount of oil.

Dipping

A dipping sauce has no oil. This is because the food that is being dipped is often deep-fried. Think of egg rolls and tempura. Salt that balances the oil is in the dipping sauce. It is the placement of the oil that defines the method. Without oil, a dipping sauce is very lightweight. Composed primarily of equal parts salt seasoning and cooking liquids, herbs and spices are optional when the salt seasoning and cooking liquids are interesting.

Dipping Sauce

TECHNIQUE

Step 1. *Mix salt seasoning and cooking liquid*

The ratio is 1 part salt seasoning to 2 parts cooking liquid. Mix well, using taste/smell when inventing.

Dollop

A dollop sauce is heavy with oil. Oil/fat is the binder. Think of mayonnaise, guacamole, and pesto. These sauces go "plop" from a spoon. They move easily around hot grain and pasta, and are used as dips, spreads, and tapenades.

Dollop Sauce

Step 1. *Blend oil with cooking liquid*

For mayonnaise, the protein and cooking liquid (tofu and cider vinegar) are blended very well before oil is drizzled into the blender while processing. The ratio of oil to cooking liquid is about 20:1. When making guacamole, the avocado (oil) is blended, and the cooking liquid (lemon juice) is mixed into the oil.

Step 2. *Salt to fit*

If the oil isn't already laden with salt (as it is with olives), use whichever kind of salt makes sense.

Marinade

All marinades are second-stage methods in plant cookery, because grain, vegetables, and beans must be cooked before they are open enough to take in the cold sauce. Marinades are famous cold sauces for salad dressings and bathing liquids for first-stage cooked vegetables, grain, and beans.

A marinade's oil to cooking liquid ratio is different for each primary element. Grain and dense vegetables like starchy roots—potatoes, beets, and carrots—will balance the intensity of a cooking liquid over time. In marinades for lightweight vegetables like lettuce or zucchini, the oil ratio is higher, which provides more protection from intense cooking liquids like vinegar and lemon and lime juice. When you salt a bean marinade, you must use enough salt to fit the beans plus the cold sauce, because beans do not use salt in the first-stage method, unlike the other primary elements.

Marinade

Step 1. *Select the bowl to fit*

The size of this bowl will fit the primary element plus enough decorative vegetables to fill half of the bowl. In a round-bottomed bowl the total amount of cold sauce is between one-half and one inch from the bottom. In a square-bottomed container, the total amount of cold sauce will be less than one inch.

Step 2. *Begin with oil*

Oil is the first ingredient because it is easy to see how many layers there are in the bowl. Too much oil in a grain marinade makes the dish feel heavy; too little in a lightweight vegetable dish and the marinade might be too intense, overwhelming the dish. The amount of oil is one layer for grain, two for beans, and three for vegetables.

Step 3. *Cooking liquid*

When improvising a cold sauce, taste the oil and smell the cooking liquid categories for selection. If ingredients in the dish are known, then herb/spice may go into the oil before the cooking liquid. The amount of cooking liquid for grain is 5 parts, for protein it is 3 parts, and for vegetables it is 1 or 2 parts.

Step 4. *Herb/spice*

Herbs and spices go into the cold sauce to fit the layers of both primary and decorative elements. This might make the cold sauce look like a paste, but keep going. Make sure there is a heavy hand with this element, because grains need it and beans like it. A lightweight touch of herb/spice to fit an inch of cold sauce will not be enough to impact a marinade method for the primary elements of grain and beans. This is not the place to be timid.

Step 5. *Salt to fit*

The layers of salt will be to fit the cold sauce, unless it is a bean marinade; then you need to take into consideration the layers of the entire bowl of primary and decorative ingredients. Sea salt is used when there are numerous ingredients in the cold sauce and if the dish is to remain simple and light in color. Salt seasonings, such as miso, diluted in the cooking liquid, and tamari/shoyu or umeboshi, are acceptable as a salt. Care should be taken when using umeboshi. Because it is sour, it matches best with non-sour cooking liquids. Avoid using it with vinegar. Lemon or lime juice may work under unique circumstances.

CHAPTER THREE

PRIMARY ELEMENTS AND RECIPE SKETCHES

This chapter demonstrates how the language of cooking is used to communicate culinary ideas from one person to another through the use of recipe sketches. Many of the dishes were invented during our improvisation classes at the school. Some of them are what I call "rep" dishes, short for repertoire, or those dishes that are worth repeating. The recipe sketches are not necessarily complete dishes, even though they go through an entire cooking method, because primary elements may be either a major component of a dish or a decorative ingredient. For example, teriyaki sea vegetables are delicious as a side dish, but they may also be used decoratively, like a condiment, with first-stage cooked grain. Braised beans, delicious by themselves, may also speckle a grain or vegetable dish. If primary elements share a major role equally, they must be taken through at least the first stage of cooking by themselves, and then put together into forms, such as a side dish, casserole, roll, or stuffed creation.

The focus of a dish will always be at least one primary element. I am inspired by their history—knowing that plants transmute nutrients in the earth, making iron, copper, magnesium, calcium, and gold into stunning grain, vegetables, and beans, and that with sun, air, and water plants manufacture vitamins and fiber, water and fat. They maintain the quality of blood, enhance immunity, and act as a thermostat for the body's heating and cooling system. One way to interpret their value is a microscopic view of the nutrients isolated in a laboratory. Another way is what I call energetic nutrition, which perceives a food's wholeness, how it grows, its shape, water content, color, texture, and taste. Most of our plants today are from ancient wild food sources. Ancestors used these plants as medicine and in rituals.

Reading a Recipe Sketch

- Title of dishes may be literal or abstract.

- Form for the dish follows the title. It gives suggestions on how to use the dish in a meal.

- Primary elements: These are nearly equal in amount and importance. If grain, protein, and vegetable are in the primary element line, depending on the form and cooking method, they will all be cooked in the same cooking method, together. If there is more than one primary element line, they should be cooked separately and the dish assembled when each one is finished.

- Pretreatment, first-stage, and second-stage methods: These are the steps for assembly found in chapter 2.

- Decorative ingredients mean that there is only enough to speckle the dish. Sometimes these are integral to the cooking method, so they appear before the supporting elements. Sometimes they go in after the primary element is fully cooked, right before serving, in which case this category will be listed at the end of the sketch.

- Cut: This is a guideline to help describe the visual. The first cut is for the first vegetable in the primary element line, the second cut for the second element, and so forth. Or one cut may suit all.

- Oil, herb/spice, cooking liquid, and salt are supporting elements for the cooking method and primary elements. These are listed in order of when they go into a dish according to the cooking method.

VEGETABLES

This primary element brings color to an otherwise brown cuisine. Knowing how a vegetable grows helps me cook it. Classification of vegetable families for cooking differ from a gardener's botanical name because they relate to the way vegetables grow in relation to the sun and earth, instead of the seed's genetics. Their relationship to earth and sky, darkness and light, guides me in cooking them. In general, when one family member isn't available, another may be substituted for the same style of dish. Vegetables that grow above the ground eat the sun. Sun equals fire. Above-the-ground vegetables require less cooking than root, sea, and fungus families that live in dark and damp environments. In the absence of direct sunlight, they benefit from more fire, longer cooking times. Cooking times are also influenced by the amount of cooking liquid in the vegetable and in the pot. The family members often share similar taste. For example, roots may be sweet when cooked, their starches rising to the occasion, even if they start out pungent or bitter. Like learning who to invite to a table, putting vegetables from the same family together takes practice. Sometimes they fight or cancel each other out. But they often sing beautifully together. Vegetables have strong personalities of their own, unlike grain and beans. Tables 1.1 and 1.2 (pages 202 and 204) are charts of tastes for primary and supporting elements. The herb/spice elements are not as important for vegetables as they are for grain and beans, except with infusion methods like boiling, braising, and marinating. It's important to have vegetables of all sizes on hand to be able to use an entire vegetable in a dish. Once cut, vegetables begin to die, so it's thoughtful to consider the size of a carrot or onion going into the dish.

ROOT FAMILY

Roots store nutrients for their leaves and stalks. Their flesh grows long or short, big or small, tapered, round, or oval. The wild version of these plants were foraged with primitive digging tools by our ancestors who identified them by their green tops. Originally they were used more for medicine than culinary dishes. Carrots originated in Afghanistan and Egypt, then traveled to Europe over the centuries, where they were cultivated for culinary and medicinal uses. Wild carrots were black, purple, white, green, or yellow. They didn't become orange until the 1700s, when Dutch horticulturists bred the vegetable to honor the royal family and the House of Orange. This is the current color of carrots, although purple varieties are returning. The Greeks regarded carrots as a love medicine to make men more ardent and women more yielding. Dioscorides, one of the fathers of the *Materia Medica*, said that the Greeks used carrot leaves to treat cancerous tumors. He concocted broths of wild carrot seed to relieve urinary retention and to stimulate menstruation. According to Chinese medicine, carrots were used to treat whooping cough in children, quench thirst, heal burns, and sharpen night vision.

> oot vegetables are mysterious. They grow in the dark, clinging to earth by little hairs through which nutrients feed the root. I appreciate their bright colors, dynamic individual tastes, and how much they like to be comforted by fire. I think of eating the beauty of gold and copper, the strength of iron and zinc, and feel most like a wizard when I cook them.

Beets came from Germany and northeastern Europe. Wild burdock, a thistle plant grown in many parts of the world, was overlooked for culinary uses by most of Europe, but was widely used in Japan. Jerusalem artichokes began as a native American plant and traveled to Italy to become popular. Rutabaga has been traced to the seventeenth century and was thought to be a turnip-cabbage hybrid from Bohemia (part of Slovakia). It traveled to Britain and Scandinavia, where it received its current name. Irish folklore tells a Halloween story about turnips and the history of the jack-o'-lantern. When Jack tricked the Devil into climbing a tree, he carved a cross on the trunk, preventing the Devil from coming down. The Devil made a deal with Jack to keep him from going into hell after he died if only Jack would remove the cross from the tree. Eventually Jack died and he didn't go to hell or heaven. He was forced to wander around the earth with a sin-

gle candle to light his way. The candle was placed in a turnip to keep it burning longer. Pumpkins replaced turnips in the 1800s when the Irish came to America. Turnips are loaded with vitamin C and, like daikon, prevent stagnation, discharging mucus that tries to build up.

Sunchokes, also called Jerusalem artichokes, "the good carbohydrate," are oddly sweet, and offer a high percentage of fiber and three grams of protein in a one-cup serving. Wild yam has been used medicinally to reduce bad cholesterol, increase good cholesterol, and balance hormones. Naturalists say that beets prevent tumors. Burdock purifies blood, raw lotus root reduces heat, and yucca, the root of a succulent cactus, is therapeutic for inflammation, joint pain relief, establishing healthy flora in the gastrointestinal tract, and asthmatic relief.

Selecting and Storing

Fresh roots harvested in late summer/fall are plump and firm with their full water content. I purchase roots with the greens intact when I want to eat the greens. Carrot tops are lovely to look at, but the carrot no longer living in the soil is the sole support for the life of the greens and the root will loose its flavor to keep the greens looking fresh. Produce sellers often cut into the root to remove the greens and repeat fresh cuts where the greens were attached. I prefer to see a not-so-clean, securely sealed root than a botched amputation in a fresh cut. Once a root has been trimmed below the attachment line, it loses moisture, texture, and flavor. When roots are old from being in the soil too long, or are grown in depleted soil, their centers become woody and extra-fibrous, and it may be difficult to slide a knife through or pull flavor from them. Store roots in a dark, cool place. Potatoes, sweet potatoes, and yams should not be stored below 55°F (12.7°C). Roots are not cleaned before they are stored; they should be scrubbed with a brush before cooking.

BEET ROOT (sweet)

I have been trained to think of beets as deep red and bloody. The beautiful pink candy-striped and delicious golden varieties feel like imposters.

Sweet by nature, beets have a dominant personality, and yet they are extremely versatile. Often beets are marinated or pickled, which infuses sour and salty to balance their intense sweetness. Beets bleed profusely when cut, either before or after cooking. Even though I have a built-in cutting counter, I cut beets on a portable wood cutting board that I can scrub in the sink. For fun, I lightly dab the beet blood on my hands and use it to blush the color of my lips and cheeks.

Glazed Beets

GARNISH

Primary element: beet

First-stage method: teriyaki

Cut: small matchstick

Oil: light sesame

Cooking liquid/sweetener: rice syrup

Salt: tamari

Dilled Beet Root and Greens

SALAD

Primary element: beet

First-stage method: steep

Cut: whole

Second-stage method: marinate

Cut: large dice

Cold sauce: marinade (1 part oil : 2 parts cooking liquid)

Oil: sunflower

Herb/spice: dill weed

Cooking liquid: cider vinegar

Salt: sea salt

Decorative: steeped beet greens

Maple Ginger Beets

CONDIMENT FOR GRAIN

Primary element: beet

First-stage method: teriyaki

Cut: small dice

Oil: toasted sesame oil

Cooking liquid/sweetener: maple syrup

Salt: sea salt diluted in ginger juice

Herb/spice: fresh ginger

Orange Pecan Tang

SIDE DISH

Primary element: beet

First-stage method: braise

Cut: large matchstick

Oil: light sesame

Cooking liquid: orange juice, raspberry vinegar

Herb/spice: orange oil

Salt: chickpea miso

Decorative: roasted, glazed pecans

Roasted Beet Marinade

Primary element: beet

First-stage method: roast

Cut: medium wedge

Second-stage method: marinate

Cold sauce: marinade

> (1 part oil : 2 parts cooking liquid)
>
> *Oil:* olive
>
> *Herb/spice:* fresh basil, fresh garlic, freshly ground black pepper
>
> *Cooking liquid*: fresh lemon juice
>
> *Salt:* sea salt

Decorative: pressed red onions, yellow bell peppers, parsley

Triple Sweet

Primary element: beet, onion

First-stage method: teriyaki

Cut: small half-moon, fan

> *Oil:* olive
>
> *Cooking liquid:* mirin
>
> *Salt:* umeboshi

Beet Chips

Primary element: beet

First-stage method: roast

Cut: thin, even circles/rounds

> *Oil:* olive
>
> *Herb/spice:* garlic granules
>
> *Salt:* sea salt, umeboshi

Classic Beets with Tarragon

Primary element: beet

First-stage method: pressure steam

Cut: whole

Second-stage method: marinate

Cut: small wedge

Cold sauce: marinade

> (1 part oil : 2 parts cooking liquid)
>
> *Oil:* olive
>
> *Herb/spice:* garlic, fresh tarragon (lots of both)
>
> *Cooking liquid:* balsamic vinegar
>
> *Salt:* sea salt

Spicy Beets

Primary element: beet

First-stage method: roast

Cut: thin rounds

> *Oil:* toasted sesame oil
>
> *Herb/spice:* cardamom, cayenne
>
> *Salt:* sea salt

Barbecued Beets

Primary element: beet

Pretreatment: smoke

First-stage method: braise

Cut: large wedge

> *Oil:* ghee
>
> *Cooking liquid:* tomato purée or tomato juice, water
>
> *Herb/spice:* garlic, ginger, prepared mustard, drop of liquid smoke
>
> *Salt:* rice or red miso

Variation on a Theme #3

Primary element: beet

First-stage method: braise

Cut: thin wedges

Oil: olive

Cooking liquid: raspberry vinegar, water

Herb/spice: fresh ginger

Salt: umeboshi vinegar

Braised Beets #4

SIDE DISH

Primary element: beet

First-stage method: braise

Cut: medium matchstick

Oil: olive

Cooking liquid: Madeira wine, balsamic vinegar, water

Herb/spice: fresh basil, fresh garlic

Salt: sea salt

Valentine's Day

SOUP

Primary element: beet, onion

First-stage method: pressure cook, cream-style soup

Cut: large wedges (quartered is best)

Oil: olive oil

Herb/spice: cardamom

Cooking liquid: cashew milk (1 part nuts : 16 parts water)

Salt: sea salt

Traditional Borscht

SOUP

Primary element: onion, beet

First-stage method: boil, loose vegetable soup

Cut: medium-small dice

Oil: light sesame or ghee

Herb/spice: dill weed (optional)

Cooking liquid: water, grape juice, cider vinegar

Salt: sea salt

Borscht with Cabbage

SOUP

Primary element: onion, beet, cabbage

First-stage method: boil, loose vegetable soup

Cut: medium-small dice, shredded

Oil: light sesame or ghee

Herb/spice: garlic, caraway

Cooking liquid: water, vegetable stock or bouillon cube

Salt: vegetable salt

Elegant and Hot

SALAD

Primary element: beet, cabbage, pear

First-stage method: press

Second-stage method: marinate

Cut: spiralized beet, shredded cabbage, fine matchstick pear

Oil: sunflower or hazelnut

Herb/spice: curry blend, cayenne

Salt: sea salt

Cooking liquid: fresh lime juice

Decorative: toasted hazelnuts

Big Red

Primary element: beet

Decorative: apple, green onion, pressed

First-stage method: press

Cut: grated, or very fine julienne or matchstick

> *Herb/spice:* lemon zest
>
> *Salt:* sea salt
>
> *Cooking liquid:* fresh lemon juice

BURDOCK ROOT (bitter/odd)

Wild burdock root needs a posthole digger and a strong arm to remove it from where it grows. Large, broad leaves fan low to the ground, while beneath the earth, hairy taproots run perpendicular holding the 8–14-inch root tightly in the soil. The best-looking burdock is the circumference of a thumb, 12 inches or more in length, and too firm to bend tip to tip. Wild burdock has dark skin, making it a good accent color in compositions. Pale-skinned commercial burdock, also known by the Japanese name *gobo,* grows in sandy soil, allowing easy removal. I don't peel the skin. Scrubbing it well is sufficient. In cooking, burdock demands a large portion of oil. If burdock is part of a mixed-vegetable dish, it goes into the oil first, even before onions, to seal its strong, sharp flavor.

Strong Root Group

SIDE DISH

Primary element: burdock, onion, carrot

First-stage method: slow cook

> *Oil:* light sesame
>
> *Salt:* sea salt, tamari

Tempura Root Stew

MAIN PLATE

Primary element: burdock, onion, carrot, celery, parsley root

First-stage method: pressure steam

Second-stage method: tempura

Third-stage method: boil, stew

Cut: large fan, medium owl cut, large diagonal

> *Binder:* tempura batter (corn flour, brown rice flour, white spelt or unbleached white wheat flour, arrowroot flour)
>
> *Cooking liquid:* water, kombu/ginger stock
>
> *Salt:* sea salt, tamari or shoyu
>
> *Herb/spice:* fresh parsley

Decorative: braised or deep-fried tofu, fresh parsley

Trinkets

CONDIMENT OR SNACK

Primary element: burdock

First-stage method: teriyaki

Cut: julienne or pencil

> *Oil:* light sesame
>
> *Cooking liquid/sweetener:* rice syrup
>
> *Herb/spice:* fresh ginger juice
>
> *Salt:* tamari

Chunks of Earth

SIDE DISH

Primary element: burdock, onion, parsnip

First-stage method: bake

> *Oil:* toasted sesame oil
>
> *Salt:* sea salt, umeboshi

Burdock Slivers #2

Primary element: burdock

Cut: julienne or pencil

First-stage method: teriyaki

> *Oil:* olive
>
> *Cooking liquid/sweetener:* agave
>
> *Herb/spice:* crushed fennel seed
>
> *Salt:* umeboshi

Deep Down and Creamy

SOUP

Primary element: onion, burdock

First-stage method: pressure cook, cream-style soup

Decorative (base binder): cauliflower

> *Oil:* sunflower
>
> *Herb/spice:* nutmeg, garlic
>
> *Cooking liquid:* water, Merlot wine
>
> *Salt:* sea salt, tamari

CARROTS (sweet)

A fresh carrot is firm and mostly sweet. Carrot's taste misses the mark when its inner circles are yellow, causing it to be fibrous and bitter even when cooked. Scrubbing the outside of a carrot to remove loose dirt and an occasional embedded stone is easy with a vegetable brush. The only time peeling a carrot feels appropriate is when the aesthetic quality of the dish requires a smooth and glossy look. After first-stage steeping or pressure steaming, the loose skin of the carrots is brushed at a 22-degree angle by my knife. Carrot tops, edible and almost palatable, are often discarded. They are dense in matter and bitter in taste. Braising impacts their flavor in a good way for use as a condiment, but I most enjoy eating them when they are coated with a lacey tempura batter, where the beautiful green, branchlike leaves glisten like a tree whose leaves have been caught in an early ice storm.

Carrots in Rosemary Olive Paste

SIDE DISH

Primary element: whole baby carrots

First-stage method: roast

Cut: small owl cut

> *Oil:* green olives, crushed or blended
>
> *Herb/spice:* fresh rosemary
>
> *Salt:* olives, umeboshi

Pressed Carrots

SALAD

Primary element: carrot

First-stage method: press

Cut: grated

> *Decorative:* golden raisin
>
> *Herb/spice:* fresh cilantro
>
> *Salt:* sea salt
>
> *Cooking liquid:* fresh lime juice

Functional Tastes

SIDE DISH

Primary element: carrot

First-stage method: pressure steam

Second-stage method: refry

> *Oil:* light sesame
>
> *Herb/spice:* ground fennel, black pepper
>
> *Salt:* umeboshi vinegar

Carrot and Ginger

Primary element: carrot, onion

First-stage method: pressure cook, cream-style
soup

Cut: large owl, large fan (quartered onion)

Decorative: orange bell pepper, fresh pear

    Oil: hazelnut

    Herb/spice: ginger, ground coriander

    Cooking liquid: mango juice, water

    Salt: sea salt

Fire in the Bowl

SALAD

Primary element: carrot

First-stage method: steep

Second-stage method: marinate

Cold sauce: marinade (1 part oil : 1^1/$_2$ parts
cooking liquid)

    Oil: sunflower

    Cooking liquid: raspberry vinegar

    Herb/spice: fresh dill weed

    Salt: sea salt, chickpea miso

Decorative: red bell pepper, yellow bell pepper,
glazed toasted almonds

Glazed Carrots with Roasted Pecans

SIDE DISH

Primary element: carrot

First-stage method: teriyaki

    Oil: light sesame

    Cooking liquid/sweetener: brown rice syrup

    Salt: umeboshi

Decorative: roasted pecans

Oven Party

SIDE DISH

Primary element: carrot, leek, parsnip,
burdock, rutabaga

First-stage method: bake

    Oil: light sesame

    Salt: sea salt, tamari

CELERIAC/CELERY ROOT
(pungent/bitter)

This root appears to be swollen, with features
resembling Jabba the Hutt's looks and Sarah
Brightman's voice. Soil clings to and grips the
crevices. If the root won't come clean when
scrubbed with a vegetable brush, use a knife to
slice and shave off the mica-looking crystals held
deep in the folds of the body. With the dirt and soil
removed, celeriac has a delectable light yet powerful, almost pungent, taste. Celeriac is related to
celery, but the celery plant is a stalk family member. This vegetable, most common in Europe,
originated around 1600 in Italy and Switzerland. It
is equally delicious prepared both raw and cooked.

Cream of Celeriac

SOUP

Primary element: celeriac, onion, celery stalk

First-stage method: pressure cook, cream-style
soup

Decorative: shallot, leek

    Oil: sunflower

    Cooking liquid: cashew milk
        (1 part nuts : 18 parts water)

    Salt: sea salt, umeboshi

    Herb/spice: freshly ground pink peppercorns

Savory Slabs

SIDE DISH

Primary element: celeriac

First-stage method: roast

Cut: board cut, $^3/_4$-inch x $^1/_4$-inch slabs

Oil: light sesame

Herb/spice: whole fennel seed

Salt: sea salt

Tangy Trio

SIDE DISH

Primary element: celeriac, carrot, apple

First-stage method: press

Decorative: green onion, dried Turkish apricot

Cut: large grated, slivers

Herb/spice: lime zest

Salt: sea salt

Cooking liquid: fresh lime juice

Complex Simplicity

SIDE DISH

Primary element: celeriac

First-stage method: teriyaki

Cut: any, not too thick

Decorative: capers

Oil: olive

Cooking liquid/sweetener: mirin

Herb/spice: fresh ginger juice

Salt: caper brine

In My Mother's House

SIDE DISH

Primary element: celeriac, purple onion

First-stage method: braise

Decorative: red grapes

Cut: small cubes

Oil: olive or ghee

Herb/spice: ground cardamom

Salt: tamari

Cooking liquid: balsamic vinegar, grape syrup

Beauty in the Beast

SIDE DISH

Primary element: celeriac

First-stage method: slow cook

Cut: long, thick matchstick

Decorative: green onion

Oil: hazelnut

Herb/spice: celery leaf

Salt: sea salt, umeboshi

DAIKON (pungent/sweet)

Daikon is the name of a long white Japanese radish. At its best, the flesh is smooth, very white, and will snap if bent. This vegetable is pungent raw and smelly sweet when cooked. It is one of the few roots that works in the vegetable stir-frying method. Steeping daikon magnifies its translucent quality. I like to eat daikon greens, when they look vital; I prepare them like other leafy green vegetables. Daikon becomes limp when it loses its water. Braising rehydrates it with character.

Tangy Grated Daikon

CONDIMENT

Primary element: daikon

First-stage method: press

Decorative: carrot

Cut: grated

    Cooking liquid: fresh lemon juice

    Herb/spice: lemon zest, fresh thyme

    Salt: umeboshi

Brilliantly Brown

SIDE DISH

Primary element: daikon, leek

First-stage method: braise

Cut: half-moon, diagonal

    Oil: toasted sesame

    Salt: rice miso

    Cooking liquid: fresh lemon juice, Marsala wine, water

    Herb/spice: ginger, lemon zest

Friends

MAIN PLATE

Primary element: daikon, carrot, parsnip, celeriac, and leek

First-stage method: boil, stew

Decorative: first-stage cooked chickpeas, millet

Cut: owl, cubes

    Oil: coconut

    Herb/spice: kaffir lime leaf, fresh cilantro

    Cooking liquid: water, coconut milk

    Salt: sea salt, chickpea miso

Decorative: roasted seitan

Shiny Daikon

SIDE DISH

Primary element: daikon

First-stage method: teriyaki

Decorative: green onion

    Cut: thin matchstick

    Oil: light sesame

    Cooking liquid/sweetener: agave

    Salt: umeboshi

Daikon Pickles

CONDIMENT

Primary element: daikon

First-stage method: pickle, paste method

Cut: $1/2$-inch rounds or boards

    Herb/spice: garlic, ginger

    Salt: barley miso

A Big Crunch

SALAD

Primary element: daikon, napa cabbage, purple cabbage

First-stage method: press

    Herb/spice: arugula, orange zest

    Salt: sea salt

    Cooking liquid: fresh orange juice

Speckled Gems

SIDE DISH

Primary element: daikon

First-stage method: roast

    Oil: olive

    Salt: sea salt

    Herb/spice: marjoram

Miso

Primary element: onion, daikon

First-stage method: boil, loose vegetable soup

    Oil: toasted sesame

    Cooking liquid: kombu ginger stock

    Herb/spice: ginger

    Salt: sea salt, miso

Decorative: slivered green onion, cubed tofu

Soft and Tangy

Primary element: daikon

First-stage method: slow cook

Cut: long diagonal

    Oil: light sesame

    Salt: sea salt, umeboshi

JICAMA (sweet)

Jicama, translated from Spanish to English, means "edible root vegetable." Other names are Mexican potato, yam bean, Mexican turnip, and Mexican yam. Jicama is more often served raw than cooked. When it is fresh, jicama's body, which is 85 percent water, has smooth skin without dark spots. Removing the thin skin reveals a crisp and starchy vegetable with more water and fiber than the common potato. Mostly I prepare jicama without fire, according to its south-of-the-border tradition. This root stays crisp in fire cooking methods.

The Classic

Primary element: jicama

First-stage method: press

Decorative: fresh cilantro

    Herb/spice: fresh cilantro

    Salt: sea salt

    Cooking liquid: fresh lime juice

Pink Heat

Primary element: jicama

First-stage method: pickle, brine method

Decorative: red onion

Cut: wedges

    Salt: sea salt

    Herb/spice: red pepper flakes, garlic

Cool Combo

Primary element: jicama

First-stage method: press

Second-stage method: marinade

Decorative: olives, tomato

    Oil: olive

    Herb/spice: garlic, fresh basil

    Cooking liquid: fresh lemon juice

    Salt: sea salt

Unlikely Method

Primary element: jicama, sweet red bell pepper, onion

First-stage method: roast

   Oil: olive

   Herb/spice: garlic granules, curry powder

   Salt: vegetable salt

KOHLRABI (mild/sweet)

Technically, kohlrabi bulbs do not grow beneath the earth line, but they function like root vegetables in dishes. Most of their flavor is in the leafy green portion of the plant. Braising brings flavor to the bulb, which adds fiber to soups and stews. Kohlrabi has a very mild character that takes on the flavor of other ingredients. Use kohlrabi with other vegetables as if it were a root. Any of the recipe sketches for roots may be applied to kohlrabi.

LOTUS ROOT (odd/sweet)

The lotus plant roots itself in muddy waters, calming the edges of a pond or lake. Beauty runs through this entire plant, its root, stalks, leaves, flower, and seeds. Lotus root is one of 80 varieties of the water lily plant. Tubes grow consecutively in vertical order. A simple cut at right angles to the bulbous root reveals an internal snowflake design. Like the structure of spokes on a wheel, lotus root tubes provide structure for water to flow on the inside of this plant. When snapped off, each individual tuber snaps off its neighbor. Lotus root skin is not so tough to make it inedible, but removing it leaves a creamy white color, which is more appealing. I use lotus root more for its visual and textural contribution than its taste. It remains crisp through all cooking methods.

Chips

Primary element: lotus root

First-stage method: press

Second-stage method: deep-fry

Cut: thin circles

   Oil: safflower

   Salt: sea salt, umeboshi

Far East

Primary element: onion, lotus root

First-stage method: braise

Decorative: roasted red bell pepper

Cut: thin slivers, lotus circles

   Oil: toasted sesame

   Cooking liquid: orange juice

   Salt: sea salt

   Herb/spice: fresh ginger, orange flower water, fresh cilantro

Lemon Wings

Primary element: lotus root

First-stage method: teriyaki

Cut: thin half-moon

   Oil: light sesame

   Cooking liquid/sweetener: agave

   Herb/spice: lemon zest, lemon oil, saffron

Lotus Tempura

Primary element: lotus root

First-stage method: steep

Cooking liquid: water

Herb/spice: turmeric

Salt: umeboshi

Second-stage method: tempura

Batter: equal parts brown rice flour, white sweet rice flour, arrowroot

Cooking liquid: Lapsang Souchong tea

Oil: safflower, optional red palm

Cold sauce: dipping

Salt: tamari

Cooking liquid: pomegranate syrup, water

White Lotus Soup

Primary element: lotus root

First-stage method: boil, clear soup

Cut: peel, grate, or slice paper thin

Decorative: slivered red onion

Cooking liquid: kombu/spice stock, onion skin

Herb/spice: ginger, star anise, garlic, fresh cilantro

Salt: tamari, sea salt

Primary element: buckwheat noodles

First-stage method: boil

Primary element: tofu

First-stage method: steep

Cooking liquid: kombu/spice stock

Herb/spice: ginger, star anise, fresh garlic

Salt: tamari

Simple Complexity

Primary element: onion, lotus root, carrot, burdock

First-stage method: slow cook

Oil: light sesame

Salt: sea, tamari

Chinese Red, White, and Green

Primary element: lotus root

First-stage method: steep

Cut: $1/4$-inch-thick half-moon

Cooking liquid: vermouth, water

Herb/spice: garlic

Salt: sea salt

Second-stage method: marinate

Decorative: red bell pepper, black sesame seed, fresh cilantro

Cold sauce: marinade ($1/2$ part oil : $1^1/2$ parts cooking liquid)

Oil: toasted sesame

Herb/spice: green chile paste, fresh cilantro

Cooking liquid: mirin, rice vinegar

Salt: sea salt, white miso

PARSNIP (sweet)

I think of parsnips as white carrots. They grow, look, and cook like carrots, only they are sweeter and I've never used them raw. They have a potent taste and work well grouped with other vegetables, especially if the others are pungent or bitter. Alone, they are like candy. Unlike carrot tops, the parsnip leaf is not palatable. The healing properties of parsnips include clearing the liver and gallbladder of obstructions, promoting perspiration, and lubricating the intestines, among others.

Simply Sweet

Primary element: parsnips

First-stage method: steep or pressure steam

Second-stage method: refry

Cut: whole, half the length

  Oil: light sesame, touch of dark sesame

  Cooking liquid: none

  Salt: sea salt, tamari, or umeboshi

Chips

SIDE DISH, SNACK

Primary element: parsnip

First-stage method: roast

Cut: $1/4$-inch diagonal

  Oil: safflower

  Herb/spice: optional

  Salt: sea salt, umeboshi

Five Tastes

SIDE DISH

Primary element: parsnip

First-stage method: braise

Cut: diagonal half-moon

  Oil: olive

  Cooking liquid: sherry wine, vinegar, water

  Herb/spice: cardamom, cayenne

  Salt: tamari

Mixed Company

SOUP

Primary element: onion, carrot, parsnip, turnip, celery stalk, red bell pepper

First-stage method: boil, loose vegetable soup

Cut: diced, soup spoon size

  Oil: olive

  Herb/spice: fresh garlic, fennel seed, marjoram, black pepper (finish)

  Cooking liquid: water

  Salt: sea salt

Sweet Mountains of Mash

SIDE DISH

Primary element: parsnip, onion

Pretreatment: sauté

First-stage method: pressure cook, hand blend

Decorative: black sesame seeds

Cut: large owl, onion quartered

  Oil: light sesame

  Cooking liquid: water or light nut milk

  Salt: sea salt

Going Solo

SOUP

Primary element: onion, leek, parsnip

First-stage method: pressure cook, cream-style soup

Cut: large cut

  Oil: olive or ghee

  Cooking liquid: cashew milk (1 part nuts : 12 parts liquid)

  Salt: sea salt

POTATO (sweet)

*W*hen entering into a short-term relationship with the potato, I first ask it, "What would you like to be? Stuffed? Mashed? Roasted? Boiled in oil? Breaded and fried? Or do you wish to sit in a cool bath of power spices or healing herbs? Are you a one-night stand or will you last a week?"

Potatoes, like consumers, come in a variety of colors, shapes, and sizes: the voluptuous russet, thick skinned and generously flaky in character; delicate white potatoes with porcelain skin and a more cohesive interior than the russet; and the reds—small, blushing and large, pockmarked; or the buttery yellow-gold and blue-purple. Potatoes wait in a cool, dark corner of my kitchen so that they are less likely to turn green or sprout. It's chlorophyll that makes potatoes green and solanine, the nightshade component, that makes the skin bitter. Both develop when the potato is exposed to light. I wouldn't want to eat a potato that couldn't sprout because then there is something wrong with its reproductive power. If it does sprout, remove the sprout before it grows. If the skin turns green, remove it to prevent bitterness. The skin holds important nutrients, but the potato's leaves and stems are toxic.

Basic

SIDE DISH

Primary element: russet potato

First-stage method: roast

Cut: keep whole (fork puncture halfway through the cooking method), or cut into large matchsticks or cubes

Oil: olive or ghee

Salt: sea salt

Potato Leek

SOUP

Primary element: Yukon Gold potato, leek, onion

First-stage method: pressure cook, cream-style soup

Cut: large diagonal (half)

Oil: olive or ghee

Herb/spice: fresh garlic

Cooking liquid: white wine, water, optional nut milk (1 part nuts : 16 parts water)

Salt: sea salt

No Mayo Potato Salad

SIDE DISH

Primary element: red potato

First-stage method: steep

Second-stage method: marinate

Cut: whole, cube

Decorative: diced red onion, diced celery

Oil: hazelnut

Cooking liquid: cider vinegar

Herb/spice: prepared mustard, fresh tarragon

Salt: sea salt

Herb Mashed Potatoes

Primary element: potato

Pretreatment: sauté

First-stage method: pressure cook, hand blend

Cut: large diagonal

Oil: ghee, olive oil

Cooking liquid: cashew milk (1 part nuts :
8 parts cooking liquid)

Herb/spice: fresh garlic, fresh thyme

Salt: sea salt or vegetable salt

Potato Patties

Primary element: potato

First-stage method: press

Second-stage method: refry

Decorative: roasted and peeled green chile

Cut: grate, dice

Oil: safflower

Herb/spice: oregano

Salt: sea salt

Comfort

Primary element: potato, leeks

First-stage method: slow cook

Cut: half circles

Oil: olive and/or ghee

Herb/spice: fresh thyme, fresh parsley

Salt: sea salt, umeboshi

The Ultimate

Primary element: small red or yellow potatoes

First-stage method: steep

Second-stage method: roast

Cut: whole

Oil: olive or ghee

Herb/spice: lemon oil

Salt: sea salt or vegetable salt

French Fries

Primary element: russet potato

First-stage method: salt, soak in ice water,
towel dry

Second-stage method: deep-fry

Third-stage method: deep-fry

Cut: large matchstick

Oil: safflower

Salt: vegetable or sea salt, umeboshi

Lemon Braised Potatoes

Primary element: potato

First-stage method: braise

Cut: small cube

Oil: safflower

Cooking liquid: fresh lemon juice, water

Herb/spice: fresh garlic, dried oregano

Salt: tamari

RADISH (pungent)

I eat radishes raw for a snack when my mouth is dry. The radish juice easily penetrates any stuffy feeling, quenching my thirst while loosening up any congestion in my head.

Radish roots add color and spice. Sized small, medium, or large, shaped round or fashioned after an icicle, their crisp, juicy, and hot personality comes in a rainbow selection of purple, red, pink, or white. During an improvisation class, we discovered that radishes transform beautifully under fire. Radish seeds are famous for sprouting into baby green leaves. They wake up a salad or live-food soup.

Light Fire

SOUP

Primary element: red radish
First-stage method: blend, cold
    Oil: macadamia nut
    Cooking liquid: nut milk (1 part nuts : 8 parts rejuvelac)
    Herb/spice: fresh mint
    Salt: umeboshi

Tops and Bottoms

CONDIMENT

Primary element: red radish and radish greens
First-stage method: press
Cut: thin circles
    Herb/spice: lemon zest
    Cooking liquid: fresh lemon juice
    Salt: sea salt

Surprise

CONDIMENT

Primary element: red radish
First-stage method: teriyaki
Cut: matchstick or wedges
    Oil: hazelnut
    Herb/spice: fresh thyme
    Cooking liquid/sweetener: agave
    Salt: sea salt

Cold Poppers

SALAD

Primary element: red radish
First-stage method: steep
Cut: whole
Second-stage: marinate
Cold sauce: marinade
    Oil: hazelnut
    Herb/spice: fresh thyme, orange zest
    Cooking liquid: fresh orange juice
    Salt: umeboshi
Decorative: roasted hazelnuts

Red Balls of Fire

SIDE DISH OR DECORATIVE
FOR ANOTHER VEGETABLE

Primary element: red radish
First-stage method: roast
Cut: whole
    Oil: pumpkin seed
    Herb/spice: ground sumac or chili powder, garlic granules
    Salt: sea salt

Pickled Radish

Primary element: red, purple, white radish

First-stage method: pickle brine

Cut: small wedges

Herb/spice: fresh rosemary

Cooking liquid: raspberry vinegar, water

Salt: sea salt

RUTABAGA (pungent/sweet)

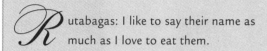

utabagas: I like to say their name as much as I love to eat them.

The rutabaga is a complex vegetable because of its pungent, bitter, and sweet taste. Rutabagas prefer to grow in cold climates and to be cooked for a long time. It is tempting to use sweet spices with rutabagas, but I refuse to pretend this hearty vegetable is a dessert and won't use cinnamon or cloves, unless they keep company with pungent spices as well. I am not alone in appreciating this amazing root. Cumberland, Wisconsin, honors them in a festival once a year, and rutabaga fans in Forest Lake, Oregon, have created an association to carry the legend.

Saturday Afternoon

SIDE DISH, SNACK

Primary element: rutabaga

First-stage method: roast

Cut: cube

Oil: dark sesame

Salt: sea salt

Pocket Pouches

SIDE DISH, SAVORY PASTRY

Primary element: leek, rutabaga

First-stage method: slow cook

Second-stage method: baked in phyllo dough or pastry

Cut: matchstick

Oil: light sesame or ghee

Salt: sea salt

Herb/spice: optional

The Golden Child

STEW

Primary element: onion, carrot, rutabaga, cabbage

First-stage method: boil, stew

Cut: wedge, owl, cube

Decorative: cooked chickpeas, quinoa, fresh peas

Oil: coconut

Herb/spice: kaffir lime leaf or lemongrass, curry powder

Cooking liquid: water, coconut milk

Salt: sea salt, miso

Toast Rub

SPREAD

Primary element: rutabaga

First-stage method: sauté, pressure cook

Second-stage method: blend, spread

Cut: quartered

Oil: walnut

Herb/spice: herbes de Provence

Salt: sea salt

Decorative: Umeboshi roasted pecans

Sunday

Primary element: leek, carrot, rutabaga, potato, tomato, celery, cabbage
First-stage method: boil, loose vegetable soup
Cut: small dice
Decorative: wild rice
   Oil: olive
   Herb/spice: garlic, paprika, bay leaf, pepper
   Cooking liquid: water, red wine
   Salt: vegetable salt or vegetable bouillon

SUNCHOKE (sweet/bitter)

This vegetable is a gnarly surprise. I imagine these tubers were foraged by ancestors before the age of cultivation. In addition to the translation of the Italian name *girasole articiocco,* they acquired another name, Jerusalem artichoke, even though this plant flowers like a sunflower, not an artichoke. Sunchokes grow in damp, low areas in many parts of the world. Originally a Native American plant, it was used like the modern potato. I cook them until soft to bring out the most flavor, but many people enjoy slivers of this vegetable as they would slivers of crisp bamboo shoot.

Baked with Fennel

Primary element: sunchoke
First-stage method: bake
Cut: diagonal halves
   Oil: olive
   Herb/spice: fennel seed
   Salt: sea salt

Elevation

Primary element: leek, carrot, sunchoke
First-stage method: braise
Cut: diagonal
   Oil: olive
   Herb/spice: fresh tarragon, garlic
   Cooking liquid: fresh lemon juice, water
   Salt: umeboshi

Summer Song

Primary element: sunchoke, tomato, fresh corn
First-stage method: boil, stew
Cut: small dice
Decorative: shallot, noodles, teriyaki seitan
   Oil: light sesame
   Herb/spice: paprika, bay leaf, dried oregano
   Cooking liquid: tomato juice, water, red wine (optional)
   Salt: sea salt, miso

Taste of Earth

Primary element: sunchoke, onion
Hot sauce: vegetable
   Oil: olive, pine nut
   Cooking liquid: pine nut milk made with water and Pinot Grigio or other white wine (1 part nuts : 10 parts cooking liquid)
   Salt: sea salt, tamari

Garlic Balls

SIDE DISH

Primary element: sunchoke
First-stage method: roast
Cut: leave whole
  Oil: safflower
  Herb/spice: garlic granules
  Salt: vegetable salt, tamari
Decorative: fresh cilantro

Cream of Sunchoke

SOUP

Primary element: onion, sunchoke
First-stage method: pressure cook, cream-style
  soup
Decorative: purple bell pepper
  Oil: olive
  Herb/spice: kaffir lime leaf
  Cooking liquid: thin coconut milk
  Salt: sea salt

TURNIPS (pungent/bitter/sweet)

I rarely say "turnip" without thinking about the nursery rhyme phrase, "Once there were three . . . who went to see the king. One had a rose, one had a ring, and one had a turnip to give to the queen."

A half dozen roasted turnips is my afternoon snack. Their leaves are generically delicious greens, but the root of this plant has lovely complexity. When turnips are fresh and fully cooked,

they become sweet with pungent overtones. Raw turnips are more pungent than sweet and might have a bitter note if they are old. Turnips in a mixed dish generally merge well, although I avoid combinations with beets.

The Easy Chair

SIDE DISH

Primary element: turnip
First-stage method: roast
Cut: wedges
  Oil: olive
  Salt: sea salt

Pillows

SIDE DISH

Primary element: turnip
First-stage method: pressure steam
Second-stage method: refry
Cut: wedge
  Oil: light and dark sesame
  Herb/spice: optional
  Salt: tamari

Go Green Cream

SIDE DISH

Primary element: turnip
First-stage method: pressure steam or roast
Second-stage method: bake in sauce
Cut: diagonal, in half
Hot sauce: nut
  Oil: cashew
  Herb/spice: fresh garlic, green onions
  Salt: chickpea miso

Many Tastes

SIDE DISH

Primary element: turnip, leek

First-stage method: braise

Cut: matchstick, diagonal

Oil: olive

Herb/spice: fennel seed, shallot

Cooking liquid: raspberry vinegar, water, mirin

Salt: white miso, sea salt

Group Therapy

SIDE DISH

Primary element: red onion, turnip, savoy cabbage

First-stage method: slow cook

Oil: safflower

Salt: sea salt

Smoke and Cream

SOUP

Primary element: leek, turnip

Pretreatment: smoke turnips

First-stage method: pressure cook, cream-style soup

Oil: light sesame

Herb/spice: fresh oregano

Cooking liquid: water, white wine

Salt: sea salt

SWEET POTATO AND YAMS
(sweet)

Yams and sweet potatoes brighten dishes and provide comfort with their smooth texture. Whether they stand alone or merge with others, their starchy nature provides substance to a dish. Yams and sweet potatoes are entirely different plants. For culinary reasons, they share the same place in my mind for how to use them. Both of these vegetables grow in warm, semitropical climates. Their identities change from country to country and person to person. Yams, which are part of the vine family, take longer to grow than sweet potatoes, which are a root. Yams have a higher starch content, which makes them good candidates for being milled into a flour that could potentially be used as a gluten-free binder. Among the hundred varieties of yam, one has been reported to have grown as large as 600 pounds. Yams are a common food in Africa. The Senegalese word *nyami* was eventually shortened to yam. When native Africans were transported to the United States and saw the similarities between yams and sweet potatoes, they began using the terms interchangeably.

I don't understand why most recipes add sugar to this already sweet food. Another pet peeve of mine is the culinary pattern of using pumpkin pie spices, cinnamon, or allspice with meaty orange vegetables like sweet potatoes, yams, or winter squashes. It confuses my palate when dinner tastes like dessert.

Chips

SIDE DISH, SNACK

Primary element: yam

First-stage method: press

Second-stage method: deep-fry

Cut: thin rounds

Oil: safflower, coconut, palm oil

Salt: finely ground sea salt (molcajete)

Almost Candy

Primary element: garnet yam

First-stage method: roast

Cut: whole (puncture halfway through cooking)

> *Oil:* olive
>
> *Salt:* sea salt

For a Cold Day

STEW

Primary element: onion, sweet potato, rutabaga, sunchoke, yellow bell pepper

First-stage method: boil, stew

Decorative: frozen peas, red beans

Cut: bulky

> *Oil:* sunflower
>
> *Herb/spice:* curry powder
>
> *Cooking liquid:* water
>
> *Salt:* sea salt, tamari

Decorative: seitan

First-stage method: braise

> *Oil:* sunflower
>
> *Salt:* tamari/shoyu
>
> *Cooking liquid:* water, fresh lime or lemon juice
>
> *Herb/spice:* ground cumin

Smoky

SPREAD

Primary element: sweet potato

Pretreatment: smoke

First-stage method: pressure steam

Second-stage method: refry

Cut: whole, mashed

> *Oil:* light sesame
>
> *Salt:* tamari

Sweet and Sour

SIDE DISH

Primary element: yam

First-stage method: braise

Cut: medium cubes

> *Oil:* hazelnut
>
> *Salt:* miso
>
> *Cooking liquid:* pineapple juice, cider vinegar, water
>
> *Herb/spice:* freshly ground pink peppercorns

YUCCA ROOT (sweet)

*T*his vegetable reminds me of working with clay, where the more water I use to form a pot, the more it stretches. When my vegetarian friend called me from the hospital asking for food, she hadn't eaten in more than a week; medication had burned a hole in her stomach. The hospital offered her vegetarian chili, but spicy beans didn't seem right for her condition. I made two yucca dishes. One to drink like a cream soup or slurry, the other a basil patty to give her a substance to chew. Within 24 hours she reported that food was staying in her body. Had yucca mended the hole?

The root of the yucca cactus commands attention for its fat, long, tuberous shape that has little taste of its own. Its delicate coppery brown skin, usually waxed for safe shipping and storage, is firmly bonded to the white starch. A cablelike chord runs the length of the root. This is removed, either cut out before cooking or after a first-stage cooking method when it is easier to see. Yucca is a dry plant. Growing in desert conditions, yucca responds well to braising and other methods that add liquid and flavor. Native Americans work the root to make a soapy broth for skin and hair by peeling yucca and mashing it in clean water. The fibers are then milked and strained. Native Africans who escaped slavery to live with the Carib Indians (in the Caribbean) grate the root, press it to remove the juice, which is toxic raw, and dry the fiber for use in bread.

Chips

SIDE DISH, SNACK

Primary element: peeled yucca root

First-stage method: press

Second-stage method: deep-fry

Cut: thin rounds on diagonal

Oil: safflower/coconut or palm

Salt: finely crushed sea salt

Infusion

SIDE DISH

Primary element: yucca root

First-stage method: braise

Decorative: sun-dried tomato, optional

Cut: long, thin matchstick

Oil: olive

Cooking liquid: white balsamic vinegar, extra-dry vermouth

Herb/spice: minced fresh garlic, freshly ground pink peppercorns

Salt: sea salt

Mushroom Sage Patties and Sauce

MAIN PLATE

Patties

Primary element: yucca root

First-stage method: pressure steam

Second-stage method: refry

Decorative: cremini mushrooms, shallot

Cut: small cubes, mashed, minced

Oil: light sesame

Herb/spice: minced fresh sage

Salt: tamari

Sauce

Primary element: white kidney beans

Hot sauce: bean

Oil: cashew as nut milk

Herb/spice: fresh garlic, fresh sage

Cooking liquid: nut milk made with bean juice and water (1 part nuts : 8 parts cooking liquid)

Salt: sea salt

Velvet Cream

SOUP

Primary element: yucca root, yellow onion

First-stage method: pressure cook, cream-style soup

Decorative: yellow bell pepper

Cut: large

Oil: sunflower

Herb/spice: shallot, lemon thyme, lemon oil

Cooking liquid: cashew milk made with water and Chardonnay (1 part nuts : 20 parts liquid)

Tones of Eastland

Primary element: yucca root, cleaned and cubed

First-stage method: braise

Oil: walnut

Salt: chickpea miso

Cooking liquid: apple juice

Herb/spice: garlic, turmeric, cumin

Amber Clusters

SIDE DISH, CONDIMENT

Primary element: yucca root

First-stage method: teriyaki

Oil: toasted sesame

Cooking liquid/sweetener: agave

Salt: umeboshi

ONION FAMILY

There is rarely a dish that would not make good use of an onion family member. It is easier to cook with onions than to eliminate them from dishes. I have been asked to cook without them for spiritual retreats where replacing onions with asafetida (a gum resin in the herb/spice category) is customary. I just leave them out.

The edible portions of onions grow where earth and sky meet, neither fully below nor completely above the earth line. When they are young, green shoots rise above the soil line and the bulb swells. When the greens are dry, there is usually a beautiful round onion sitting halfway into the earth, holding on by its delicate roots. Green onions are pulled in a row of growing onions to make room for the round onion body. Leeks grow like green onions, the large white portion buried and the leaves pulled upward by the sun, which turns them green.

Onions, one of the oldest foods, predates recorded history. The wild plants were foraged on many continents, although it is believed that they originated in the Middle East and Asia. Onions were one of the first cultivated crops. They were easy to store, transport, and plant. The structural design of an onion, a circle within a circle, symbolized eternity to the Egyptians. They were placed in their tombs and upon alters, treated as art, and used as tools in mummification. Egyptologists who observed that onions were strategically placed on the Pharaoh's body speculate that their magical properties were used to prompt the dead to breathe again or, because onions are known for their strong antiseptic and therefore magical qualities, the Egyptians felt they would be handy in the afterlife. From the Middle Ages through early American history, onions were used as a remedy for headaches, snakebites, and hair loss. They were used in cough syrups and poultices, the skin was an ingredient in dyes, and they were used for rent payments and wedding gifts. Onions produce energy in the body, generating warmth and improving circulation. I picture the potency of onions cleaning my arteries, warming my lungs, helping to extricate toxins, and reducing the influence of any unfriendly viral, fungal, or bacterial invasion. This means increased circulation, lower blood pressure, and prevention of blood clots. Onions add both moisture and fire (warmth) to any dish. Early nomadic desert societies used onions to prevent thirst. When cooked, onion's sweetness rivals any natural sugar; when raw, the taste of onions is pungent. Even though eating raw onions can improve the good HDL cholesterol levels, they can be difficult to digest unless they are pressed and/or wilted first.

When dicing, slicing, or mincing an onion, keep the root end intact until the body of the onion has been diced; then the root end can be randomly chopped. Keeping the root end connected to the body of the onion guarantees fewer tears. I hold matches in my mouth (with the tips facing away from my teeth) so that the sulfur on the striking end repels the naturally occurring sulfur in the onions. Wood-stick matches or entire matchbooks are both used. The more sugar in my blood, the more matches I need to use.

Selecting and Storing

Among the different kinds of onion there are sweet, eat-them-now varieties, and pungent, long-storage keepers. Sweet onions contain more water, grow in warm climates, require less time in the light, and do not store well. I keep them in the refrigerator. Northern climate onions spend more time in the soil and contain less water. They will keep for several months without refrigeration when stored in a cool, dark place. In the fall, my garage is suitable. I look for onions that are firm, especially at the top. Keepers have thick skin. Once they begin to sprout, a green shoot transforming them, their life force is on its way out.

RED ONION (pungent)

Red onions are usually a first choice over the yellow or white varieties to function as a raw decorative ingredient. This is the only onion I cut into, use a small part of, wrap in plastic, and store in the refrigerator. If a red onion is cooked, using the entire onion is not a problem. Raw or cooked, the flavor of red onions is slightly milder than white or yellow onions.

Marvelous Mauve

SIDE DISH

Primary element: red onion

First-stage method: teriyaki

Cut: large fans

Oil: olive

Cooking liquid: 1 part cane sugar : 2 parts water

Herb/spice: fresh lemon thyme

Salt: umeboshi

Familiar Tastes

MAIN PLATE

Primary element: red onion

First-stage method: slow cook

Cut: slivers or small fans

Primary element: gluten

First-stage method: braise

Oil: olive

Salt: tamari/shoyu

Cooking liquid: red wine, water

Herb/spice: fresh garlic, fresh ginger

Primary element: potato

Pretreatment: sauté

First-stage method: pressure cook

Oil: ghee or olive

Cooking liquid: cashew milk (1 part nuts : 8 parts liquid)

Salt: sea salt

Herb/spice: freshly ground black pepper

Pickles

SIDE DISH

Primary element: red onion

First-stage method: miso paste pickle

Cut: medium fans

Salt: barley miso

Herb/spice: sage

Purple on Purple

SALAD

Primary element: purple cabbage, red onion

First-stage method: press

Second-stage method: marinate

Cut: shredded, slivers

Oil: mayonnaise

Cooking liquid: fresh lemon or orange juice

Herb/spice: minced fresh garlic

Salt: sea salt

Rosemary Roasted

SIDE DISH

Primary element: red onion

First-stage method: roast

Cut: large fans

Oil: olive

Salt: sea salt

Herb/spice: minced fresh rosemary

YELLOW ONION (pungent/sweet)

There are several versions of yellow onions, from sweet, short-storage Vidalia and Walla Walla to pungent, longer-keeping Spanish. Raw Vidalia onions, grown in and around Vidalia, Georgia, are touted to be as sweet as apples. Identify them by their paper-thin skin and thick, flat bodies. Similarly sweet onions are Maui (hailing from Hawaii) and Noonday (from Noonday, Texas). These are perfect pressed for salsa or as a decorative element in potato and pasta salads. Washington State takes pride in the Walla Walla. Sweet and watery, it is interchangeable with the Vidalia. The yellow Spanish onion, used mostly for fire methods, has firm skin and a dry body; it is more pungent than sweet in taste. The skins of yellow onions impart a beautiful golden color when boiled with cooking liquid. If boiled for more than 10 minutes, however, they will make a dish extremely bitter and difficult to balance.

Crusted Moon Roasted Pepper Sauce

SIDE DISH

Primary element: onion

First-stage method: steep

Second-stage: encrusted, roasted

Cut: peeled, whole, large fans

Oil: roasted pumpkin seeds

Salt: tamari

Herb/spice: chili powder

For the second stage, dip the onion into an arrowroot wash (arrowroot mixed with a small amount of water) and then into roasted and crushed tamari pumpkin seeds. Roast the onion so the seeds will adhere.

Primary element: roasted red bell pepper

Hot sauce: vegetable

Herb/spice: fresh garlic

Cooking liquid: cashew cream made with water and Merlot (1 part nuts : 4 parts cooking liquid)

Salt: sea salt, light miso

French Onion

Primary element: onion

First-stage method: boil, loose vegetable soup

Cut: paper-thin slivers

   Oil: olive

   Herb/spice: garlic, shallot, fresh thyme

   Cooking liquid: vegetable stock (onion, onion skin, thyme), wine

   Salt: sea salt, tamari

Decorative: sourdough crouton

Onion Butter

SPREAD

Primary element: onion

First-stage method: slow cook

Cut: slivers

   Oil: ghee or olive

   Salt: sea salt

WHITE ONION (pungent/sweet)

White Bermuda and white Spanish onions have both reached weights of up to three pounds. I imagine one three-pound onion would make enough onion rings for 10–15 people. These are the best onions for dishes where the shape of the ring needs to remain intact during cooking. Small white onions are lovely steeped whole, scooped, stuffed, and roasted.

For Salad Greens

SALAD

Primary element: onion, fennel

First-stage method: press

Second-stage method: marinate

Cut: half rings

   Oil: sunflower seed

   Herb/spice: parsley, cumin, cardamom

   Cooking liquid: fresh lime juice

   Salt: chickpea miso, sea salt

Decorative: tamari roasted sunflower seeds

Braised

SIDE DISH

Primary element: onions

First-stage method: braise

Cut: fans

   Oil: light sesame

   Salt: rice or barley miso

   Cooking liquid: fresh lemon juice, wine, water

   Herb/spice: lemon zest/oil, pimenton (smoked paprika)

Curried Onion Rings

SIDE DISH

Primary element: onion

First-stage method: tempura

Cut: rings

Binder/batter: corn flour, brown rice flour, unbleached spelt, arrowroot

   Cooking liquid: ice-cold sparkling water

   Herb/spice: curry powder

   Oil: safflower

   Salt: dipping sauce and/or finely ground sea salt

GREEN ONION (pungent)

When people are learning a sport or a business, usually young people, they are called "green." An onion seed's first visible growth sends up green shoots. Given enough room to grow, it matures into a full adult onion. The green shoots make this onion refreshing and delightful. There is no reason to discard the greens and eat the white part alone. Green onions are a little stronger in flavor than chives and are used in the same way, decoratively. I use the entire length of the green onion. If one green onion looks too big for the amount needed, a thinner one is usually close by. I even like to use the delicate white roots when they are clean. If only a small quantity of onion is needed, leeks are often too big to be used whole; green onions are the perfect alternative.

Simple Simon

Primary element: rehydrated dried shiitake
    mushroom, green onion, baby bok choy
First-stage method: stir-fry
Cut: $1^1/_2$ inch log, large squares
  Oil: olive
  Salt: vegetable salt
  Cooking liquid: iced mushroom water from
    soaking

LEEK (sweet/pungent)

Leeks look like giant green onions. The white part of the leek grows in the dark, protected from light by being surrounded with soil. The green rises upward, developing chlorophyll from its interaction with the sun. Soil and sand move into the crevices where the green and white halves meet. There are two ways to clean leeks, depending on the cut. If the vegetable is going into a cooking method that uses oil, then it is cut before it is washed in a colander; otherwise the vegetable will be cooked whole. To wash a whole leek, let water run down the leaves and into the center while carefully peeling the leaves away, trying not to break them. The green part of a leek can contribute to a dish if its color will not interfere. For example, blending the leek greens in a cream of carrot soup would turn it brown.

Not On Its Own

SIDE DISH

Primary element: leek
First-stage method: steep
Second-stage method: marinate
Decorative: roasted red pepper or tomato, roasted
    almonds
  Oil: olive
  Herb/spice: fresh basil, fresh garlic
  Cooking liquid: cider vinegar, fresh orange
    juice
  Salt: sea salt

Circle Chews

SIDE DISH

Primary element: leek
First-stage method: roast
Cut: $^3/_4$-inch circles
  Oil: hazelnut
  Salt: sea salt, umeboshi

Elegance in Pastry

Primary element: leek

First-stage method: slow cook

Second-stage method: bake in phyllo

Decorative: bean pâté

    Oil: ghee or olive oil

    Herb/spice: fresh thyme

    Salt: sea salt, tamari

Hot sauce: nut

    Oil: pine nut

    Herb/spice: fresh garlic

    Cooking liquid: water

    Salt: chickpea miso

Soft Silhouette

SIDE DISH

Primary element: leek, onion, carrot

First-stage method: bake

Cut: diagonal, fans

    Oil: light sesame

    Salt: sea salt

Decorative: roasted, glazed cashews

Tang

DECORATIVE FOR BLACK RICE

Primary element: leek

First-stage method: braise

Decorative: mushrooms

Cut: small

    Oil: olive oil

    Cooking liquid: fresh lemon juice

    Herb/spice: herbes de Provence, garlic

    Salt: umeboshi

GARLIC (pungent)

Garlic, famous in the herb/spice category, performs as a major ingredient in the recipe sketches that follow. There are festivals in honor of this ancient food that is loaded with healing properties and surrounded by folklore. There are two opposing views about garlic: some say it is beneficial; others say it is to be avoided. Due to its intense pungency and ability to linger in the blood system for more than a day, garlic has been reputed to guard against "evil" (illness), thwart vampires, build the fire of courage in Roman soldiers, and strengthen Egyptian slaves. Garlic's alleged power as an aphrodisiac has caused it to be put on a list of prohibitions by some religious practices. I have heard the root end of the garlic clove should be removed because it adds bitterness, but I see no reason to do this. I don't mind a little bitterness and prefer to use the whole clove.

First Course

SOUP

Primary element: chayote or zucchini, onion, fresh garlic

First-stage method: pressure cook, cream-style soup

Cut: large

    Oil: olive

    Herb/spice: lemon zest, fresh garlic

    Cooking liquid: water, fresh lemon juice

    Salt: sea salt

Cold Garlic Cream Sauce

DOLLOP SAUCE

    Oil: mayonnaise

    Herb/spice: fresh garlic

Gives Punch to Grain

Primary element: fresh garlic

First-stage method: braise

Cut: fans

Oil: toasted sesame

Salt: tamari

Cooking liquid: mirin, fresh lemon juice

Herb/spice: ginger

Dipping Oil for Bread

SAUCE

Oil: olive

Herb/spice: fresh garlic, fresh rosemary

Cooking liquid: balsamic vinegar

Salt: sea salt

Alive

SPREAD

Primary element: soaked almonds, peeled

First-stage method: blend

Second-stage method: ferment

Cooking liquid: water, fresh lemon juice

Herb/spice: garlic

Salt: miso

Purple Meets Brown

SAUCE

Hot sauce: nut

Oil: pecan

Herb/spice: fresh garlic

Cooking liquid: water

Salt: chickpea miso

Garlic Olive Tapenade

DOLLOP SAUCE

Primary element: peeled roasted whole garlic, pimiento, green onion

Cold sauce: dollop, blend

Oil: olive (green or black)

Herb/spice: fresh sage

Cooking liquid: Madeira wine

Salt: olive

SHALLOT (pungent/bitter)

Shallots are positioned between onion and garlic. Their intensity raw is over-the-top, but their strength decreases nicely when they are cooked. In a bean pâté they manage to turn bitter. Shallots do not soften quickly. They are best used in long-cooking dishes or minced to respond to the heat more quickly. Pressure cooking them in soups and sauces is beneficial.

Threesome

CONDIMENT

Primary element: shallot, leek, red or yellow bell pepper

First-stage method: teriyaki

Cut: very small circles, small dice

Oil: olive

Cooking liquid/sweetener: mirin

Salt: umeboshi

Classical Beauty

Primary element: shallot, tomato

First-stage method: braise

Oil: olive oil

Cooking liquid: Madeira wine

Herb/spice: fresh basil

Salt: sea salt

VINE FAMILY

Squashes and melons that grow on vines have a shell/skin and a meaty body and seed cavity. The vines crawl on the surface of the earth, connected by plant umbilical chords. Melons and summer squashes hold water and minerals in a lightweight fiber—perfect for hot summer days. They need little time in the pot, if they are cooked at all. Summer squashes grow quickly, are not larger than the span of my hand, and they have more water content and less flavor than winter squashes. Winter squashes take time to mature and are harvested in the fall; they taste best if they experience a cold spell. Winter squashes provide more nutritional benefits when they are fully cooked. Although their cooking times vary, their meat will be soft like room temperature butter on a summer day. Melons are not just the fruit of the vine family. Their texture differs from winter and summer squashes and their fiber doesn't break down and become soft and smooth. Because winter squashes are more fibrous, they benefit from using a form of oil.

Archeologists discovered vine seeds and stems in early Egyptian and Roman excavations, but these were thought to be gourd shells and melons rather than the meaty squashes we cook today. Even when Christopher Columbus and Francisco Pizarro brought luscious Native American squash seeds home to Spain, Europe had no interest. But China and Japan took the seeds to heart and have developed varieties of their own. Speculation links the early relationship between Mexico and China as a possible source of seeds traveling to Asia. Native Americans have been cultivating squash since the beginning of recorded time. It has a prominent position in the famous "three sisters" tradition where corn (grain element) and beans (protein element) and squash (vegetable element) are planted in near proximity to support each other's growth. The cornstalk supports climbing beans, which are surrounded by a hill of big squash leaves, which shade the ground to keep moisture available to all three plants. Native American belief in the fertility of this food is reflected in their saying, "Plant a squash seed by your door and you will have a large family." The Pilgrims abbreviated the Native American words "askutasquash" and "isquouter-squash" to simply "squash."

Winter squashes are good sources of carbohydrates, natural sugar, vitamin A, and energy that is warm and soothing. Summer squashes are the opposite. They cool the body and deliver water and a quick supply of nutrients, especially vitamin C. Squash juice is purported to remove the sting from skin burns. Winter squashes and pumpkin seeds have a reputation for expelling worms from the intestinal track. Chinese melons have been reported to aid type 2 diabetes.

Winter squash resists even a heavy knife. I need to use a locked elbow-to-hip technique to cut through them. The tip of my knife is aligned with my wrist and elbow, and then my elbow is tucked tightly into my hip bone. The squash is held by my claw hand (left hand) on the cutting board, my legs are slightly bent, and my right leg is parallel to and behind the left. In this position the power of my hip as it thrusts forward and the blade of the knife sliding through the squash makes a difficult job easy. The meat of winter vine vegetables is separated from their seeds. If seeds in summer squash are large enough to remove, it means the vegetable is overgrown and tough. Whether or not you want to eat the skin of winter squashes depends on the color and cooking method of the finished dish. Winter squash cavities are perfect for stuffing with other primary elements. Before stuffing, it must first be completely roasted by itself. These large cavities are thick. Puncturing the squash meat with a fork before applying oil and salt lets the sugar juices rise into the cavity, make a puddle, and sink back down into the meat. With this technique it is important not to place the squash upside down; an upright cavity will collect the sugar juices of the squash for a richer flavor.

Selecting and Storing

Winter squashes take up too much room in a refrigerator and would begin to rot with moisture and no airflow. Therefore my first choice for storage is on a cool porch or in a garage during the fall and winter months. Left on the kitchen counter for more than a month, their meat will dry out. I'll cook them anyway, in a braised dish, soup, or sauce. Often pale green lines indicate an unripe, winter squash, and it will lack flavor. To tell if a winter squash is ready to eat, I might snap off the stem and hope to see juice and a bright orange color. Summer squashes might last a week in the refrigerator, but they are best cooked as close to picking time as possible. Their naturally bitter flavor increases the longer they sit; too large and they are pithy. I compare the size with the distance between my outstretched third finger and thumb, which spans about eight inches. To determine freshness, try the fingernail test; if a fingernail enters the skin easily with no resistance, the squash is fresh.

ACORN SQUASH (winter/sweet)

A good acorn squash will not need brown sugar and butter. The fiber of this squash can be stringy, but when the meat is orange-gold and the skin is deep dark green, there is a chance that this deep-ridged winter squash will be naturally sweet and buttery. The gold variegated versions of this football-shaped squash are equally delicious. Cut into quarters, thirds, or halves, acorn squashes invite stuffing after they are roasted. It is important to roast the squash facing up so its sweet juices are collected in the bowl of the body.

Acorn Stuffed with Spicy Seitan

MAIN PLATE

Primary element: acorn squash

First-stage method: roast

Cut: in half, seeded, poked with a fork

    Oil: light sesame

    Salt: sea salt

Primary element: gluten

First-stage method: teriyaki

Cut: thin strips

    Oil: light sesame

    Herb/spice: cayenne (use with caution)

    Cooking liquid/sweetener: brown rice syrup

    Salt: umeboshi

Hot sauce: flour

Binder: brown rice flour

    Oil: light sesame

    Cooking liquid: water

    Herb/spice: bay leaf, thyme, ground coriander

    Salt: tamari or shoyu

Decorative: minced fresh parsley

BANANA SQUASH (winter/sweet)

It takes two arms to hold a banana squash, which can grow as large as 12 pounds. The thick skin of these winter squashes is not as palatable as other varieties, so I usually discard it after cooking or remove it before. To cook banana squash whole, first I have to find one. Since most grocery stores cut and wrap banana squash in one-pound portions, I search for it at farmers' markets. For Thanksgiving, picture creamy, pink-skinned banana squash, cut in half lengthwise, scooped out like a boat, roasted, and stuffed with Smokey Sage Stuffing (page 196) and served with Purple Meets Brown sauce (page 119).

BUTTERCUP SQUASH
(winter/sweet)

Buttercup squashes have square heads. They are my favorite winter squash because after the effort of cutting and cleaning there is plenty of bright, moist, orange meat. The dark green skin is tasty and easily removed, which is important if I'm making a creamy soup. I think of buttercup as one of the most versatile and dependable winter squashes.

A Sweet Caper

SIDE DISH

Primary element: buttercup squash, onion

First-stage method: braise

Cut: cubes, large dice

Oil: hazelnut

Salt: caper brine

Herb/spice: lemon zest, fresh rosemary

Cooking liquid: fresh lemon juice, caper brine, water

Decorative: capers

BUTTERNUT SQUASH
(winter/sweet)

Butternut squashes are in the market all year round. I don't expect them to taste their best in spring or summer. Pale skin and chartreuse-colored lines running the length of this gourd-shaped vegetable often indicate the meat's flavor is weak. Like most starchy squashes, their sweetness increases when they have on-the-vine exposure to cold. Butternut is the most flexible squash for cooking. Its thin skin is easily eaten or removed.

Fall

SIDE DISH

Primary element: butternut squash

First-stage method: bake

Cut: skinned, cubed

Oil: sesame

Salt: sea salt

Herb/spice: fresh rosemary (optional)

Cream of Squash

SOUP

Primary element: butternut squash

First-stage method: pressure cook, cream-style soup

Decorative: onion, red bell pepper

Cut: large

Oil: light sesame

Herb/spice: coriander seed, fresh cilantro

Cooking liquid: cashew milk made with water and white wine (1 part nuts : 15 parts cooking liquid)

Salt: sea salt

PRIMARY ELEMENTS AND RECIPE SKETCHES

HOKKAIDO SQUASH (RED KURI), KABOCHA SQUASH (winter/sweet)

These traditional Japanese squashes, identified by their flat, elliptical shape and hearty gray-green or reddish-orange skin, have dry, rich, flaky meat. *Kabocha* is the Japanese word for winter squash or pumpkin. I love their chewy texture when roasted and enjoy eating their skin, which resembles a potato skin. These versions of winter squash provide heft to a dish, making them good additions to stew and other mixed-vegetable dishes.

Drunken Squash

SIDE DISH

Primary element: Hokkaido squash
First-stage method: braise
Cut: cubes
> *Oil:* olive
> *Herb/spice:* fresh rosemary
> *Salt:* umeboshi
> *Cooking liquid:* dry vermouth, water

SPAGHETTI SQUASH (winter/sweet)

Spaghetti squash is a winter squash with more form than taste. After a first-stage method, this winter squash appears to look like noodles. Many people are impressed by its texture. I am not impressed by its taste. So if asked to cook it, I use infusion methods, like braising and marinating, once the meat of the squash is soft enough to separate it from its shell-like skin. This is the only vegetable that requires a simple first-stage method like pressure steaming to prepare it for more flavors.

Funny Noodle Squash with Sauce

(SIDE DISH)

Primary element: spaghetti squash
First-stage method: pressure steam
Cut: in half lengthwise, seeds removed
Second stage: braise
Decorative: diced mushroom, red and yellow bell pepper, diagonally slivered green onion
> *Oil:* olive
> *Salt:* umeboshi
> *Cooking liquid:* Marsala wine
> *Herb/spice:* minced garlic, fresh thyme

Hot sauce: nut
> *Oil:* cashews
> *Cooking liquid:* water
> *Salt:* chickpea miso
> *Herb/spice:* star anise

CUCUMBER (melon/bitter/sweet)

Cucumber varieties have skin that is smooth or bumpy, thick or thin. Their bodies may be long, short, or curly. Some have large, annoying seeds; others do not have any seeds that are visible. Their colors are green or yellow. I look at the skin and seeds to decide how to eat them. The green variety with sturdy skin is made more palatable by cutting off the ends and rubbing the cut piece on the body of the opposite end. Like the magic of bubbles rising in a bath tub, a dense white foam will appear. Although cucumbers may feel smooth to the fingers, their bitter taste can be rough on the tongue. Not all cukes do this. The "defoaming" process makes the taste sweeter and the skin more edible.

Mixed Vegetables

Primary element: cucumber, yellow
 bell pepper, celery

First-stage method: press

 Salt: sea salt

 Herb/spice: lemon zest

 Cooking liquid: fresh lemon juice

Kosher-Style Dill Pickles

SIDE DISH

Primary element: pickling cucumber

First-stage method: hot brine pickle

Cut: whole

Herb/spice: whole peppercorns, bay leaves,
 garlic cloves, fresh dill seed, fresh dill weed

 Cooking liquid: hot salt brine (1 cup salt :
  1 gallon water)

 Salt: sea salt

Cool

SALAD

Primary element: English cucumber

First-stage method: press

Second-stage method: marinate

Cut: half-moon diagonal

 Oil: soaked almonds

 Cooking liquid: almond cream made with
  rejuvelac (1 part nuts : 2 parts cooking
  liquid)

 Salt: umeboshi

 Herb/spice: minced fresh mint

PATTYPAN SQUASH
(summer/sweet)

With their elliptical bodies edged with petal-shaped curves, pattypan summer squashes are visually inspiring. Usually bright yellow or deep green, and smaller than the palm of my hand, pattypan squashes are easily cooked whole, which enhances their subtle flavor.

Kebobs

SIDE DISH

Primary element: pattypan squash, mushroom,
 red bell pepper

First-stage method: steep

Second-stage method: marinate

Third-stage method: grill

Cut: whole, large wedges (quartered)

 Oil: light sesame

 Cooking liquid: fresh orange juice, raspberry
  vinegar

 Herb/spice: fresh thyme

 Salt: miso

Tastes of Summer

SIDE DISH

Primary element: pattypan squash

First-stage method: broil

Decorative: tomato

Cut: thin circles

 Oil: olive

 Herb/spice: fresh basil

 Salt: vegetable salt

GOLD BAR ZUCCHINI
(summer/sweet)

This is the perfect name for the most valuable summer squash. With its brilliant, deep yellow color, mild sweet taste, and long shape, gold bar zucchini invites creativity. Before or after cooking, this long vegetable may be cut in any number of shapes: owl, long diagonal, julienne, half-moon diagonal, or dice.

GREEN ZUCCHINI (summer/bitter)

Zucchini, the most famous summer squash, is often used with garlic and basil to balance its bitter nature. Deep and variegated, green zucchini is similar to gold bar zucchini, and they may be used interchangeably in dishes.

CROOKNECK SQUASH
(summer/sweet)

The neck on this summer squash is usually half the size or smaller than its body. When they are small, these squashes are aesthetically pleasing cooked whole. Because of the curve of the neck, cutting crookneck squash is best approached in the same fashion as a concave shape—in half lengthwise first. If the arch is either facing up or down on the board, a knife will easily go from tip to bottom, creating two equal halves.

Yellow and Gold

SIDE DISH

Primary element: gold bar zucchini
First-stage method: roast
   Oil: sunflower
   Salt: vegetable salt
   Herb/spice: curry powder

Elegant Mix

SIDE DISH

Primary element: gold bar zucchini, leek
First-stage method: slow cook
Cut: diagonal
   Oil: Olive
   Herb/spice: fresh garlic
   Salt: sea salt, tamari/shoyu
Note: This may be put in a crust or phyllo pastry, with or without a sauce.

POD/SEED FAMILY

Like a shooting star, corn, peas, string beans, and green beans have a very short lifespan. They are brilliant within the first 24 hours from harvest, then they begin to hibernate, either naturally, by drying in their pods, or by kitchen preservation or cooking methods.

When they are harvested young and fresh, they are cooked and served as vegetables. When they stay connected to the earth until the pods are dry, corn becomes grain and peas and beans function as protein elements. The fresher they are, the more vitamins and water they contain. Water content dictates the cooking methods. These seeds are nourished and protected by a silk/husk and shell/pod.

Many seeds originated in South America, found their way to Europe, and then arrived in the United States. Corn, however, is all-American. Corn and beans, two of the "three sisters," appeared in the Aztec culture around 10,000 BCE. Corn exploded onto the eating scene as a hybrid around 1500, was traded up through the American Southwest by 1100, and made it all the way to the Northeast Woodland tribes by 200 AD. Soybeans originated in China around the first century BCE. One famous way they are served is known as edamame, the Japanese name for fresh soybeans. The soybeans are boiled in their pods with salt and squeezed out of their pods when they are served.

The watery nature of both fresh corn and legumes supports healthy kidney function, balanced sexual activity, strong teeth and gums, a hearty appetite, and good digestion. Legumes contain more protein than corn, and blue corn has more protein than yellow corn. This family provides complex carbohydrates, large amounts of potassium, and vitamins A and C.

Selecting and Storing

The best way to select these vegetables is in a garden. Produce at a farmers' market is usually picked within 24 hours before being sold. These vegetables turn to starch after 48 hours, even when kept in a cooler. If stored in cold water, their crispness can be maintained, but replacing their natural juices with water is not appealing. These vegetables must snap (green beans), crunch (peas), and pop (corn) to be considered fresh. I poke fresh corn on the cob with my fingernail to see if it will squirt. Finding a worm in a corncob top where the silk is brown and dry indicates few, if any, chemicals were used. If the worm has chosen this food, it may be good. If a worm bores through the top of the cob, just slide a knife through that portion of the cob and discard it.

CORN (sweet)

A Native American riddle that references roasted corn on the cob offers advice to young ones: "Bring to your elders the girl with the watery teeth. Her odor will be fragrant when they remove her garments." Corn on the cob tastes best pressure steamed, steeped, or roasted in its husk. Boiling corn is overkill. Steeping and pressure steaming take one-fourth the time and energy and taste 110 percent better. Dried sweet corn tastes like candy.

Better than Boiling

SIDE DISH

Primary element: fresh corn on the cob
First-stage method: steep
   Salt: sea salt, umeboshi

A Mirror

SOUP

Primary element: fresh corn off the cob, onion
First-stage method: boil, clear soup
Cut: whole corn kernels, diced onion
   Cooking liquid: fresh corncob without kernels in kombu stock
   Salt: sea salt, tamari or umeboshi
   Binder: kudzu (1 tablespoon : 1 quart cooking liquid)

Yellow Chowder

Primary element: fresh corn off the cob, onion

First-stage method: pressure cook, cream-style soup

Base binder: cauliflower

Oil: olive or ghee

Herb/spice: optional

Cooking liquid: cashew milk (1 part nuts : 8–12 parts cooking liquid)

Salt: sea salt, umeboshi

Decorative: roasted potato cubes, bell pepper

Tango

SIDE DISH

Primary element: fresh corn off the cob

First-stage method: braise

Decorative: green onion, cherry tomato

Oil: olive

Herb/spice: fresh oregano

Salt: tamari

Cooking liquid: white balsamic vinegar

Living Wafer

CRACKER

Primary element: fresh corn off the cob, sprouted quinoa

First-stage method: blend

Second-stage method: dehydrate

Oil: soaked nuts

Herb/spice: fresh herbs

Salt: sea salt or soaked sea vegetable

PEA (sweet/bitter)

There are three kinds of fresh peas, and they come in large and petite sizes. English garden peas are round, firm, and must be removed from their pod. The Asian snow pea is flat, thin, and delicate. Its edible pods contain miniature peas. The third kind, the snap pea, is a combination of the other two, with an edible pod and removable, pebble-size peas (that I don't remove). Peas thrive in a cool climate. Edible pods are held together by a strong, stringlike fiber. These tough strings are removed so you don't feel you are chewing on dental floss. The top of the pod usually has a knob where it attaches to the bush. I put my thumb on this knob and break it off just enough to pull the strings down and away from the pod. Then they are ready to eat raw or take to a first stage.

Tradition

MAIN PLATE

Primary element: snow pea, shiitake mushroom, green onion

First-stage method: stir-fry

Cut: large

Decorative: deep-fried tofu

Clear sauce: (1 tablespoon kudzu : 1⁺ cup liquid)

Oil: toasted sesame

Herb/spice: fresh garlic, Chinese five spice

Cooking liquid: ginger/kombu stock

Salt: sea salt, tamari/shoyu

Primary element: black forbidden rice

First-stage method: steep

Herb/spice: sliced ginger

Cooking liquid: water

Salt: sea salt

For the Fairies

SALAD

Primary element: snap pea

First-stage method: steep

Second-stage method: marinate

Cut: whole

  Oil: safflower

  Cooking liquid: fresh lemon juice

  Herb/spice: lemon zest

  Salt: vegetable salt

The Mimic

SIDE DISH

Primary element: any pea

First-stage method: braise

Cut: halved, lengthwise

  Oil: olive

  Herb/spice: ground cardamom

  Salt: chickpea miso

  Cooking liquid: mirin, water, rice vinegar

GREEN BEANS AND
STRING BEANS (sweet/bitter)

The difference between green beans and string beans is the former grows on the vine a little longer. They both hold the nutritional potential of a bean seed in their pod. String beans are long and thin, crisp and sweet. They don't keep well. To capture and store the freshness of this vegetable, freezing is better than canning. Green beans, like soy, fava, and lima beans, are easier to cook and digest fresh than their dried versions. Fresh, out-of-the-pod fava beans act like bigger, tougher English peas, and it is appropriate to use them interchangeably in dishes. Once out of the pod, these large, flat seeds require either soaking or steeping to remove a second skin that is as tough as horsehide. It is a bit labor intensive but worth the work. With the skins removed, fava beans split into small ovals, almost chartreuse in color. These are ready for second-stage methods where the herb/spice, salt, and other supporting elements finish the dish.

> *W*hen I grow beans in the summer, they are lucky to make it into a dish. I usually eat them between the garden and kitchen.

Summer Special

SALAD

Primary element: green or string beans

First-stage method: steep

Second-stage method: marinate

Cut: whole, owl

Decorative: apple, roasted glazed pecans

Cold sauce: marinade (1 part oil: $1^1/_2$ parts cooking liquid)

  Oil: pumpkin

  Cooking liquid: peach juice, cider vinegar

  Herb/spice: fresh basil

  Salt: sea salt

Trilogy in Cream

Primary element: green, yellow, purple string beans

First-stage method: steep

Cut: whole, long diagonal

Hot sauce: nut

Oil: pine nut

Herb/spice: fresh garlic

Cooking liquid: water, white wine

Salt: chickpea miso

Green Glazed

Primary element: green or string beans

First-stage method: teriyaki

Cut: log

Oil: toasted sesame

Herb/spice: fresh ginger

Cooking liquid/sweetener: rice syrup

Salt: tamari

Salt: tamari

Cooking liquid: balsamic vinegar, mirin

Mediterranean Flash

Primary element: purple or green string beans or fresh fava beans removed from pod

First-stage method: braise

Cut: diagonal

Oil: olive

Herb/spice: fresh garlic, fresh basil

Cooking liquid: blended fresh tomato, Marsala wine

Salt: light miso, sea salt

House of Yellow Glass

Primary element: green, yellow, or purple string beans

First-stage method: tempura

Cut: whole

Batter: sweet rice flour, brown rice flour, unbleached white, arrowroot

Herb/spice: optional dash of turmeric

Cooking liquid: sparkling water

Oil: safflower

Cold/dipping sauce: (1 part salt : 2 parts cooking liquid)

SEA VEGETABLE FAMILY

Sea vegetables differ from land plants in a variety of ways. Land plants gain their nutrients from the soil in their specific growing area. Sea vegetables breathe the ocean's nutrients directly into their leaves through water. The ocean is not just any water; all land plants eventually find their way to the ocean. Seaweed absorbs 77 minerals from the ocean. The nutritional power of this "superfood" is further enhanced when it is grown in a cool, clean, nontoxic environment. The cold ocean is best for harvesting sea vegetables (weeds of the sea), but it is not specific to one continent. Although Japan and Korea have incorporated sea vegetables into their cuisine, sea vegetables are harvested on many coasts including the American northwest, Britain, Ireland, Scandinavia, and Asia. Kelp, a generic term for about 8,000 species of leafy green, brown, and red algae, is too vague a word for culinary purposes. Variations of new sea vegetables are regularly entering the marketplace to add to the current popular selection. Arame, hijiki, wakame, nori, and sea palm are only a few of the sea vegetables harvested for cooking. They are interchangeable in the recipe sketches that follow.

> *S*ea vegetables make me think about the earth being a container for the ocean. If I could consume the power of everything that grows in the earth—trees, flowers, wild grasses, ornamental plants, and the worldwide supply of fruits and vegetables—the result would be sea vegetables.

I have seen people who eat a steady diet of sea vegetables strengthen their nervous system, grow a beautiful head of hair, and drop pounds. In addition to calcium, iron, and many other healthful minerals and trace minerals, sea vegetables are rich in iodine, especially the sea vegetable bladderwrack. In the 1800s bladderwrack was used to balance the thyroid, preventing swelling and obesity; it was considered dangerous if overdosed. Sea vegetables' superpower is no secret to people eating a variety of them regularly. They are difficult to overeat, and it's easy to know when you've had enough. A single serving may only be a tablespoon, due to the intensity of this mineral-rich vegetable. Using sea vegetables as a decorative element is beautiful, practical, and easy. First they need to be so delicious that the dish could stand on its own. Then, placed with a cooked main grain or vegetable dish, it becomes a condiment or decorative vegetable. Their black and green shiny color is both a nutritional and color statement. Wakame and arame work well in raw dishes, especially with the marinade method. That is the only time marinating is a first-stage cooking method.

Selecting and Storing

Sea vegetables are very delicate; the most common way to find them, unless one is a forager, is dried. Occasionally this process will leave some sea salt glistening on the leaf. This is preferred to dried sea vegetables that have been rinsed in fresh water. Once they are soaked, I rub my fingers over them gently to see if the surface is slippery or slimy. Slippery sea vegetables are acceptable to eat; slimy ones are not. When sea vegetables are large, they are often cut after harvesting, like arame. Or when they are small, like nori flakes, they are pressed into sheets. Sea vegetables should be stored in a dark, dry place. They have a long shelf life.

AGAR (mirror)

Agar (also known as agar-agar) fascinates me. Scientists use it to stabilize substances in order to study them under a microscope, because agar, unlike gelatin, which is animal protein, is not protein based and won't break down the substance that is being studied. Agar is used as a binding agent for gelled desserts, but it is not heat sensitive like gelatin, which requires a cool environment to remain stable. Agar gels at room temperature. It has multiple uses including as a clarifying agent in winemaking and brewing and as a filler during the manufacture of cloth and paper. It is also used in dentistry, cosmetics, film, and adhesives. Industry utilizes agar in powder form. I do not advise using the powder for culinary functions because it is highly processed and the ratios as a binder are more difficult to master. Bars and flakes are featherweight. To make agar, manufacturers gather several species of red algae in cold temperatures, boil them, set them into blocks, and freeze them to extract excess moisture.

Agar provides substance with no flavor. It gives shape to other ingredient categories. Used with or without nut milk, agar creates a clear, custardlike gel. The ratio of cooking liquid to agar is 3 cups cooking liquid to 1 bar agar for a not-too-firm gel. More liquid would make a substance that is too soft to hold a molded shape. For agar flakes, the ratio is 1 tablespoon flakes to 1 cup liquid. I usually make that a heaping tablespoon. It is important to soak the agar bar in water before combining it with other ingredients to cook. Flakes need to soak also, but it is difficult to separate the rehydrated flakes from the soaking water. It is best to soak the flakes in the thinnest cooking liquid of the dish for about 15 minutes before they are combined with other ingredients. Whether the soaked bar is torn into flakes after soaking, or the flakes have soaked in the dish's cooking liquid, the agar needs to dissolve completely in the boiling method before it can take form, which will happen as it cools. The entire amount of agar may be cooked in a small amount of cooking liquid and then added to ingredients that won't be cooked, as with Guacamole Ring (page 132) and Living Spinach Custard (next column).

Pineapple Cranberry Fluff

Primary element: soaked agar bars, fresh or canned pineapple

First-stage method: boil

Cooking liquid: blended fresh or canned pineapple and its juice, blended fresh cranberry, Triple Sec liqueur (optional)

Decorative: fresh cranberry

   Herb/spice: orange oil

   Salt: sea salt

Decorative: roasted, glazed pecans

Tomato Aspic

Primary element: soaked agar

First-stage method: boil

Decorative: pressed and slivered green onion, minced cilantro

   Cooking liquid: tomato-based vegetable juice

   Herb/spice: minced fresh garlic, freshly ground black pepper

   Salt: sea salt

Party Beans

Primary element: anasazi beans

First-stage method: pressure cook

   Cooking liquid: beer

   Herb/spice: ancho chile, chipotle chile, epazote

Second-stage method: braise

Decorative: agar, red bell pepper, onion

   Oil: corn oil

   Herb/spice: garlic

   Cooking liquid/sweetener: bean juice, agave

   Salt: sea salt

Living Spinach Custard

Primary element: soaked spinach, boiled agar

First-stage method: blend, boil

   Oil: soaked pine nuts

   Herb/spice: lemon zest, ground nutmeg

   Cooking liquid: water, fresh lemon juice, pine nut milk (1 part nuts : 8 parts liquid)

   Salt: sea salt

Guacamole Ring

Primary element: blended avocado, soaked agar

First-stage method: boil agar

Decorative: cilantro

Cooking liquid: fresh lemon juice, water

Herb/spice: garlic

Salt: sea salt

ARAME (salty)

Arame is a "beginner's" sea vegetable; it's best for guests who aren't familiar with or don't like seaweed. Arame pieces are shredded off a large, thick frond, which dilutes the impact of the "sea taste" found in other sea vegetables. After arame has been taken through an entire cooking method by itself, its mild flavor and almost-black color work well to decorate a dish. To make 6–8 servings of arame (about $3/4$ cup total, or 1 tablespoon/9 grams per serving), soak $1/2$ ounce (13 grams) dried arame in $8\,3/4$ ounces (240 grams) water.

Sea Salad #1

Primary element: soaked arame, yellow and red bell pepper

First-stage method: marinate

Cut: slivers

Decorative: deep-fried tofu

Oil: peanut butter

Herb/spice: fresh garlic, lime oil, ginger, tamarind, cayenne

Cooking liquid: fresh lime juice, kombu-galangal stock, agave

Salt: tamari

Everyman's

Primary element: soaked arame

First-stage method: teriyaki

Oil: light sesame

Cooking liquid/sweetener: mirin

Herb/spice: minced fresh garlic

Salt: umeboshi

DULSE (salty)

One of the most famous sea vegetables, in shades of red, dulse grows attached to ocean rock in coastal Canada and Ireland. After being sun-dried, dulse is crushed into flakes to be used in condiments, soups, or mixed-vegetable dishes. It tastes more strongly of minerals than of the sea. My favorite use for dulse is smoked and crushed with sesame seeds as a condiment.

HIJIKI (salty)

Hijiki is thick, dark, and bold, with a dynamic taste—not for the sea vegetable novice. I feel the entire sea in this vegetable. Pitch-black hijiki contrasts beautifully with the white of tofu as well as with green and orange vegetables. By using hijiki in a mixed-vegetable dish or as a decorative vegetable, the intense taste is balanced. To make 6–8 servings (about 1 tablespoon per serving), soak $1/4$ cup ($1/2$ ounce/14 grams) dried hijiki in $8\,3/4$ ounces (240 grams) water for 15–20 minutes, depending on the thickness of the hijiki.

Black Streaks

SIDE DISH

Primary element: soaked hijiki, onion, carrot, parsnip

First-stage method: slow cook

Cut: slivers, julienne

Oil: light sesame

Salt: sea salt, tamari

Golden Crisp Disks

APPETIZER

Primary element: soaked hijiki, green onion

First-stage method: tempura

Batter binder: brown rice flour, corn flour, unbleached white, arrowroot

Cooking liquid: beer

Oil: safflower

Cold sauce: dipping (1 part salt seasoning : 2 parts character liquid)

Salt: chickpea miso

Cooking liquid: fresh lemon juice, water

Tradition

CONDIMENT

Primary element: soaked hijiki

First-stage method: teriyaki

Oil: toasted sesame

Cooking liquid/sweetener: agave

Herb/spice: ginger juice

Salt: tamari

KOMBU (salty)

Kombu is the one sea vegetable that I use the most and eat the least. Known as "the giant," it grows at the rate of almost a foot a day and can reach lengths of 400 feet or more. It's not just fast growing, it is strong, thick, and has many uses. Kombu goes into the cooking methods for soup stock and first-stage beans. It sits in the bottom of a pressure cooker when I pressure steam vegetables, and sometimes accompanies first-stage grain. Kombu brings out the best of other ingredients, and its properties help make vegetable protein easier to digest. Too much kombu exposes the taste of sea. In bean cookery, the ratio is one inch of kombu to one cup of dried beans. In stock, use one inch for each quart of liquid. Despite its leathery texture, I will eat kombu in a dish where it adds flavor and the color is compatible. For example, with red or black first-stage beans, kombu's green color doesn't interfere like it might with chickpeas or white beans. With light-colored beans like these, kombu should be removed after cooking. Kombu boiled in stock may be removed or cut into slivers and used as a decorative element for soup.

Flakes

CONDIMENT

Primary element: kombu

First-stage method: deep-fry

Cut: break into 1–2-inch pieces, crush kombu with crushed red pepper flakes after cooking

Oil: safflower

Herb/spice: crushed red pepper flakes

Utility

Primary element: kombu, soba noodles, baby bok choy

First-stage method: boil, clear soup

    Cooking liquid: kombu spice stock, water

    Herb/spice: galangal, kaffir lime leaf, lemongrass

    Salt: sea salt, tamari/shoyu

Cut: slivers

Decorative: tofu

Second-stage method: braise

    Oil: light sesame

    Cooking liquid: mirin

    Salt: tamari/shoyu

Decorative: slivered green onion, toasted nori

NORI (salty/sweet)

Nori has become world famous through its use in sushi. It begins as a thin, purple, tangled laver (red algae) that is pressed into sheets with a rough side and a smooth side. The rough surface goes toward the inside of a sushi roll so rice can grip it; the exterior side is smooth and shiny, allowing a knife to slide through it easily. Although toasted (green) nori is readily available, toasting raw (purple) nori (or retoasting green nori to freshen it) is easy. Put two sheets together, rough sides touching, and pass the shiny side of the sheets quickly over an open flame. Purple will turn to green and an aroma reminiscent of camping by the sea will travel through the air. Nori is ready to eat when it turns green. Holding it up to a light will reveal the spots that still need to be toasted. When it is done, crisp nori becomes a snack, condiment, or sheet for making sushi rolls. The most important advice for cooking with nori is don't let it get wet. Wet nori becomes slimy, difficult to work with, and grossly unappealing.

Treats

Primary element: nori

First-stage method: dry roast

Second-stage method: roast, lightly brush on mixture of following:

    Oil: dark sesame

    Cooking liquid: mirin

    Salt: tamari

    Herb/spice: cayenne

SEA PALM (salty)

Extra cooking liquid is required to cook sea palm longer than other sea vegetables because its ribbed pattern creates a sturdy ribbon shape. Sea palm has the most exquisite chewy texture and color, which is a combination shade of black and emerald green.

Daily Fare

Primary element: sea palm, onion

First-stage method: braise

Cut: slivers, strips

    Oil: hazelnut

    Herb/spice: orange zest

    Cooking liquid: orange juice, soaking water from sea palm

    Salt: umeboshi

Classic Flavors

Primary element: sea palm
First-stage method: marinate
Decorative: red onion
Cut: paper-thin slivers
    Oil: toasted sesame
    Cooking liquid: mirin, rice vinegar
    Herb/spice: ginger juice
    Salt: miso

WAKAME (salty)

Wakame became popular with ordinary people in the eighteenth century. Until then it was only available to the wealthy. It has become so popular that there has been an increase of cultivated wakame, although naturally grown and harvested sea vegetables are available through a number of companies. Wakame has a delicate temperament. Unlike the black sea vegetables, this green one performs with a light energy body. Thin, broad leaves attach to a strong center. The core is edible when fully soaked, which takes 15–20 minutes. Sometimes wakame is slimy after soaking, which indicates poor quality. Rub soaked wakame between two fingers to determine if you have a clean, healthy batch. Broad leaves easily capture sea life in their wings. In the 1970s, I would find itty-bitty sea horses and barnacles at the bottom of the soaking liquid. Today the sea vegetables are much cleaner.

Sea Salad #2

Primary element: soaked wakame, cucumber, celery
First-stage method: marinate
Cut: half-moon, long diagonal
    Oil: tahini
    Cooking liquid: fresh lemon juice, water
    Herb/spice: garlic
    Salt: umeboshi

Branches

Primary element: soaked wakame
First-stage method: tempura
Cut: large
Binder for batter: sweet rice flour, brown rice flour, arrowroot, unbleached white
    Cooking liquid: sparkling water
    Oil: safflower
    Salt: dipping sauce

Loose Miso

Primary element: soaked wakame, onion, carrot
First-stage method: boil, loose vegetable soup
Cut: small squares, slivers, julienne
    Oil: dark sesame
    Cooking liquid: kombu/spice stock
    Herb/spice: ginger
    Salt: sea salt, miso

This family began as wild plants. Their lineage originated before the fifth century BCE. Kale, one of the first recorded members of this family, was cultivated for its large, broad, curly leaf. By the first century AD, horticulturists had developed the kale leaf into a tighter head. Since bigger was considered better at that time, large heads of cabbage were developed. By the eighteenth century, small heads were the fashion in France and Belgium. Cabbage buds were grown and harvested near Brussels, Belgium, hence brussels sprouts. Edible leaves include the tops of roots, cabbages, wild greens, and simple, flat, broad leaves from many plant varieties. They are usually shades of green, ranging from pale, almost-white celadon to rich, dark green-black tones. A pan brimming with greens will shrink to one layer by the end of cooking. The firmer the green, the more cooking liquid is required.

Leafy greens prefer growing in cold temperatures. Some grow through snow. Although they have a reputation for creating a strong odor while cooking and after digestion, I find them appealing for their bold character and potent nutritional benefits. They are rich in minerals and vitamins: folate, iron, magnesium, phosphorus, calcium, potassium, copper, manganese, riboflavin, thiamin, vitamin A, vitamin C, vitamin K, and vitamin B_6. They also contain notable amounts of fiber. Dandelion, nettles, fiddlehead ferns, and lamb's-quarters, often regarded as useless weeds, are potent vegetables picked in the wild. Wild greens may be used like the other vegetables in the leaf family. When these plants are found in the wild, I pay attention to their "season," harvesting them when they are best. Dandelion, the most common, easy-to-harvest wild food, is best in the spring, before it produces its notorious yellow flower. Nettles are harvested with gloves to avoid a sting, usually in the late spring as the weather warms. Lamb's-quarter shares its name with wild spinach, pigweed, and goosefoot. It grows as a common garden weed, best harvested in summer. Orache grows in and around rocks near the coastline. It is a late bloomer to be harvested in late summer. The delicate fiddlehead fern grows at the top of an ostrich fern and is best harvested between April and May.

Leafy vegetables have three basic personality types—soft, sturdy, and crisp. The ones with soft leaves, like spinach, beet greens, Swiss chard, and amaranth greens, cook quickly into a fine, delicate texture. Sturdier versions that contain a high water content are used to add elegance, as with lettuce, chicory, endive, and radicchio. The largest category of greens belongs to the cruciferous collective; they have coarse fibers that create a crisp texture, and include kale, collards, cabbage, brussels sprouts, mustard greens, the Chinese choy family, and kohlrabi.

Selecting and Storing

Look for a good water content indicated by crisp leaves, tight heads, and even coloring without brown spots. These greens do not keep for long periods and respond well to special care. Wash loose leaves in a large amount of water so that sand and dirt can fall away. Then lift them out of the cold bath and either spin dry or towel dry. Laying them in paper or cloth towels and placing them in a plastic bag in the refrigerator will keep them crisp for almost a week. After they are washed, they can also be used immediately in cooking or salads. Tight heads are cleaned by removing the outer leaves and soaking, if insects are present. For longer storage, freezing is an option, but dehydrating will hold the energetic nutrition better.

AMARANTH (bitter)

In my opinion, all leafy greens respond to the same cooking methods. Amaranth greens are a large, broad, tender leaf, similar to flat spinach. In addition to the powerhouse of nutrients available in all leafy greens, amaranth greens are a good source of protein and niacin.

When I was introduced to amaranth greens it was love at first sight. It was Saturday morning at the farmers' market, with the typical produce filling the stands. Seeing amaranth greens for the first time pulled me like a magnet into a farmer's booth; I thought it was perfection and then some. I had heard about a man whose knowledge of the soil produced brilliant vegetables. It turned out that this was his booth—The Plant Man himself. With his hands bunching amaranth like a bouquet of flowers, I asked, "Are you Richard, the famous seed man?" He explained that amaranth seed for greens is different from the grain variety. His partner told me that millet greens are equally beautiful.

BRUSSELS SPROUTS
(pungent/bitter)

Brussels sprouts taste best when grown and harvested in cool weather. They grow year-round, but picking them in warm weather will make them bitter. With a tighter head than cabbage, they hardly look like leafy greens, but I think about each leaf separate from the head and apply the cooking methods for leafy greens, adjusting the amount of water for their density. To clean brussels sprouts, slice across the core end and let the outer leaves come off. Brussels sprouts are round and constructed like onions, so I cut them like onions. I put each one upside down, keeping the core intact and facing me, while I cut it in half or wedges. If they will be cooked whole, scoring the core will help them cook evenly.

Soft Inside

SIDE DISH

Primary element: brussels sprouts
First-stage method: roast
Cut: whole
    Oil: light sesame
    Salt: sea salt or umeboshi

Complex Flavors

SIDE DISH

Primary element: brussels sprouts
First-stage method: steep
    Cooking liquid: water
    Herb/spice: rose water
    Salt: sea salt
Second-stage method: marinate
Cut: whole, quartered
    Oil: safflower
    Cooking liquid/sweetener: raspberry vinegar, agave
    Herb/spice: rose water, cumin, chili powder
    Salt: sea salt
Decorative: roasted pecan

Strong Meets Strong

Primary element: brussels sprouts

First-stage method: braise

Cut: quarter fans

> *Oil:* ghee or olive
>
> *Salt:* sea salt
>
> *Cooking liquid:* water, fresh lime juice
>
> *Herb/spice:* fresh garlic, prepared mustard

BOK CHOY AND OTHERS
(bitter/sweet)

Most Chinese greens may be used interchangeably in dishes. Choys, the Chinese version of collard greens, have been part of Chinese cuisine since the fifth century. Seeds migrated to Europe and America in the late eighteenth century. Chinese vegetable businesses sprouted in response to fading railroad work and the end of the gold rush. The most well-known and boring of Chinese greens is bok choy; it has thick, crunchy stems with light to dark green wide leaves. Other names for this vegetable include Chinese white cabbage, Chinese chard, Chinese mustard cabbage, and pak choi. I find no pleasure in the larger vegetable, but the baby bok choy, with lighter green leaves and stems, is tender and bittersweet. Use one plump bunch of baby bok choy per serving in a mixed-vegetable dish, and two or three small bunches in a single-vegetable dish. The stems are as delicious to eat as the leaves.

Floating in a Cloud

Primary element: baby bok choy, tofu, rice noodles

First-stage method: boil, clear soup

Decorative: green onion slivers, fresh corn kernels, shiitake mushroom

Cut: diagonal

> *Cooking liquid:* kombu/spice stock, coconut milk
>
> *Herb/spice:* ginger, lemongrass
>
> *Salt:* sea salt, white miso

Lumps on Leaves

Primary element: baby bok choy or other leafy green

First-stage method: braise

Cut: medium squares

> *Oil:* olive
>
> *Salt:* umeboshi
>
> *Cooking liquid:* water
>
> *Herb/spice:* fresh garlic

Primary element: gluten

First-stage method: teriyaki

Cut: strips

> *Oil:* olive
>
> *Cooking liquid/sweetener:* mirin
>
> *Salt:* umeboshi

Twist on a Classic

Primary element: baby bok choy, onion, celery, yellow or red bell pepper

First-stage method: stir-fry

Cut: large squares, boats, slash-back

    Oil: toasted sesame

    Herb/spice: fresh garlic, fresh ginger, lemon zest

    Salt: sea salt

    Cooking liquid: iced lemon water

Decorative: umeboshi roasted cashews

BEET GREENS (bitter/odd)

Beet greens pull energy from the root to stay alive, and it is usually for the root that I purchase beets with greens, so removing their top is the first step. The stalk is cut from the root above the bulb. When beets are picked and sold within 24–48 hours, the greens are often vibrant and good to eat. Baby beet greens are often part of the salad mix found in upscale grocery markets. These thinnings are pulled in the field to make room for beet roots to grow large. The stalks take a little longer to cook than the tender beet leaf, so they go into the pot first, before the leaf.

COLLARD GREENS (bitter)

As part of the cabbage family, collard's name is born from the Anglo-Saxon word *coleworts,* which means "cabbage plants." The most significant difference between collard greens and kale is not in nutritional benefits or taste but in how they grow. Collard's flat broad leaf and warm climate contrasts with kale's curly leaf and cool growing environment. Collard greens make good wraps for other primary elements in the roll form. Its reputation as Southern food, soul food, and food of the poor keeps collard greens from being used in high cuisine. I consider collard greens an upgrade to spinach because they are tender with a stronger substance and have a preferred nutrient profile.

Green Pie

Primary element: onion, collard greens

First-stage method: slow cook

Cut: small squares or shredded

    Oil: olive oil

    Herb/spice: dried basil

    Salt: sea salt

Primary element: feta cheese, tofu

First-stage method: blend

Cut: coarse, mashed with hands

    Oil: olive oil, feta

    Herb/spice: fresh basil

    Salt: feta, umeboshi

Primary element: phyllo pastry

First-stage method: bake

    Oil: olive oil

    Salt: umeboshi

Rolled Greens

Primary element: collard greens

First-stage method: steep

Primary element: basmati rice

First-stage method: steep

Second-stage method: braise

Decorative: green onion, tomato, braised black bean

Oil: light sesame

Salt: tamari/shoyu

Cooking liquid: mirin

Herb/spice: pimenton (smoked paprika)

Primary element: butternut squash, onion

Hot sauce: vegetable, pressure cook

Oil: light sesame

Herb/spice: chipotle chile (smoked jalapeño chile)

Cooking liquid: water

Salt: sea salt

HEAD CABBAGES (sweet/pungent)

This plant was named *Brassica oleracea* variety *capitata,* which means "cabbage of the vegetable garden, with a head." Green, purple, curly savoy, and the wide open leaves of napa (Chinese cabbage) are easily interchangeable in most dishes. Purple cabbage is a touch drier than green. Cabbage merges well with all ingredients except beans. Why risk potential digestive combustion? This is one of the best vegetables to have on hand. It keeps for long storage in cool weather, especially when there are no cuts into the head. When my dish doesn't use the entire head, I cut through the root end, release the outer leaves from the bottom, and cut them for a dish that requires only a small amount. The remaining cabbage head, still whole, is stored without plastic and refrigerated; it doesn't bleed.

Everyday Food

Primary element: purple cabbage

First-stage method: slow cook

Cut: squares or shredded

Oil: olive

Herb/spice: garlic

Salt: sea salt, umeboshi or tamari

Fresh Shades of Green

Primary element: napa cabbage

First-stage method: press

Cut: squares or shredded

Decorative: cucumber

Salt: sea salt

Herb/spice: fresh cilantro, lime zest

Cooking liquid: fresh lime juice

Old World in a Bowl

Primary element: savoy cabbage, onion, leek, potato

First-stage method: boil, loose vegetable soup

Cut: small squares, cubes

Oil: light sesame

Herb/spice: fennel seed, thyme, garlic

Cooking liquid: water

Salt: sea salt

Pale and Soft

Primary element: green cabbage

First-stage method: pressure steam

Cut: large wedge

> *Salt:* sea salt, umeboshi

Hot Pepper Kraut

CONDIMENT

Primary element: prepared sauerkraut

Second-stage method: refry

Decorative: green onion

Cut: slivers

> *Oil:* light sesame
>
> *Herb/spice:* crushed red pepper flakes
>
> *Salt:* sauerkraut liquid

Kimchee

CONDIMENT

Primary element: napa cabbage

First-stage method: pickle, press

Cut: large squares

> *Herb/spice:* fresh garlic, ginger, jalapeño chile or cayenne
>
> *Salt:* sea salt

Mellow

SIDE DISH

Primary element: green or purple cabbage

First-stage method: braise

Cut: squares

> *Oil:* olive
>
> *Salt:* chickpea miso, sea salt
>
> *Cooking liquid:* Marsala wine, water
>
> *Herb/spice:* fresh tarragon

Slaw

SALAD

Primary element: green and purple cabbage, carrot

First-stage method: press

Second-stage method: marinate

Cut: shred, grate

Decorative: green onion, walnuts, currants

> *Oil:* light sesame
>
> *Herb/spice:* fresh dill weed
>
> *Cooking liquid/sweetener:* cider vinegar, agave
>
> *Salt:* sea salt

Gold and Green

SIDE DISH

Primary element: green head or napa cabbage

First-stage method: stir-fry

Cut: medium squares

> *Oil:* sunflower oil
>
> *Herb/spice:* curry powder
>
> *Salt:* sea salt
>
> *Cooking liquid:* iced white wine

CHICORY, RADICCHIO (bitter)

Chicory, endive, and escarole often masquerade in each other's names. Seed packages sold with a mix of these plants used for quick greens such as European salad mix and mesclun help to confuse customers. I use radicchio and chicory leaves the same way I use dandelion or endive to replace or accent a lettuce dish. Their intense bitter quality helps balance a sour dressing. Radicchio, a red version of Italian green chicory, also grows into a loose head. In addition to the general nutrient base of the leaf family, chicory offers 3 grams of protein in each 1 cup (180 grams) serving.

Elegant and Clean

Primary element: curly or Belgian endive

First-stage method: raw and/or steep

Second-stage method: marinate (no oil)

Cut: across root end, release the leaves

Decorative: slivered and pressed red onion

> Cooking liquid: mirin, rice vinegar, orange juice
>
> Salt: chickpea miso
>
> Herb/spice: fresh orange zest and/or fresh cilantro (optional)

Mixed Bitters

Primary element: romaine lettuce, radicchio, fresh fennel

First-stage method: press

Second-stage method: marinate

Cut: tear, medium pieces

Decorative: pineapple, pressed red onion slivers

Cold sauce: marinade (1 part oil : 4 parts cooking liquid)

> Oil: tahini
>
> Herb/spice: fresh garlic, freshly ground cardamom
>
> Cooking liquid: pineapple juice, cider vinegar, water
>
> Salt: sea salt

Just Fine

Primary element: radicchio

First-stage method: braise

Cut: small squares

> Oil: hazelnut
>
> Salt: tamari
>
> Cooking liquid: fresh lemon juice, agave, water
>
> Herb/spice: freshly ground black pepper, lemon zest

KALE (bitter)

Tribes from Asia Minor and the eastern Mediterranean each claim to have cultivated this ancient leaf cabbage. Many names apply to this primitive vegetable, which is used in various countries. The Greek and Roman term *coles* refers to the cabbage family. *Kale* is the Scottish word; *kohls* the German. No matter the name, this powerhouse green vegetable has a sturdy leaf, wavy, curly, long, or wide. Sometimes I remove the stems to make a more gentle dish, but mostly they stay in place during cooking methods that don't use oil. When the stem looks transparent, the greens are finished cooking. Cooking the leaves with the stems intact retains their flavor and nutrients. Stems can be removed after cooking. To examine the tenderness of a leaf while I'm shopping, I nibble before I buy. Kale is a keeper in the leafy green family. Refrigerate kale without washing it. If leaves lose moisture and become limp during storage, that doesn't stop me from braising them or dropping them into a loose vegetable soup.

Green Meal

Primary element: kale

First-stage method: blend, cold

Decorative: radish, apple, quinoa sprouts

  Oil: soaked almonds

  Herb/spice: fresh mint

  Cooking liquid: rejuvelac

  Salt: smoked dulse (optional)

Another World

Primary element: kale

First-stage method: braise

Cut: large squares

  Oil: olive

  Herb/spice: garlic, ground coriander

  Salt: tamari/shoyu

  Cooking liquid: balsamic vinegar, pomegranate syrup, water

Leaf, Fruit, and Root

Primary element: kale, carrot, roasted red bell pepper

First-stage method: steep

Second-stage method: marinate (1 part oil: $1^1/_2$ parts cooking liquid)

  Oil: light sesame

  Cooking liquid: orange juice, raspberry vinegar

  Herb/spice: ginger juice

  Salt: sea salt, chickpea miso

Decorative: roasted almonds

Delightful Duo

Primary element: kale, potato, onion

First-stage method: slow cook

Cut: small squares, cubes

  Oil: ghee or olive oil

  Herb/spice: freshly ground black pepper

  Salt: sea salt, umeboshi

Italian Stir-Fry

Primary element: onion, kale, gold bar zucchini

First-stage method: stir-fry

Cut: medium

  Oil: olive

  Herb/spice: fresh garlic, fresh basil

  Salt: sea salt

  Cooking liquid: ice water, lemon juice

KOHLRABI (neutral/sweet)

This vegetable has two distinct parts, making its identity confusing. Leaves shoot up from the bulb at the base of the plant. Often the bulbs are sold as roots because they resemble turnips when peeled and the greens are discarded. Even though the bulbs do not grow below ground, kohlrabi may be cooked as a root vegetable. Developed in Germany from the kale plant to have shorter, thicker stems, the kohlrabi plant was named by botanists *Brassica oleracea*, variety *caulorapa*, with the last word meaning "stem turnip." The greens have a more interesting taste than an overgrown bulb, which when small is mild and slightly sweet. Ideally, kohlrabi should be harvested when the greens are brilliant and the bulbs are small.

LETTUCE (bitter/sweet)

I see lettuce as liquid minerals held in fiber. The more color, the more nutritional value. A healthy bunch of lettuce is full of water. The Latin name for lettuce is *Lactic sativa,* the root word "lac" means "milk." It is interesting that lettuce, the second most popular vegetable worldwide, is rarely cooked, has a short life, and little possibility for long-term storage. I think of lettuce as either soft or crisp. Soft-leaf varieties—butterhead lettuce (Boston and Bibb), red leaf, and green leaf—grow as individual leaves attached to a stalk, or form a loose head that spirals like a rose. The cuplike shape of each leaf makes these good for a roll/wrap form. Two crisp lettuces—romaine, also known as Cos, and the white tight-head, known as iceberg—are usable both cooked and raw. Iceberg lettuce, originally named crisphead, is a modern version of an ancient wild seed. Cultivated in California in the early twentieth century, ice was used to pack and ship the lettuce, hence the modern name. Its most concentrated component is water; with a great imagination, you may notice its slightly sweet taste.

Winter Way with Greens

Primary element: green and red leaf lettuce, cucumber, fresh fennel or celery
First-stage method: press
Cut: shredded, diagonal
> *Herb/spice:* lemon zest
> *Salt:* sea salt
> *Cooking liquid:* fresh lemon juice

Warm Salad

Primary element: green onion, red radish, romaine lettuce
First-stage method: braise
Cut: slivers, large squares
> *Oil:* olive
> *Herb/spice:* fresh garlic
> *Salt:* umeboshi
> *Cooking liquid:* fresh lemon juice, water
Decorative: glazed roasted pecans

Minestrone One

Primary element: sweet onion, gold bar zucchini, carrot, tomato, romaine lettuce
First-stage method: boil, loose vegetable soup
Cut: small squares, cubes
Decorative: mini pasta, white navy beans
> *Oil:* olive
> *Herb/spice:* dried basil, bay leaf, fresh basil, freshly ground black pepper
> *Cooking liquid:* vegetable bouillon or vegetable stock
> *Salt:* vegetable salt

MUSTARD GREENS (pungent/bitter)

Mustard greens are both bitter and pungent. The spicy quality of mustard greens softens when cooked. Their color, which is more like celery than kale, makes this ingredient a good decorative vegetable. It is often too intense to be used as a single primary element.

Impact

Primary element: mustard greens

First-stage method: braise

> *Oil:* olive
>
> *Cooking liquid:* fresh lemon juice, Marsala wine, water
>
> *Salt:* chickpea miso

Green on Green

SALAD

Primary element: mustard greens, napa cabbage, celery

First-stage method: press

Decorative: green onion, cucumber

Cut: optional

> *Herb/spice:* fresh parsley, fresh tarragon
>
> *Salt:* sea salt
>
> *Cooking liquid:* mirin, fresh lime juice

One of Many

SIDE DISH

Primary element: onion, purple cabbage, red bell pepper, mustard greens

First-stage method: stir-fry

Cut: medium squares

> *Oil:* toasted sesame
>
> *Herb/spice:* fresh ginger
>
> *Salt:* sea salt
>
> *Cooking liquid:* ice water

SPINACH (bitter/odd)

History links the origins of spinach to Persia, where dishes made with it were composed with yogurt and garlic. From Nepal it moved to China, where it is still known as the "Persian green." Spinach is easy to work with if it is clean. It has short stalks that keep it close to the ground, and the curly varieties often collect sand and fine soil in the cavities. The tender leaves cook quickly and are delicious pressed. Spinach has many valuable nutrients, but it also is proportionately high in oxalic acid, which inhibits the assimilation of calcium. To me, spinach seems wimpy when compared with collards and kale.

Quick

SIDE DISH

Primary element: spinach

First-stage method: slow cook

Cut: big

> *Oil:* olive
>
> *Herb/spice:* garlic, lemon zest
>
> *Salt:* sea salt, umeboshi

Walnut Spinach Pesto

DOLLOP SAUCE

Primary element: spinach

First-stage method: blend

> *Oil:* walnuts, walnut oil
>
> *Herb/spice:* fresh basil
>
> *Cooking liquid:* vermouth
>
> *Salt:* sea salt, umeboshi

Green Eyes

Primary element: onion, leek, spinach (use one-third cooked spinach, or two-thirds blended raw spinach)

First-stage method: pressure cook, cream-style soup

Decorative: cauliflower

Cut: large

Oil: hazelnut

Herb/spice: shallot

Cooking liquid: hazelnut milk made with water and white wine (1 part nuts : 16 parts liquid)

Salt: sea salt

SWISS CHARD (bitter)

Swiss chard, also called silverbeet or perpetual spinach, was originally cultivated from the wild sea beet, which is found in and near rock formations with proximity to the sea. Swiss chard is a tall, wide, wavy green leaf, with a thick-ribbed, crunchy, edible stalk that comes in white, red, or yellow. Chard belongs to the same family as beets and spinach, and its texture and taste are a blend of both. Chard combines the soft quality of beet greens and the slightly odd flavor of spinach leaves. It has good concentrations of vitamins K, A, C, and E, magnesium, manganese, potassium, iron, and oxalic acid, which inhibits calcium absorption. Swiss also contains respectable amounts of vitamins B_1, B_2, and B_6, copper, calcium, protein, phosphorous, zinc, folate, biotin, niacin, and pantothenic acid.

Mediterranean Marinade

Primary element: Swiss chard

First-stage method: steep

Second-stage method: marinate

Cold sauce: marinade (1 part oil : 1 part cooking liquid)

Oil: olive

Cooking liquid: cider vinegar

Herb/spice: fresh or dried basil, lemon zest

Salt: sea salt

Something Saucy

Primary element: Swiss chard

First-stage method: braise

Cut: large squares

Oil: sunflower

Herb/spice: crushed cumin seed, fennel seed, freshly ground pink peppercorns

Salt: umeboshi

Cooking liquid: coconut cream

FLOWER FAMILY

This is a small family of three—artichokes, broccoli, and cauliflower. Broccoli and cauliflower belong to the botanical cruciferous family, but they don't look like leaves. Instead, they look more like trees whose branches stretch out from the trunk. Near the top, buds flower into a tight head. It takes the cruciferous name from a four-petal leaf formation that resembles a Roman cross (crucifix). Broccoflower, a relatively recent horticultural invention, combines the features of broccoli and cauliflower into a single vegetable. I don't understand why anyone would think this could be good. Looks just aren't enough. The onion family is the only other vegetable that successfully merges with broccoli in a first-stage method. Its siblings have similar limitations. This is critical because these vegetables fight for their identity in mixed, first-stage dishes, leaving a gassy smell in their wake. Artichokes also flower at the end of a stalk, and are surrounded by leaves six feet in diameter that protect it from too much sun. Like children, their beauty is in their heart. Tender young artichokes have not yet developed the fibrous choke and tough exterior that is standard with mature artichokes.

These vegetables have a reputation for both their potent sulfur content and a nutrient profile that includes vitamins C and B_6, and the minerals potassium, manganese, iron, and calcium. The stalks are a dense version of the heads, doubling the nutrition, so I include them in my dishes. Broccoli is not for everyone. It lowers cholesterol, provides enzymes that help prevent cancer, diabetes, heart disease, osteoporosis, and high blood pressure, has abundant trace minerals, and helps improve eye conditions. It also has a natural supply of chemicals that interfere with the body's ability to use iodine, which is necessary for thyroid function. Sometimes a streak of purple colors these vegetables; it is easiest to see this streak in cauliflower. The same beneficial phytochemical that pigments red cabbage, cranberries, and red grapes is what causes this purple streak.

Selecting and Storing

Tight heads of cauliflower and broccoli are preferred. When a hand brushes the tops, they should not flake. Reject those with yellow and brown spots whenever possible. Both these vegetables keep well in the refrigerator. They will even look good to the eye after two days of sitting on a kitchen counter, but they won't taste good. It's best to select broccoli with long stalks. Artichoke leaves should squeak when one petal rubs another. These vegetables may be kept moist by sprinkling them with beads of water and storing them in a plastic bag in the refrigerator.

BROCCOLI (bitter/sweet)

The most delicious part of broccoli is not the flower but the branch. Its name, derived from the Latin word *brachium,* meaning "strong arm," gives the clue. To enjoy this part of broccoli, the thick skin needs to be removed by peeling it away from the translucent celadon branch. When broccoli is left on the plant too long, its sugars develop into a type of fiber called lignin, creating stems that will be tough no matter how long the cooking process. Broccoli rabe, native to the Mediterranean region, is also called Italian broccoli, brocoletti di rape, rapini, Chinese broccoli, and gai lon. This variety, recognized by its thin stems, tiny budding heads, and abundant leaves with jagged edges, cooks more quickly than the strong-arm branches of broccoli, and therefore requires less cooking liquid.

Broccoli is a prima donna. Whatever dish it goes into, it must be treated as a single vegetable before meeting up with other vegetables or it makes a dramatic stink.

Simpleton

Primary element: broccoli

First-stage method: roast

Cut: bite-size pieces

   Oil: olive

   Herb/spice: garlic granules

   Salt: sea salt, umeboshi

Cream of Broccoli

Primary element: broccoli, onion, leek

First-stage method: pressure cook, cream-style soup

Cut: large

   Oil: olive or ghee

   Herb/spice: fresh tarragon (optional)

   Cooking liquid: cashew milk made with water and white wine (1 part nuts : 16 parts liquid)

   Salt: sea salt

Smothered Broccoli

Primary element: broccoli or cauliflower

First-stage method: bake in sauce

Cut: bite-size pieces

Hot sauce: flour

   Binder: brown rice flour

   Oil: ghee or olive

   Herb/spice: garlic, bay leaf, freshly ground black pepper

   Cooking liquid: cashew or pine nut milk (1 part nuts : 16 parts liquid)

   Salt: vegetable or sea salt

Precious with Pasta

Primary element: broccoli, cooked soba noodles

First-stage method: steep

Second-stage method: marinate

Decorative: fresh cilantro

   Oil: light sesame, toasted sesame

   Herb/spice: fresh ginger, fresh mint, lime zest

   Cooking liquid: fresh lime juice, agave

   Salt: tamari

Pad Si Yu

Primary element: broccoli

First-stage method: slow cook

   Oil: sunflower

   Salt: sea salt

Primary element: triangle rice noodles

Pretreatment: partially soak in boiling water

First-stage method: braise

Decorative: slow-cooked broccoli

   Oil: sunflower

   Herb/spice: minced fresh garlic, fresh Thai pepper, tamarind paste

   Cooking liquid: vegetable bouillon

   Salt: tamari/shoyu

   Miscellaneous: cane sugar

Primary element: tofu

Second-stage method: braise

   Oil: sunflower

   Herb/spice: minced fresh garlic, fresh Thai pepper, tamarind paste

   Cooking liquid: vegetable bouillon

   Salt: tamari/shoyu

   Miscellaneous: cane sugar

No Name

Primary element: broccoli

First-stage method: braise

Cut: small

> Oil: olive
>
> Herb/spice: dried basil, curry powder
>
> Salt: tamari
>
> Cooking liquid: Marsala wine, water, pomegranate syrup

The Sweet Side of Bitter

Primary element: broccoli

First-stage method: teriyaki

Cut: very small

> Oil: olive
>
> Cooking liquid/sweetener: agave
>
> Salt: umeboshi

Decorative: roasted almonds

CAULIFLOWER (pungent)

I like cauliflower because it is almost white, and few vegetables are this color. Its color and texture allow it to work as a base binder in a cream-style soup or sauce. Cauliflower has more ability to merge its flavor with other ingredients than its sister broccoli. The core, shorter than a broccoli branch, tastes as good as the flowers. Cauliflower stays out of the sun's rays to keep it white. This requires much attention, which is why cauliflower commands a higher price than other, less difficult, produce. Cauliflower has a reputation for being the true aristocrat of the cabbage family, "a cabbage with a college education."

To Set on Lettuce

Primary element: cauliflower, roasted red bell pepper, steeped collards

First-stage method: steep

Second-stage method: marinate

Cut: optional for marinade; as whole as possible for steeping

> Oil: corn oil
>
> Herb/spice: none
>
> Cooking liquid: none
>
> Salt: umeboshi

All Wrapped Up

Primary element: leek, cauliflower

First-stage method: braise

Cut: bite-size pieces

> Oil: olive
>
> Herb/spice: finely ground fennel seed
>
> Salt: sea salt, light miso
>
> Cooking liquid: cashew milk (1 part nuts : 16 parts water), white balsamic vinegar, white wine

Decorative: frozen or fresh garden peas

Primary element: long-grain brown rice

First-stage method: pressure cook

> Cooking liquid: water
>
> Herb/spice: ground fennel seed
>
> Salt: sea salt
>
> Miscellaneous: small amount of kombu (optional)

Second-stage method: bake in phyllo dough

Tan, Pungent, and Moist

SIDE DISH

Primary element: cauliflower

First-stage method: bake

Cut: medium

Oil: olive

Herb/spice: whole garlic cloves

Salt: sea salt

Companion for Millet

MAIN PLATE

Primary element: onion, carrot, parsnip, cauliflower

First-stage method: bake in sauce

Cut: medium

Hot sauce: flour

Binder: brown rice flour

Oil: ghee or sunflower

Herb/spice: curry powder, kaffir lime leaf

Cooking liquid: coconut milk, water as needed

Decorative: cooked chickpeas

Para La Tortilla

SPREAD

Primary element: cauliflower

First-stage method: pressure cook

Second-stage method: refry

Decorative: green onion

Oil: light sesame

Herb/spice: freshly ground cumin, freshly ground coriander seed, fresh cilantro

Salt: tamari

Simple Beauty

SIDE DISH

Primary element: cauliflower, leek

First-stage method: braise

Cut: medium

Oil: light sesame

Salt: light miso, sea salt

Cooking liquid: mirin, water

Herb/spice: rosemary

On Its Own

SIDE DISH

Primary element: cauliflower

First-stage method: roast

Cut: bite-size pieces

Oil: olive

Herb/spice: anise seed

Salt: sea salt plus finishing salt (sea salt diluted in fresh lime juice)

ARTICHOKE (bitter/odd)

A fresh, mature artichoke is best simply pressure steamed and served with a cold sauce. I like the option of an herb/spice in the steaming water to infuse the background flavor. With knife in the slash-back position, shave the spikes at the end of the leaves, cutting them off about one-half inch from the tip. Trim the stalk about three-quarter inch from the flower head in a right angle cut and the head will stand perfectly upright in the steaming basket and on a serving plate. Baby artichokes need less trimming. They can be eaten whole, as the fibers in the center have not developed. The easiest way to eat artichokes regularly is to purchase the plain hearts in a can. The following recipe sketches begin with such a heart, which has already moved through the first stage.

Marinade at Home

Primary element: water-packed canned artichoke hearts

Second-stage method: marinate

Decorative: olives, red onion, roasted yellow bell pepper, cucumber, fresh fennel

Cut: medium bulky

Cold sauce: marinade (1 part oil : 1 part cooking liquid)

Oil: olive or hazelnut

Herb/spice: fresh marjoram, freshly ground pink peppercorns

Cooking liquid: white grape juice, cider vinegar

Salt: sea salt

Artichoke and Spinach in Cream

DIP

Primary element: water-packed canned artichoke hearts

Decorative: washed spinach

First-stage method: press spinach

Second-stage method: blend, dip

Decorative: chunks of canned artichoke hearts

Oil: pine nuts soaked in cooking liquid

Cooking liquid: rejuvelac, lemon juice, white wine (optional)

Herb/spice: fresh chives, fresh parsley, fresh garlic, lemon zest

Salt: sea salt, umeboshi

Cranberry Beauty

CONDIMENT

Primary element: first-stage cooked or canned artichoke hearts

Second-stage method: teriyaki

Decorative: fresh cranberry, finely diced candied ginger

Oil: refined walnut

Cooking liquid/sweetener: agave

Herb/spice: minced shallot, orange flower water

Salt: sea salt

To Go in Pasta

DECORATIVE

Primary element: fresh baby artichoke hearts (or canned)

First-stage method: braise

Cut: quartered

Decorative: black olives

Oil: olive

Herb/spice: garlic, fennel seeds

Cooking liquid: liquid from the canned artichokes, Marsala wine, tomato juice

Salt: sea salt

Encrusted

SIDE DISH

Primary element: artichoke hearts

Second-stage method: breaded, roasted in crushed nuts and bread crumbs (optional)

Oil: roasted, salted pecan meal

Salt: sea salt on roasted nuts

Herb/spice: dried oregano, freshly ground black pepper, paprika

Soft Infusion

SIDE DISH WITH SAUCE

Primary element: water-packed canned artichoke hearts

Second-stage method: bake in sauce

Cut: half or quarter

Hot sauce: nut

    Oil: cashew butter

    Cooking liquid: liquid from the canned artichokes

    Herb/spice: minced fresh rosemary

    Salt: umeboshi

FRUIT FAMILY

This most famous vegetable family has toxic consequences. I feel bloated when I overeat them, which is easy to do because they are often delicious.

The fruit family is all over the map. Avocado, bell pepper, and tomato originally traveled from the Aztec culture of South America. Eggplant is thought to have come from China and India, and okra from Ethiopia. Tomato and eggplant took centuries to be accepted as food. People shied away from them because they belong to a variety of the nightshade family, which includes the poisonous belladonna, Jimson weed, petunia, and tobacco. The leaves and stems of this powerful plant, which are used for sleep inducement and anesthesia, give off a sharp, unfriendly aroma. The chemical compound solanine is responsible for the characteristics of belladonna, which means "beautiful lady." The name was attached to the plant because Italian women would use belladonna to dilate their eyes, thinking big eyes would make them look more beautiful.

Before King Louis XIV encouraged its culinary acceptance, eggplant was called "bad egg," "mad apple," or "apple of madness." Tomatoes took time to be accepted also. They might have been yellow in their first home, the wild mountainous regions of the Andes—Peru, Ecuador, and Bolivia. Italy began cultivating and cooking tomatoes in the mid-sixteenth century. Fifty to a hundred years later, France incorporated tomatoes into its cuisine. Some tomato enthusiasts believed that it had aphrodisiac powers, and the French called them *pommes d'amour,* meaning "love apples." A century later, in 1781, Thomas Jefferson was growing tomato vines in his progressive garden.

Tomatoes relieve thirst and dryness and stimulate appetite. Eggplant assists in managing blood flow, helping the blood to move when it is stuck and to stop when flow is excessive. The vitamin C content of sweet bell peppers and tomatoes is highest when these foods are raw. Red peppers have more than five times the food value of red tomatoes. Primitive uses of capsaicin, the potent compound that gives chiles their fiery heat, include relieving asthma, coughs, sore throats, and toothaches. I have also heard that cayenne can stop bleeding in an emergency. One day, at the end of a long weekend program, while I was cutting beautiful white tofu, the knife slipped into my finger. I didn't feel anything, thanks to my sharp knife; it was the red on white that stopped me. I reached for the cayenne. All I knew was that it might stop the bleeding. What I didn't know was that a wavelike electric shock would move from my hand through my heart to my head. I passed out. The bleeding stopped.

The fruits that aren't nightshade related, avocado and okra, are both soothing to the lungs and stomach. Okra has a powerful nutrient profile, with avocado following close behind it. Brought to the Americas from Africa, okra means "soul," a word integrated into the beliefs and culture of Ghana. Avocado originated in Central and South America with the Mayans, Toltecs, Aztecs, Incas, and other great civilizations.

The eggplant, pepper, okra, and tomato members of the fruit family are often cooked together. To join the culinary "fruit family" a plant has to droop off a branch as it grows. The fruits are fleshy and moist, and a portion of their body is seed. Avocado, with its big seed, is mostly thought of as the oil element in a dish. They all grow in warm and slightly humid environments and have a short window for life, growing quickly. They must be eaten soon after they are picked. Their relation to the botanical nightshade family makes them beneficial in small doses.

Selecting and Storing

Fruits are best eaten when they are as close to ripe as possible. If they are picked before they are ripe, it's best to capture them in a dish before they begin to deteriorate. Refrigeration delays deterioration only slightly. Chilling arrests the best part of these vegetables, and they do not recover their peak performance, which is available only when they are stored at room temperature. Eggplants are shiny, plump, firm, and smooth skinned. You can tell the sex of an eggplant by looking at its bottom; an oval shape indicates a female and a circle indicates a male. Although I haven't counted, there are supposed to be more seeds in the female. Tomatoes, vine ripened if possible, are best when firm enough to pass a knife through without squishing the meat, which is accomplished by sliding the knife back and forth, not pressing down. Peppers should be firm and unblemished. Select okra that feels strong, is unbendable, and "glows." Of all the fruits, avocados are the easiest to control in terms of ripening. When ripe, the skin is firm but the meat beneath it will give slightly. Place onions with avocado in a brown paper bag in a warm area to expedite ripening.

AVOCADO (sweet)

Avocado belongs in the fat/oil category. When avocado is in a dish, other oils are not necessary. In guacamole, avocado is the primary element. It is not often cooked with fire because it grows in a very hot environment and does not need more fire. Avocados are most likely to be used in cold sauces, dips, and cold soups, or simply served as a decorative element. A ripe avocado is firm with a little give beneath the skin. Once the meat turns brown, its taste is no longer available.

Cool

SOUP

Primary element: avocado, pear, green onion
First-stage method: blend
> Oil: avocado meat
> Herb/spice: fresh dill weed
> Cooking liquid: juiced parsnip, rejuvelac
> Salt: optional

Guacamole

DOLLOP SAUCE

Primary element: avocado
First-stage method: blend
> Herb/spice: garlic
> Cooking liquid: fresh lemon juice
> Salt: sea salt, umeboshi

A Little Outrageous

Primary element: avocado

First-stage method: tempura

Cut: large wedge

> *Oil:* safflower
>
> *Binder:* rice flour, corn flour, unbleached spelt, arrowroot
>
> *Cooking liquid:* beer
>
> *Herb/spice:* curry powder in batter

Cold sauce: dipping

> *Salt:* tamari
>
> *Cooking liquid:* balsamic vinegar, fresh lemon juice

EGGPLANT (sweet/bitter/odd)

Eggplants thrive in heat. They require considerable fire/cooking because, as a nightshade family member, the toxic properties of solanine are then reduced. When eggplant is buttery soft, gastrointestinal upset will be less likely. Many cooks use the pressing/wilting method for eggplant before adding fire methods. This helps the transformation under fire become more complete. Salting is not necessary if eggplant is cooked thoroughly, using salt in the first-stage method as well as the second. Eggplant likes oil. It sucks it up like a sponge.

Glossy

SIDE DISH

Primary element: white eggplant

First-stage method: teriyaki

> *Oil:* sesame
>
> *Cooking liquid/sweetener:* barley malt
>
> *Salt:* sea salt

Famous

SIDE DISH

Primary element: Japanese or other eggplant

First-stage method: braise

Cut: rounds

> *Oil:* toasted sesame
>
> *Herb/spice:* fresh garlic, grated fresh ginger
>
> *Salt:* tamari
>
> *Cooking liquid:* rice vinegar, mirin, water

Big W's Relish

SPREAD

Primary element: eggplant

First-stage method: roast whole

Second-stage method: marinate

Decorative: onion

Cut: remove skin, diced small

> *Oil:* olive
>
> *Herb/spice:* freshly ground black pepper
>
> *Cooking liquid:* white balsamic vinegar
>
> *Salt:* sea salt

Smokey Pâté

SPREAD

Primary element: eggplant, first-stage cooked navy beans

Pretreatment: smoke eggplant

First-stage method: roast

Second-stage method: bake, pâté

> *Oil:* light sesame, tahini
>
> *Herb/spice:* fresh garlic
>
> *Salt:* sea salt, chickpea miso

Ratatouille

Primary element: eggplant, bell pepper, tomato

First-stage method: slow cook

Cut: medium-small cubes

Oil: olive

Herb/spice: oregano, thyme, basil

Salt: sea salt

BELL PEPPERS (sweet)

I use bell peppers to enhance the color of a dish the way dayglow (iridescent light) came forward in the late 1960s. A small portion of colored bell pepper gives its glow without imparting its taste.

Peppers are divided into two categories. The hot/pungent variety go into the herb/spice element, and the sweet bell performs as decorative element and major vegetable. Green bell peppers are immature, unripe, and challenging for the digestive system. But the colored bell peppers—yellow, red, gold, and purple—have all gone through the green stage and outgrown it. The colored varieties bring a great sweetness to any dish. In blended soups and sauces, the waxy skin of this vegetable may be removed either by dry roasting or by blanching. Dry roasting a pepper singes the skin black, creating a smoky flavor; this can be done over a flame on the stove top or under a broiler. The pepper is then placed in a plastic or paper bag where it can steam while it cools. Blanching will keep the color of a pepper bright. Drop it into boiling water for just two minutes, then plunge it into ice water; the skin will blister and you can simply peel it off.

Pungent Red

Primary element: red bell pepper

First-stage method: roast

Hot sauce: vegetable

Oil: olive

Herb/spice: dried ancho chile (rehydrated), chipotle chile

Cooking liquid: pine nut milk made with water and Shiraz red wine (1 part nuts : 16 parts liquid)

Salt: sea salt

Accent liquid: fresh lime juice (optional)

Stuffed and Sauced

Primary element: red bell pepper

First-stage method: roast

Cut: in half

Oil: light sesame

Salt: sea salt

Primary element: wild rice

First-stage method: sauté/bake

Decorative: mushroom, green onion, seitan

Oil: light sesame

Herb/spice: thyme, sage

Cooking liquid: vegetable bouillon

Salt: sea salt

Primary element: yellow bell pepper

First-stage method: pressure cook, sauce

Hot sauce: vegetable and nut

Oil: light sesame

Herb/spice: bay leaf (remove)

Cooking liquid: cashew milk made with water and optional white wine (1 part nuts : 8 parts liquid)

Salt: sea salt, chickpea miso

Sunset

Primary element: red, yellow, and orange bell peppers

First-stage method: braise

Cut: long, square, or triangle

Oil: olive

Cooking liquid: Madeira wine, water, raspberry vinegar, maple syrup

Salt: tamari

Sweet and Sour

SAUCE

Primary element: onion, orange bell pepper, yellow zucchini

First-stage method: pressure cook

Hot sauce: vegetable

Cut: large

Oil: light sesame

Herb/spice: orange zest, cardamom, star anise

Cooking liquid: orange juice, water, Marsala wine

Salt: sea salt

Accent liquid: raspberry vinegar

Just a Little

SIDE DISH

Primary element: any bell pepper

First-stage method: teriyaki

Cut: small or thin

Oil: olive

Cooking liquid/sweetener: rice syrup

Herb/spice: fresh ginger juice

Salt: umeboshi

A Family of Five

SIDE DISH

Primary element: red, gold, yellow, green, and purple bell peppers

First-stage method: stir-fry

Cut: medium triangles

Oil: olive

Herb/spice: fresh cilantro

Salt: sea salt

Cooking liquid: ice water with lime oil

OKRA (sweet)

Okra looks like green velvet stretched tightly on a tear-shaped pentagon. It's not a common vegetable, although I believe much of okra's lack of visibility has to do with people not knowing how to cook it. Fried and stewed are its most famous performances. This vegetable also benefits from being freshly picked. The seeds act like fresh corn cut from the cob and provide a crisp texture in a very slippery food. The viscous quality of okra may hinder an appetite for it, but if the supporting elements are doing their job, and the techniques are explicit, this vegetable has a future.

Teriyaki Okra

DECORATIVE

Primary element: okra

First-stage method: teriyaki

Cut: small circles

Oil: olive

Cooking liquid/sweetener: agave

Herb/spice: fresh basil

Salt: sea salt

Succotash

Primary element: okra

First-stage method: slow cook

Decorative: tomato, fresh corn, fresh lima beans

Cut: rounds

    Oil: olive or ghee

    Herb/spice: freshly ground black pepper

    Salt: sea salt

Braised Okra

CONDIMENT

Primary element: okra

First-stage method: braise

Cut: small

    Oil: light sesame

    Salt: tamari

    Herb/spice: fresh ginger juice

    Cooking liquid: fresh lemon juice, water

Gumbo

MAIN PLATE, STEW

Primary element: okra, tomato, green pepper, onion, celery, fiddlehead fern (if available), long-grain rice, roasted tofu or seitan

First-stage method: boil, stew

Hot sauce: dark roux made with rice flour or white spelt flour

    Oil: coconut butter

    Herb/spice: fresh garlic, dried thyme, bay leaf, freshly ground black pepper, cayenne

    Cooking liquid: vegetable stock

    Salt: sea salt or vegetable salt

TOMATO (sweet)

Multiple varieties keep this vegetable in the forefront of many cuisines. Lumpy shaped heirloom tomatoes in shades of red, purple, and yellow-orange have less acid compared to the globe-shaped classic red beefsteak tomato. Small round tomatoes and pear-shaped tomatoes are best used fresh and uncooked because their skin is annoying in cooked dishes. If cooking them is important, you can press them through a sieve afterward to remove the skin and seeds, but they will no longer be considered a whole food. Tomato flesh is held by its skin, and is moist and seedy like a persimmon's. When this fruit is eaten raw, with small cuts, the skin does not interfere with a dish. Removing the skin is best when cooking tomatoes whole because large pieces of skin interfere with the smooth texture of a cooked tomato. A clean cut on a tomato requires an ultra-sharp knife. My porcelain knife always slices a tomato neatly and paper thin. If I use my steel knife, I start at the back of the fruit and pull the knife to the front to prevent squishing the tomato.

He was not so old that life was slowing down, but his words felt ancient. I was purchasing equipment at a restaurant supply house in Denver. A man at the checkout was waving his arms when he found out I operated a cooking school. "Why do people put onions in tomato sauce? There are no onions in tomato sauce!" I took his recipe sketch right then and there.

Summer Special

Primary element: fresh tomato

First-stage method: broil

Cut: round slices

Oil: olive

Herb/spice: fresh thyme

Salt: vegetable salt

Cream of Tomato

SOUP

Primary element: canned crushed or tomato purée

Second-stage method: boil, cream-style soup

Decorative: finely diced onion

Oil: olive

Herb/spice: minced fresh garlic, dried basil, fresh basil, oregano, sage, bay leaf

Cooking liquid: cashew milk made with water and Madeira wine (1 part nuts : 12 parts liquid)

Salt: sea salt

No Onion Fresh Marinara

SAUCE

Primary element: fresh tomato

Pretreatment: roast or blanch

First-stage method: slow cook

Cut: peel, large dice

Hot sauce: vegetable

Oil: olive

Herb/spice: minced fresh garlic, fresh basil; other options: oregano, marjoram, cayenne

Cooking liquid: Madeira or Marsala wine, or other wine

Salt: sea salt

Tradition from Mike

SIDE DISH

Primary element: fresh tomato

Pretreatment: blanch to remove skin

First-stage method: bake

Oil: olive

Herb/spice: fresh basil, finely diced shallot

Salt: sea salt

The Little Guys

SIDE DISH

Primary element: fresh cherry or pear tomato

First-stage method: teriyaki

Cut: in half

Oil: sunflower

Herb/spice: minced fresh garlic and ginger; mixture of freshly ground coriander seed, cumin, mustard, cardamom, clove, fennel, fenugreek, ajwain, star anise, and anise seed; fresh cilantro

Cooking liquid/sweetener: agave

Salt: sea salt

Classic

SALAD

Primary element: fresh tomato

First-stage method: marinate

Cut: wedges

Oil: olive

Cooking liquid: balsamic vinegar

Herb/spice: fresh basil, freshly ground black pepper

Salt: sea salt

Braised Tomato with Friends

Primary element: fresh cherry or pear tomato

First-stage method: braise

Cut: in half

> *Oil:* toasted sesame
>
> *Herb/spice:* cardamom, chili powder
>
> *Cooking liquid:* mirin, fresh lime juice, water
>
> *Salt:* vegetable salt

Primary element: tofu

Second-stage method: roast

> *Oil:* dark sesame
>
> *Herb/spice:* curry powder or mixture of freshly ground turmeric, red pepper flakes, coriander, cumin, fenugreek, white pepper, cinnamon, fennel, nutmeg, cardamom, cloves, black peppercorns; bay leaf
>
> *Salt:* vegetable salt

Primary element: Job's tears

First-stage method: pressure cook

> *Herb/spice:* bay leaf
>
> *Cooking liquid:* water
>
> *Salt:* sea salt

STALK FAMILY

Asparagus, celery, and fennel belong to the elegant stalk family. Graceful to look at, they grow slowly and require tending to keep them moist in their sunny environment. Once these vegetables take root, shoots and stalks grow more quickly. Green, white, and purple versions of asparagus appear as growers either expose them to the sun, allowing chlorophyll to turn them green, or keep them from sun, blanching them to produce white versions of the plant. King Louis XIV demanded asparagus in December, so his gardener created a hothouse where white asparagus was born. Blue pigments called anthocyanins create the purple asparagus.

This family originated in the Mediterranean and comprises some of the oldest known foods. Records in Egyptian tombs dated 4000 BCE confirm that asparagus was cultivated at that time. The seeds and roots were treasured as medicine centuries before culinary uses for asparagus came into fashion. Wild asparagus was cultivated and accepted in culinary applications as early as 1000 BCE and was known as "sperage" and "sperach" in England. It became a major farm crop in New England in the early 1700s. In the sixteenth century, celery, still a primitive plant, was used for medicinal purposes and in the herb/spice category in cooking. By the middle of the seventeenth century, France began serving the little stalks and leaves with a marinade-style cold sauce. In the late seventeenth century and early eighteenth century, horticulturists in Italy, France, and England had removed the intensity of wild celery by planting it in darker times of the year, which made it more palatable as a primary element. Wild fennel, as tall as a human, thin, and graceful, reminiscent of dill when it flowers, also began its history as medicine. Like celery, fennel was cultivated as an herb/spice and a primary element in the sixteenth century.

The health benefits of this family cover about 30 ailments affecting eyes, throat, stomach, teeth, and sex organs. In addition, these foods protect against cancer, relieve stress, stimulate appetite, support weight loss, loosen phlegm, flush waste from the joints, increase urine flow, break up kidney stones, dispel flatulence, act as a breath freshener, and are purported to have aphrodisiac qualities.

Selecting and Storing

Stalk family vegetables are crisp and bright right out of the earth. If I need to keep them crisp for a long time, I stand them in a shallow container of water. Asparagus, best eaten within minutes of picking, is one of the most seasonal vegetables. Abundant in late spring to early summer, lower prices reflect the freshness of the crop. The life of Belgian endive may be extended by wrapping it in lightly dampened towels, putting it into a plastic bag, and refrigerating it. Stalk vegetables should have firm bodies with no browning on the tip of the leaves. Look for celery that has a good arch and no brown spots on the inside.

ASPARAGUS (bitter/odd)

Asparagus, a sophisticated vegetable in purple, white, or green, implies phallic strength. Its distinctive, earthy taste lingers in the body the day after it has been eaten. The root end is usually tough. Sometime I shave the skin near the end; other times I snap the stalk. Where it breaks determines which part of the asparagus will be tender and edible. After I break off the tough ends, I save them to make stock for a creamy asparagus soup. I like both fat and skinny varieties.

Warm Salad

SIDE DISH

Primary element: asparagus

First-stage method: steep

Second-stage method: marinate

Decorative: green onion, red bell pepper, sesame seeds

Cut: diagonal

Oil: light sesame

Herb/spice: fresh ginger

Cooking liquid: cider vinegar, maple syrup

Salt: tamari

Cream of Asparagus

SOUP

Primary element: onion, leek, asparagus

First-stage method: pressure cook, cream-style soup

Cut: large

Oil: hazelnut

Herb/spice: lemon zest

Cooking liquid: cashew nut milk made with water and optional white wine (1 part nuts: 18 parts liquid)

Salt: sea salt

Accent liquid: fresh lemon juice

Taken to the Edge

SIDE DISH

Primary element: asparagus

First-stage method: roast

Cut: whole

Oil: olive

Herb/spice: dill weed

Salt: sea salt

In Creamy Lemon Sauce

SIDE DISH

Primary element: asparagus

First-stage method: steep

Hot sauce: vegetable, flour, nut

Binders: gold bar zucchini, onion, unbleached spelt flour

Oil: safflower

Herb/spice: lemon zest

Cooking liquid: cashew milk made with water and fresh lemon juice (1 part nuts: 8 parts liquid)

Salt: vegetable salt

In Its Own Sauce

Primary element: asparagus

First-stage method: braise

Cut: long diagonal

>   *Oil:* olive

>   *Herb/spice:* garlic

>   *Salt:* chickpea miso

>   *Cooking liquid:* Marsala wine, fresh lime juice, water

CELERY (bitter/salty)

The crisp texture of celery helps balance its opposites in a meal, like eggplant or squash. Because there is so much liquid in this vegetable, very little liquid is needed when it is cooked. Celery contains molybdenum, a metal that gives strength to my vegetable knives. Its juice reduces cholesterol and stagnation in the arteries, equalizing blood pressure. Even though celery is high in sodium and potassium, which control the movement of fluids in the body, I don't use it in place of salt.

> *D*uring a cooking demonstration for about 100 people, I removed strings from the outer stalks of celery. Like dental floss, they are not chewable, especially in a raw vegetable dish. Pulling them out lets the celery's juice come forward into the dish. That night, for her husband, a lady in the audience prepared the dish I had demonstrated in class. The next day she was thrilled to report that her husband enjoyed a dish with celery for the first time in his life.

Flowery Tang

Primary element: celery

First-stage method: braise

>   *Oil:* olive

>   *Cooking liquid:* raspberry vinegar, water

>   *Herb/spice:* lavender

>   *Salt:* sea salt

Translucence

Primary element: celery

First-stage method: steep

Second-stage method: refry

Cut: whole, slash-back

>   *Oil:* olive

>   *Salt:* caper brine

Celadon in Velvet

Primary element: celery, onion

Hot sauce: clear

Cut: thin diagonal, slivers

>   *Oil:* safflower

>   *Herb/spice:* fresh garlic

>   *Cooking liquid:* kombu/star anise stock

>   *Salt:* sea salt

>   *Binder:* kudzu

Light Celery

Primary element: celery, onion, leek

First-stage method: pressure cook, cream-style
  soup

Cut: large

  Oil: hazelnut

  Herb/spice: cardamom (light hand)

  Cooking liquid: hazelnut milk (1 part nuts :
    10 parts water)

  Salt: sea salt, umeboshi

Side Kick

SIDE DISH

Primary element: celery, leek, red or yellow bell
  pepper

First-stage method: roast

Cut: slash-back

Decorative: sesame seeds

  Oil: toasted sesame

  Herb/spice: cayenne (light hand)

  Salt: sea salt

FENNEL (sweet)

*I*ts Greek name is *marathon,* meaning "to
grow thin." Fennel earned this title because
of its reputation for weight loss. As soon as I found
this out, I bought bunches at the farmers' market.
I nibble on it for my restless, nervous hunger. I
take it with me in the car, suck the juice from the
tough stems, and chew the fiber when my mouth
would like to be busy. I do believe it works.

In medieval times, the seeds (an herb/spice element and quieter to chew than the stalk) were
chewed to stop gastric rumblings during church
services. Although the taste and aroma of fennel
are sometimes mistaken for anise or licorice, the
plant is related to caraway. This fresh vegetable,
with more fiber than celery, may be prepared as a
major or decorative vegetable.

Multidimensional

SIDE DISH

Primary element: fresh fennel, leek

First-stage method: braise

Cut: small, long diagonal

  Oil: olive

  Herb/spice: lemon zest/oil

  Cooking liquid: fresh lemon juice, vermouth,
    water

  Salt: vegetable salt

Decorative: salted roasted pecans

Tuscan Influence

SALAD

Primary element: fresh fennel bulb

First-stage method: marinate

Cut: bite-size pieces

  Oil: olive

  Cooking liquid: fresh lemon juice

  Herb/spice: freshly ground black pepper

  Salt: sea salt

Decorative: blood orange segments, pomegranate
  seeds, hard Tuscan cheese (optional)

Cream of Fennel

Primary element: fresh fennel bulb, onion, leek

First stage method: pressure cook, cream-style soup

Cut: large

Oil: olive

Herb/spice: crushed fennel seed, fresh garlic

Cooking liquid: cashew milk made with water and optional white wine (1 part nuts : 12 parts liquid)

Salt: sea salt

Oven Friends

SIDE DISH, PIZZA TOPPING

Primary element: artichoke hearts, fennel, mushroom

First-stage method: roast

Cut: medium

Oil: olive

Herb/spice: dried basil, dried oregano, garlic granules

Salt: sea salt

Crunchy Delight

SIDE DISH

Primary element: fresh fennel

First-stage method: stir-fry

Cut: large diagonal

Oil: light sesame

Herb/spice: fresh basil

Cooking liquid: ice water

Salt: sea salt

A Refreshing Chew

SALAD

Primary element: fresh fennel or celery

First-stage method: press

Decorative: orange bell pepper, shredded red cabbage

Salt: sea salt

Cooking liquid: raspberry vinegar

Soft Celadon with Heat

SIDE DISH

Primary element: fresh fennel bulb

First-stage method: bake

Cut: wedge

Oil: sunflower

Herb/spice: peeled whole garlic cloves

Salt: sea salt

MUSHROOM FAMILY

One of the most intense cooking experiences that I put food through is making mushrooms squeal. To ensure they are cooked thoroughly, they go into a pan before other vegetables. Once I have tossed the oil around them, I leave the fire fairly high and only stir once or twice until they are sealed, always spreading them evenly across the surface of the pot. When they shrink, squeal, turn golden to dark brown, and wear a leathery texture, they are ready for the next step in the dish.

I look at this vast species and divide them into four functions. The culinary mushroom adds flavor, healing properties, and wonderment to dishes; the magical mushrooms are used for ceremonies that alter the mind, connect humans with other worlds, and, according to some, bring enlightenment. The third kind—deadly mushrooms—end this life. The fourth provide color, texture, and light from an array of brilliant and subdued colors that have been extracted to be used as dye for cloth and yarn. One kind of mushroom is bright enough to be used as a lantern. Another has fiber that, once dried and shredded, can be used for kindling. Recorded history links mushrooms to primitive man, who used them in ceremonies. Europe and Asia bring distinctly different mushrooms to the table. Where the mushroom originated is not clear, but folklore entertains the idea that they fell from the sky. Another theory held by peoples as diverse as the ancient Greeks, the Mayans, and Filipinos is that mushrooms emerge after bolts of lightning hit the ground.

*T*his family, more than others, separates the people who love them and the people who don't. With more grace than groupies at a rock concert, fungophiles are held captive by mushrooms. I am not one of them. But with respect and good technique, I can appreciate a good mushroom dish.

Scientists say that mushrooms are more like humans than other vegetables. Some have two genders and others have multiple genders. They grow without seeds by spores from a kind of mold. Wild mushrooms hide in forests; others are cultivated on farms or in basements, exponentially expanding. When mushrooms reproduce, they spray spores to define the area where the body will appear. Connected by underground systems, they live in community. Their growing environment is dark and moist, a breeding ground for mold. The best way to balance this fungal food is with fire, to drive away toxins. I don't eat them raw. Their healing properties are more potent when cooked.

Healing benefits include strengthening the immune system and anti-inflammatory properties, helping to reduce pain from swelling.

Mushrooms absorb oil and liquid like a sponge. If oil is in the cooking method, they require more than other vegetables. Leaving the stems attached during washing prevents water from diluting their flavor. I rinse them in a colander without plunging them, allowing only enough water to touch the outside of the mushrooms. My hands move quickly to loosen dirt. Paper towels are ready for an immediate gentle rub. Large portobello mushrooms are easily hand-wiped with a damp paper towel.

Selecting and Storing

I've had the privilege of foraging wild mushrooms with an avid fungophile. We walked in mystery on a mountain adventure close to the forest ground. Mushroom hunting requires serious study; otherwise you risk becoming gravely ill by following wrong information. So I forage in the markets where mushrooms are not wild but an interesting selection is increasingly available as mushroom farmers expand their varieties.

Select mushrooms with a dry, nonslippery surface, no bruises, and an appealing smell. Store fresh mushrooms in a paper bag open at the top, or poke holes in it so the mushrooms don't become slimy. They still don't keep well. Try to use fresh mushrooms within three days of purchase. If I am making a soup or a sauce, I prefer ripe cremini. They have a stronger smell, but this doesn't matter with cooking methods that use a major cooking liquid. I prefer to cook with dried shiitake because the flavor is stronger. Truffles that have been stored in rice will flavor the dull grain, making the storage material delicious in its first-stage method.

MUSHROOMS (odd)

The fact that entire books have been written about the subject of mushrooms demonstrates the breadth of their popularity. There are different opinions on how to eat and cook mushrooms. They grow very quickly below ground or on dead trees and living tree roots. They also die quickly, which makes drying important to capture and intensify their flavor. Fungi vary in size from a fraction of an inch to several feet wide. Because mushrooms are mostly made of water and fiber with subtle variation in taste, it's the cooking method and supporting elements that make mushroom dishes successful.

Mushroom connoisseurs enjoy the subtle flavors of the following varieties. *Black trumpet* is a lily-shaped, thin-fleshed mushroom with delicate taste and purple-gray to black color. *Button,* a standard white mushroom with little taste and more water content than others, may take longer to reach the "squeak" sound that indicates that they have reached their maximum taste. If Disney created a caricature of a mushroom, it might look like a *porcini,* with its rounded cap and thick J-shaped stem. Porcinis have a deep, musty flavor and sometimes go by other names like Polish mushroom or King Bolete. *Chanterelles* have a subtle, sharp, spicy taste and a rusty gold color; they are shaped like a vase. *Cremini* have the shape of a white button, but are darker skinned and have at least twice the flavor. When their growth is unchecked, they become the meaty *portobellos. Enoki,* harvested in the wild, are found near timberline and snowcapped mountains. They are short stemmed with a cap as wide as the stem. Cultivated enoki, also known as *golden mushroom* or *velvet stem,* grow tall in the neck of bottles. These fragile, elegant mushrooms are mostly used decoratively and have a very short life span. *Morels* feel like sponges. They are dark brown/gray and hollow. Morels need to be washed in water and cut open to purge other living things that may have settled into the morel's cavity and made it their home. *Oysters,* one of the more flavorful specialty mushrooms, are light gray and come clumped together like a fan. *Shiitake* mushrooms, also called *Chinese, black forest* or *oak mushrooms,* are very sturdy. The stems, too tough to eat, are removed, but they make great stock. Dried shiitake have more than double the flavor of fresh, which are easier to use but very mild. Reading that female pigs were used to hunt *truffles* because these fungi emit the same odor as the sex hormone of male pigs puts this highly prized food in perspective. The majority of truffles are harvested in Provence, France, between January and March. Even the mild ones have a dominant taste, which puts these fungi into the herb/spice category, even though they may be decorative.

Classic Thai

Primary element: fresh shiitake mushrooms

First-stage method: braise

Cut: leave whole, remove stems

Oil: dark sesame and olive, equal parts

Herb/spice: fresh garlic, fresh cilantro, fresh basil, crushed red pepper flakes, ground coriander, turmeric powder, mustard powder, onion powder, lemon zest

Cooking liquid: rice vinegar

Salt: sea salt and tamari/shoyu

Miscellaneous: cane or palm sugar

Decorative: sesame seeds

Porcupine

Primary element: button or cremini mushrooms

First-stage method: tempura (double dip with seasoned rice cracker crumbs in arrowroot wash)

Cut: cut stem off at cap leaving cap cavity full

Binder: brown rice flour, sweet white rice flour, arrowroot, unbleached spelt

  Cooking liquid: plain sparkling water

  Oil: safflower

  Salt: dipping sauce (tamari/shoyu and Marsala wine)

Stuffed

Primary element: button or cremini mushrooms

First-stage method: roast, cavity up

Cut: remove stems all the way into the cap, leaving cap cavity empty

  Oil: olive

  Salt: sea salt

  Herb/spice: dried basil

Second-stage method: broil

Filling: shallot, mushroom stems, celery, parsley

First-stage method: slow cook

Cut: minced

Decorative/binder: bread crumbs or cracker crumbs

  Oil: ghee or olive; optional: parmesan or feta cheese

  Herb/spice: thyme, sage, freshly ground fennel seed

  Salt: vegetable salt, tamari

  Cooking liquid: Marsala wine, fresh lemon juice

Earth and Sea

Primary element: button mushrooms

First-stage method: teriyaki

Decorative: soaked and drained hijiki

Cut: slivers

  Oil: coconut

  Cooking liquid/sweetener: mirin and agave

  Salt: tamari

  Decorative: coconut flakes

Good for Grain

Primary element: portobello mushrooms

First-stage method: braise

Cut: slivers

  Oil: safflower

  Cooking liquid: water, Madeira wine, raspberry vinegar

  Salt: umeboshi

Zen Pickles

Primary element: dried shiitake mushrooms

First-stage method: pickle, brine

Cut: whole

  Herb/spice: ginger, garlic, whole Thai chile

  Cooking liquid: water, rice vinegar, mirin

  Salt: tamari

Ready for Something

Primary element: cremini mushrooms

First-stage method: steep

Cut: whole

> *Herb/spice:* bay leaf, black peppercorn, all-spice
>
> *Cooking liquid:* water
>
> *Salt:* sea salt

Second-stage method: marinate

Cut: quartered

> *Oil:* hazelnut
>
> *Herb/spice:* fresh lemon thyme
>
> *Cooking liquid:* fresh lemon juice
>
> *Salt:* light miso, sea salt

Cream of Mushroom

Primary element: cremini mushrooms, onion, leek

First-stage method: pressure cook, cream-style soup

Decorative/binder: potato or cauliflower

Cut: large

> *Oil:* olive or ghee
>
> *Herb/spice:* thyme, freshly ground black pepper
>
> *Cooking liquid:* vegetable stock (mushroom stems, cauliflower leaves and core, onion), cashew milk made with water/stock and Merlot wine (1 part nuts: 16 parts liquid)
>
> *Salt:* sea salt, tamari

Lightweight

Primary element: button mushrooms

First-stage method: steep

Cut: whole

> *Cooking liquid:* water, mirin
>
> *Herb/spice:* bay leaf, dried thyme
>
> *Salt:* vegetable salt

Trice and David's Wedding

Primary element: caramelized cremini mushrooms, caramelized onion

Decorative: soaked dried porcini mushrooms

Hot sauce: vegetable, flour, nut, clear

Binders: mushroom, onions, brown rice flour, cashews, arrowroot

> *Oil:* olive
>
> *Herb/spice:* shallot, garlic, bay leaf, freshly ground black pepper
>
> *Cooking liquid:* vegetable stock (mushroom, onion, herb/spice), soaking water for dried porcini, red wine, cashew cream (1 part nuts : 2 parts liquid)
>
> *Salt:* sea salt, tamari/shoyu

VEGETABLE PROTEIN

*W*e need protein in our food because it constitutes the basic machinery of all life. Proteins are at the heart of all organic movement, change, and growth: the most important characteristics of life itself.

—Harold McGee, *On Food and Cooking*

Proteins are chemicals. Give the body a few to inspire it, and it will make more. This primary element creates and recreates all tissues in the physical body. One of my students who is an emergency room nurse validated, in my mind, the power of vegetable protein. I was explaining that protein is the only primary element that freezes well. But once it has been defrosted, it should not be refrozen; instead, it needs to be used as soon as possible. She quickly injected an image that stays with me today. "Oh, it's like taking an arm out of the deep freeze at the hospital. It has one chance to be reused."

Plant protein is the most misunderstood primary element in classical cooking. I don't accept fungi in place of protein, because even though a portobello mushroom might look like and mimic the texture of a burger or a slab of meat, it doesn't have the same nutrient profile as a protein element. Vegetarians find a concentrated source of protein in beans, including soybean products like tempeh and tofu, and gluten, which is the protein extracted from wheat or spelt berries. Grain also provides protein, as do some vegetables, but in these primary elements the nutritional analysis weighs in with considerably more carbohydrate than protein. In meal composition, grain and vegetables are not a source of protein. Grains and beans that are sprouted instead of cooked nearly triple their protein content, except for soybeans, which contain more protein when cooked. But even when cooked, many beans have 8.5 grams of protein in a half-cup serving. Gluten from wheat or spelt is a concentrated portion of protein extracted from the grain's web of fiber and starch. A cup of this plant protein is worth 75 grams, the highest plant protein content per reasonable serving size. It is easy to enjoy a cup of seasoned gluten. I like to combine all three forms of plant protein: seasoned gluten (seitan), beans, and nuts. Together the variety of potential dishes is endless.

BEANS

Beans migrated from Arizona along with 8-row corn, but they were such hussies that the historical record couldn't keep up with all their migrations.

—Native American Food and Soupways,
http://www.soupsong.com

Beans, like antiques, are full of history and tradition. Ancient Egyptian lore forbade eating beans because they were powerful seeds honored for their own fertility and their shape, which they thought resembled male testicles. Beans, an emblem of life, were buried with Pharaohs and temples were dedicated to them. Greeks and Romans used beans in politics for voting and in festivals to worship their gods. Powerful Roman families took the name of beans: Fabius (fava bean), Lentulus (lentil), Piso (pea), and Cicero (chickpea). Bean seeds roamed with merchants, explorers, and warriors around the world. In the Middle Ages, peasants of Europe, like those in the Great Depression, survived on "poor man's meat." Native Americans in each part of North and South America have a connection to numerous kinds of beans. Because of their powerful nutrition and great storage ability, beans have been, and still are today, a primary food for sailors (which is how the navy bean got its name) and other armies of the world.

Some beans have more carbohydrate than protein, others more protein than carbohydrate. I choose them by the importance of their color in a dish. Beans are a source of niacin, thiamin, riboflavin, vitamin B$_6$, and many other nutrients. They are also rich in complex carbohydrates and fiber. Beans are high in potassium, which is required for the normal functioning of nerves and muscles. They have more calcium and iron per cup than three ounces of cooked meat, but contain no cholesterol and have fewer calories. Beans are the best source of folate, which is required for the production and maintenance of new cells and is especially important during periods of rapid cell division and growth, such as infancy and pregnancy. In addition, beans have a perfect nutrient base for people interested in losing weight, reducing cholesterol, and/or improving digestion. Beans also help prevent anemia and may minimize some of the side effects of aging. To gain the nutritional benefits, beans need to be fully cooked and buttery soft. Beans don't need to fall apart or expand outside the boundaries of their skin, but they should not be al dente. To balance their potency, serve beans with vegetables and grain.

ANASAZI (medium)

In the southwestern four corners where Colorado, Utah, Arizona, and New Mexico meet, anasazi beans have been cultivated by the Navajo Native Americans as early as 130 AD. The name "anasazi" means "the ancient ones." These heirloom beans look like a painted horse, with red and white spots that turn a mauve-pink color when cooked. Pinto beans, a hybrid of anasazis, pale in taste, but the two may be used interchangeably in all recipe sketches.

Company for Cornbread

Primary element: first-stage cooked anasazi bean
Second-stage method: steep
  Cooking liquid: beer, bean juice
  Herb/spice: garlic, cumin, hickory smoke flavor
  Salt: sea salt

Smoked Wonders on Corn Crackers

Primary element: anasazi bean
First-stage method: pressure cook
  Cooking liquid: water
  Herb/spice: chipotle chile, ancho chile
Second-stage: smoke
Third-stage: bake, pâté
Decorative: roasted red bell pepper
  Cooking liquid: onion juice (finely grated or blended onion)
  Herb/spice: minced fresh garlic
  Oil: cashew butter
  Salt: chickpea miso, sea salt

Potato and Bean Patty

Primary element: first-stage cooked pinto/anasazi bean, steeped russet potato
Second-stage method: refry
Decorative: leek, minced
  Herb/spice: freshly ground fennel seed, freshly ground black pepper
  Salt: sea salt
  Oil: ghee or olive oil

Chili with Beans

Primary element: first-stage cooked anasazi bean with epazote; onion; yellow bell pepper; rutabaga; canned Anaheim green chile (roasted, peeled, and seeded); roasted seitan

Second-stage method: stew

Decorative: soaked, pressure cooked posole, or canned posole

Cut: diced

Oil: olive

Cooking liquid: bean juice or water, red wine

Herb/spice: garlic, oregano, ancho chile, chipotle chili powder, cumin

Salt: vegetable salt

Mexican Refried Beans

Primary element: anasazi beans

First-stage method: pressure cook

Herb/spice: epazote, ancho and chipotle chiles

Cooking liquid: beer, water

Second-stage method: braise

Decorative: onion, red bell pepper

Cut: small diced

Oil: corn oil

Herb/spice: garlic, chili powder

Cooking liquid/sweetener: bean juice, rice syrup

Salt: sea salt

Tortilla Filling

Primary element: first-stage cooked anasazi bean; oil-cured sun-dried tomato

Second-stage cooking method: blend

Decorative: oil-cured black olives

Oil: olive oil from the olives and sun-dried tomato

Cooking liquid: fresh lime juice

Herb/spice: crushed red pepper flakes, fresh cilantro

Salt: olives

ADZUKI (short–medium)

This very old bean has many names: adzuki, aduki, asuki, azuki, chi dou (Mandarin), feijao, field pea, hong xiao dou (Mandarin), red oriental, and Tiensin red. It looks like a mung bean with a square-shaped body and a white sliver on its side. Even though the protein is doubled in the sprouted raw bean compared with the cooked bean, adzukis have more carbohydrate value than other beans, which explains why this bean is often sweetened and used in traditional Asian dessert dishes.

Ah So

Primary element: first-stage cooked adzuki beans, leek

Second-stage method: braise

Decorative: carrot

Cut: thin rounds

Oil: toasted sesame

Cooking liquid: sake

Salt: tamari

Red and Gold

SIDE DISH

Primary element: first-stage cooked
    adzuki beans, winter squash, onion
Second-stage method: braise
Cut: cubes, diced
   Oil: toasted sesame
   Herb/spice: fresh ginger, fresh cilantro
   Cooking liquid: bean juice, coconut milk,
       water, fresh lime juice
   Salt: miso

Summer

SALAD

Primary element: first-stage cooked adzuki beans,
    steeped pattypan squash, roasted red bell
    pepper
Second-stage method: marinate
Cut: small fans, diced
Decorative: arugula
   Oil: olive
   Cooking liquid: mirin, raspberry vinegar
   Salt: sea salt
Decorative: roasted sunflower seeds

Easy Going Down

SOUP

Primary element: first-stage cooked adzuki beans
Second-stage method: boil, bean soup
Decorative: leek, any bell pepper, carrot
Cut: small dice
   Cooking liquid: bean juice, water
   Herb/spice: cumin, coriander, cardamom,
       crushed red pepper flakes
   Salt: sea salt, tamari

BLACK BEANS (turtle, medium)
(soy, medium–long)

Black turtle beans are oval, dry, and small compared to black soybeans, which are round and moist. Soybeans are usually long-cooking beans, but the black soy has the flexibility to be cooked like a medium-term bean if it is cooked for an extra 30 minutes. Black soybeans feel like velvet in the mouth and have a better taste than yellow soybeans. Black turtle beans, commonly used in Mexican dishes, absorb flavors more easily than soybeans, whose innate fat requires a heavy hand with herb/spice.

Delicious Disks

SIDE DISH

Primary element: first-stage cooked
    black turtle beans
Second-stage method: refry, patty form
Binder: crushed corn flakes
   Oil: olive
   Herb/spice: shallot, fresh basil
   Salt: sea salt

Shaped Velvet

MAIN PLATE OR APPETIZER

Primary element: first-stage cooked black
    soybeans with seeded ancho
Second-stage method: bake, pâté
Decorative: roasted pumpkin seeds
   Oil: tahini
   Herb/spice: crushed green peppercorns,
       shallot
   Salt: red miso

Shiny Pebbles

DECORATIVE

Primary element: first-stage cooked black turtle beans

Second-stage method: braise

Oil: olive

Herb/spice: fresh garlic, fresh cilantro

Salt: tamari

Cooking liquid: bean juice, red wine

Red and Black

MAIN PLATE

Primary element: first-stage cooked black turtle beans, first-stage pressure cooked wehani rice

Second-stage method: refry, patty form

Decorative: red bell pepper, green onion

Cut: minced

Oil: light sesame

Herb/spice: garam masala (coriander, cardamom, black pepper, cinnamon, caraway, cloves, ginger, nutmeg), orange flower water, garlic

Salt: sea salt

Cooking liquid: fresh lime juice

Smooth Moves

SAUCE

Primary element: first-stage cooked black soybeans

Hot sauce: bean

Decorative: leek, roasted red bell pepper, cilantro

Oil: olive (optional)

Herb/spice: garlic

Cooking liquid: water, mirin

Salt: sea salt, tamari

Accent liquid: raspberry or blackberry vinegar

Stolen

SOUP

Primary element: first-stage cooked black turtle beans

Second-stage method: boil, bean soup

Decorative: onion, bell pepper, green chile

Cut: minced

Cooking liquid: bean juice, water, coconut milk

Oil: coconut milk

Herb/spice: fresh garlic, lime zest, cayenne (optional)

Salt: sea salt

Accent liquid: fresh lime wedges

Salsa

SALAD

Primary element: first-stage cooked black turtle beans

Second-stage method: marinate

Decorative: steeped fresh corn or canned corn, English cucumber, cherry tomato, yellow bell pepper

Cut: same size of bean, diced

Oil: olive

Cooking liquid: fresh lemon juice

Herb/spice: fresh garlic, jalapeño chile, fresh cilantro

Salt: sea salt

PEAS (black-eyed, medium) (green pea, long)

In 1835, Hans Christian Andersen's fairy tale *The Princess and the Pea* referred to a whole dried green pea (protein, not vegetable). In the story, a princess tried to sleep upon 20 mattresses plus 20 eiderdown comforters, but reported a sleepless night and bruised body due to the hard, dried pea that had been placed beneath the lot. Living at an altitude of more than 5,000 feet elevation, I do not even try to cook whole dried peas because I haven't figured out how to make them soft enough. This is also true for split peas. At sea level they cook beautifully, once the foam is removed. Black-eyed peas grow in a warm, moist climate, which creates a softer nature than the cold environments of green peas. Their delicate skin is thinner than other beans.

Orange Eyes

SIDE DISH

Primary element: first-stage cooked
    black-eyed peas
Second-stage method: braise
Decorative: winter squash, onion
Cut: diced small
    Oil: hazelnut
    Cooking liquid: apple juice, water
    Herb/spice: cumin, garlic

Pâté in Pink

SPREAD

Primary element: first-stage cooked
    black-eyed peas
Second-stage method: bake, pâté
Decorative: Turkish apricots, pecans
Cut: diced small
    Oil: sesame tahini
    Herb/spice: shallot, amaretto, freshly ground
        black pepper
    Salt: white or chickpea miso, sea salt

Rosemary Lemon Peas

SIDE DISH

Primary element: first-stage cooked black-eyed
    peas
Second-stage method: steep
    Herb/spice: fresh rosemary, lemon zest
    Cooking liquid: bean juice, white wine
    Salt: sea salt, tamari

Pea Patty

SIDE DISH

Primary element: first-stage cooked black-eyed
    peas
Second-stage method: refry
Decorative: fresh cilantro (optional)
    Oil: olive or ghee
    Herb/spice: garlic granules, fresh cilantro
    Salt: sea salt

CHICKPEAS/GARBANZO BEANS (long)

Chickpeas appear to be round and square at the same time. They are an extremely seductive bean with an abundance of natural fat. Well-cooked chickpeas will be smooth like butter. There should be no crunch. Most first-stage canned chickpeas do not compare to the smooth quality of those that are cooked at home in a pressure cooker. All chickpea dishes will be successful if the first-stage method is done well. These beans benefit from soaking.

Dilled

Primary element: first-stage cooked chickpeas

Second-stage method: marinate

Decorative: green olives

  Oil: olive

  Cooking liquid: olive brine

  Herb/spice: fresh dill weed

  Salt: olive brine

Golden Sweet

Primary element: first-stage cooked chickpeas

Second-stage method: bake, pâté

Decorative: onion, yellow and red bell pepper

  Oil: raw cashew butter

  Salt: chickpea miso, sea salt

  Herb/spice: ginger juice

Minestrone Two

Primary element: first-stage cooked chickpeas, onion, carrot, celery, savoy cabbage, fresh tomato (optional)

Second-stage method: boil, loose vegetable soup

Cut: small dice

  Oil: olive

  Herb/spice: fresh garlic, dried basil, oregano, fennel seed, thyme, fresh basil, black pepper

  Cooking liquid: chickpea juice, water or vegetable stock, Marsala wine

  Salt: sea salt, finishing salt (optional)

Decorative: pasta spirals or other noodle

Falafel

Primary element: chickpeas

Pretreatments: soak 12 hours, drain, blend

Decorative: fresh cilantro or parsley

  Miscellaneous: light handed baking powder to fit

  Herb/spice: fresh garlic, ground cumin, crushed red pepper flakes

  Salt: vegetable salt

First-stage method: deep-fry

  Oil: safflower

Cold sauce: marinade

  Oil: tahini

  Herb/spice: fresh garlic crushed in water

  Cooking liquid: garlic water, fresh lemon juice

  Salt: sea salt

Gold and Green in Lemon

Primary element: first-stage cooked chickpeas, spinach

Second-stage method: steeped in sauce

Hot sauce: flour/nut

Binder: brown rice flour

  Oil: coconut milk

  Cooking liquid: coconut milk, fresh lemon juice

  Herb/spice: shallot, curry powder, lemon zest

  Salt: sea salt

World Flavors

Primary element: first-stage cooked chickpeas

Second-stage method: braise

Oil: olive

Salt: umeboshi vinegar

Cooking liquid/sweetener: fresh lemon juice, chickpea liquid, agave

Herb/spice: garlic, cumin, paprika, black pepper, fresh cilantro

A Symphony

CASSEROLE

Primary element: first-stage cooked chickpeas, leek, carrot, rutabaga, turnip

Second-stage method: bake

Hot sauce: flour, short method

Binder: rice flour

Oil: light sesame

Herb/spice: bay leaf, garlic

Cooking liquid: bean juice, water

Salt: sea salt

Shades of India

SOUP

Primary element: first-stage cooked chickpeas

Second-stage method: boil, bean soup

Decorative: carrot, onion

Oil: light sesame

Herb/spice: cardamom, garlic

Cooking liquid: chickpea juice, water, or vegetable stock

Salt: sea salt

Hot Pepper Hummus

SPREAD

Primary element: first-stage cooked chickpeas

Second-stage method: blend

Oil: tahini, olive oil as garnish (optional)

Herb/spice: garlic, crushed red pepper flakes or cayenne

Cooking liquid: fresh lemon juice, chickpea liquid to thin (optional)

Salt: sea salt, umeboshi

KIDNEY BEANS (medium–long)

Shaped like a kidney and about an inch long, these plump beans come in white (cannellini) and dark red. They are famous in the American dish three-bean salad that also contains chickpeas and string beans. Kidney beans were added to the roster of red beans in 1551, distinguishing it from other varieties of common beans. The red kidney is particularly good for stimulating and strengthening the immune system, if it is fully cooked. Uncooked beans cause a type of food poisoning that includes vomiting and diarrhea; although these symptoms are temporary, the intensity of them is directly related to the amount of beans eaten. It is prudent but not essential to soak and parboil (cook briefly in boiling water) this bean before pressure cooking it in the first stage. If the beans are not soaked, they should be cooked for 90 minutes in the pressure cooker. White kidney beans are 30 percent less toxic than red.

Kidneys have a delicate skin, so if soaking is chosen, it is important to have the first-stage cooking liquid only to the top of the beans in the pressure cooker.

Duo

Primary element: first-stage cooked kidney beans

Hot sauce: bean, nut

Binders: kidney beans, almonds

   Herb/spice: optional

   Cooking liquid: bean juice

   Oil: almond butter

   Salt: umeboshi

Off White

Primary element: first-stage cooked white kidney
   beans

Second-stage method: bake, pâté

Decorative: onion, leek

   Herb/spice: herbes de Provence

   Oil: cashew butter

   Salt: chickpea miso, sea salt

Kidney Bean Chili

Primary element: first-stage cooked kidney beans,
   fresh corn, tomato, tomatillo, onion

Second-stage method: boil, stew

Cut: cubes, diced

Binder: cooked white rice

   Oil: olive

   Herb/spice: garlic, chili powder, garam
      masala (coriander, cardamom, black
      pepper, cinnamon, caraway, cloves,
      ginger, nutmeg)

   Cooking liquid: spicy tomato juice

   Salt: sea salt

Decorative: green or black olives

Red Sauce and Black Rice

Primary element: first-stage cooked kidney beans,
   roasted red pepper

Hot sauce: bean, vegetable

   Cooking liquid: bean juice, beer

   Herb/spice: shallot

   Oil: corn

   Salt: sea salt

Primary element: black forbidden rice

First-stage method: pressure cook

Second-stage method: refry

Decorative: leek, fresh or frozen corn

   Oil: corn

   Herb/spice: shallot

   Salt: umeboshi

August Harvest

Primary element: first-stage cooked kidney beans,
   fresh corn, tomato, tomatillo, onion

Second-stage method: braise

Cut: small cubes

Decorative: green or black olives

   Herb/spice: garlic, chili powder, garam
      masala (coriander, cardamom, black
      pepper, cinnamon, caraway, cloves,
      ginger, nutmeg)

   Oil: olive

   Cooking liquid: bean juice, water, Madeira
      wine

   Salt: sea salt

Blood Sweet

Primary element: first-stage cooked red kidney
  beans

Second-stage method: braise

Decorative: red onion, roasted red pepper

Cut: small diced

  Oil: olive

  Cooking liquid: Madeira wine, water or bean
    juice

  Salt: dark barley miso

  Herb/spice: fresh cilantro

White, Red, and Green

SALAD

Primary element: first-stage cooked white kidney
  and red kidney beans, steeped fresh green
  beans

Second-stage method: marinate

Cut: diagonal

  Oil: olive

  Herb/spice: fresh basil, black pepper

  Cooking liquid: white balsamic vinegar

  Salt: sea salt

Decorative: tamari roasted pumpkin seeds

WHITE BEANS (medium)

Three small white beans—lima, navy, and Great
Northern—never really look white when cooked;
they are more off-white or ivory. They do provide
a light background color for pâté, and are especially supportive for yellow/orange tints. Lima
beans, flat and almost kidney shaped, are named
for Lima, Peru. Navy beans, oval in shape, are the
smallest white bean. Great Northern beans look
and taste similar to navy beans, but they are larger.
These are very common beans used in French and
Mediterranean cooking.

Friends in Summer

SIDE DISH

Primary element: first-stage cooked lima beans,
  tomato, fresh corn

Second-stage method: braise

  Oil: olive oil

  Herb/spice: garlic, oregano

  Cooking liquid: tomato juice, bean juice

  Salt: sea salt

Fun with Kumquat

SIDE DISH

Primary element: first-stage cooked lima beans

Second-stage method: braise

Decorative: kumquat, roasted hazelnuts

  Oil: hazelnut

  Herb/spice: ginger

  Cooking liquid: mirin, orange juice, rice
    vinegar, bean juice

  Salt: sea salt

Delicate Tastes

SALAD

Primary element: first-stage cooked lima beans,
  fresh fennel bulb

Second-stage method: marinate

  Oil: walnut oil

  Herb/spice: black pepper, parsley

  Cooking liquid: cider vinegar

  Salt: sea salt

Curry Bean and Potato Patty

Primary element: first-stage cooked white beans, steeped Yukon Gold potato

Second-stage method: refry

Decorative: green onions or chives

Cut: minced

Oil: olive oil

Herb/spice: curry powder

Salt: vegetable salt

Wrap It Up

Primary element: first-stage cooked Great Northern beans

Second-stage method: refry

Decorative: green onions, cherry tomato

Oil: olive oil

Herb/spice: garlic, basil

Salt: sea salt, umeboshi

Primary element: large collard greens

First-stage method: steep

Cooking liquid: water

Salt: sea salt

Primary element: wild rice

First-stage method: pressure cook

Herb/spice: cinnamon stick

Cooking liquid: vegetable bouillon

Salt: sea salt

Hot sauce: nut

Oil: pine nuts

Cooking liquid: water, white wine

Salt: chickpea miso

Cream of White Bean

Primary element: first-stage cooked white beans

Second-stage method: boil, bean soup

Decorative: roasted parsnip, parsley

Cut: small cubes, minced

Oil: almond milk

Cooking liquid: almond milk (1 part nuts : 15 parts water)

Herb/spice: bay leaf, fennel seed, thyme

Salt: sea salt

No Cream Basil

Primary element: first-stage cooked white beans

Hot sauce: blend, bean

Oil: olive oil

Herb/spice: fresh garlic, fresh basil, cayenne, shallot (optional)

Cooking liquid: water, bean juice, sake or dry sherry

Salt: sea salt

Flag Colors

Primary elements: first-stage cooked cannellini beans, steeped kale, cucumber

Second-stage method: marinate

Cut: squares, dice

Oil: olive

Herb/spice: fresh oregano, Dijon mustard

Cooking liquid: cider vinegar

Salt: sea salt

Decorative: sesame seeds

Variation of Boston Baked Beans

Primary element: first-stage cooked navy beans

Second-stage method: bake in sauce

Decorative: onion

Cut: small dice

Hot sauce: vegetable

Binder: tomato paste

Oil: olive oil or ghee

Herb/spice: garlic, ginger, prepared mustard, horseradish (optional), liquid smoke

Cooking liquid/sweetener: bean juice, cider vinegar, barley malt or molasses

Salt: brown rice miso

Miscellaneous: organic brown sugar

MUNG BEANS (short)

Cooked whole, these small olive-green seeds turn into a boring mush. If the skin is removed, the mush is yellow mung, called moong dal in Indian cuisine. These beans cook quickly and are easily digested. Mung are one of the few beans that fully transform during the sprouting process, using the entire seed. These long, crisp sprouts are famous used as a refreshing decorative element or major ingredient in Asian cuisine. Raw mung beans may be ground into flour, mixed with water, and rolled into clear bean thread noodles.

FAVA BEANS

Fava's nickname, "horse beans," indicates the strength of their hide—too tough to eat whether fresh, dried and cooked, or from a can. Even treated as a long-term bean, I could not make the dried bean soft. Cooking them fresh out of the pod, I discovered their secret and understood why fava beans are named after great Roman warriors. Fava beans have a layer of armor surrounding the vulnerable meat. It needs to be removed before this protein can be enjoyed, which is easily done after the beans are steeped. These are best eaten as a pea or green bean dish. Refer to the dishes in the Pod/Seed Family (page 125-129).

GLUTEN

Gluten is a strange and simple food. Pure protein is extracted from wheat or spelt berries by removing the starch and fiber. Born from a mild-tasting grain, gluten has little flavor, but its strands are open to many cooking methods that use herb/spice, oil, and interesting liquids that transform this plain food into something so exquisite the name changes to "seitan" in Japan, "kofu" in China, and "wheat meat" in the United Kingdom and United States. For thousands of years gluten-based dishes have been created in the cuisines of China, Japan, Korea, Russia, and the Middle East. More recently, Seventh-day Adventists and Mormons have adopted gluten as part of their vegetarian protein source. In Chinese restaurants, gluten dishes may be called "Buddha food," referring to a pacifist Buddhist monk who developed gluten dishes as a meat substitute.

The nutritional benefits of gluten dishes are only valuable if the body can digest gluten. I prefer using spelt over wheat because it is more tender and easier to digest. Gluten contains approximately 23 grams of protein in a one-third cup serving and no fat. The preparation options for this primary element are endless because it can undergo almost any first-, second-, or third-stage cooking method. For example, braising may be used as a first-stage method or a second-stage method after steeping. Alternatively, roasting could be a first-stage method or a second-stage method after baking in a broth. Combining methods will have a positive effect on the flavor and texture.

Selecting and Storing

Prepared seitan is available from several companies. Some add bean flour to the raw gluten to boost the protein and have a grain/bean combination. Others use traditional flavors—ginger and kombu with tamari/shoyu as the salt seasoning. Although tempted by the light-colored chicken-style and dark-colored beef-style, I prefer to make my own. Commercial seitan products often are made with gluten flour, which makes the texture extremely chewy; also, because gluten flour has no spaces for flavor to enter the way that fresh gluten does, commercial seitan is less flexible.

Fresh gluten is delicate and will only keep refrigerated for a few days. It should be stored in water and covered; for longer storage, it may be frozen. Salt acts as a preservative, so when I store complete seitan dishes, they will contain salt/salt seasoning and will keep for about a week. I don't really know exactly how long they will keep, though, because such delicacies rarely make it to storage.

To make fresh gluten, first select either whole grain spelt or wheat flour, or a mixture of up to half and half whole grain flour with unbleached white flour. Mix the flour with water and knead into a ball of dough, as if making bread. Work the dough until smooth and let it rest in a bowl. You can use the same bowl from the original mixing so you don't have to wash the bowl first. Cover the ball with water, and let it rest. A minimum of 20 minutes resting time, either with or without water, helps develop the gluten strands. Knead the dough in the water until the starch water is so thick there isn't any room for more. The ball of dough is now soft and shapeless. Slide it into a colander with large holes. Alternating warm and cool water, allow it to fall through the dough, washing away starch and bran. Lift the batterlike substance, folding it toward the center, over and over as the shapeless form comes back into a ball. Press lightly until all the starch water is gone, and then press the gluten ball until it is firm and the water runs clear. Open and close the gluten strands as the ball takes shape.

Raw gluten will take the shape of whatever it is stored in. If I am cooking it in a skillet, I want the pieces fairly thin, between $1/4$ and $1/3$ inch thick. When simmered with a steeping method, the pieces will expand in accordance with the amount of liquid. The more liquid, the longer it will take to cook. Steeping a large piece or slab will firm the seitan so it can be easily cut for a second stage. These cuts can be as small or large as necessary for the dish. The book *Cooking with Seitan* by Barbara and Leonard Jacobs details the making of seitan.

Protein Drops

SIDE DISH

Primary element: whole and unbleached white spelt gluten

First-stage method: steep

Cooking liquid: spiced water (fennel, turmeric, cardamom)

Second-stage method: roast

Oil: sunflower

Salt: chickpea miso

Herb/spice: dried basil, turmeric

Comfort

Primary element: spelt gluten

First-stage method: braise

> *Oil:* olive
>
> *Salt:* tamari
>
> *Cooking liquid:* red wine, water
>
> *Herb/spice:* minced fresh garlic, grated fresh ginger

Primary element: cauliflower

First-stage method: bake in sauce

Cut: bite-size pieces

Hot sauce: flour

Binder: rice flour

> *Oil:* olive
>
> *Cooking liquid:* cashew milk (1 part nuts : 16 parts water)
>
> *Herb/spice:* fresh garlic, freshly ground black pepper, bay leaf
>
> *Salt:* sea salt

Two Steps

Primary element: whole grain and unbleached white spelt gluten

First-stage method: steep

Cut: small pieces

> *Cooking liquid:* water, Madeira wine
>
> *Salt:* umeboshi
>
> *Herb/spice:* cardamom

Second-stage method: deep-fry

> *Oil:* safflower

Mustard Morsels

Primary element: whole spelt gluten

First-stage method: braise

> *Oil:* light sesame
>
> *Cooking liquid:* white wine, water
>
> *Herb/spice:* Dijon mustard
>
> *Salt:* chickpea miso

Savory Loaf

Primary element: whole wheat and unbleached white spelt gluten

First-stage method: steep

Cut: medium pieces

> *Cooking liquid:* water, red wine
>
> *Salt:* tamari
>
> *Herb/spice:* bay leaf

Second-stage method: roast

Cut: coarse chopping blade to ground beef texture

> *Oil:* olive

Third-stage method: bake in oiled loaf pan

> *Binder:* dry roasted rolled oats
>
> *Oil:* cashew or almond butter
>
> *Herb/spice:* garlic, thyme, prepared mustard, freshly ground black pepper
>
> *Salt:* tamari

Primary element: squash, onion

Hot sauce: vegetable

> *Oil:* olive
>
> *Cooking liquid:* water
>
> *Salt:* sea salt, umeboshi
>
> *Herb/spice:* fresh ginger slices, removed after cooking

Three Tastes

Primary element: whole spelt gluten

First-stage method: braise

Oil: corn oil

Cooking liquid: mirin, water

Salt: tamari

Herb/spice: onion powder, cayenne, cumin, oregano

Crisp and Chewy #1

MAIN PLATE

Primary element: whole and unbleached white spelt gluten

First-stage method: teriyaki

Cut: very thin strips

Oil: toasted sesame

Cooking liquid/sweetener: rice syrup

Herb/spice: fresh ginger juice

Salt: tamari/shoyu

Crisp and Chewy #2

MAIN PLATE

Primary element: whole spelt gluten

First-stage method: teriyaki

Cut: very thin strips

Oil: safflower

Cooking liquid/sweetener: barley malt

Herb/spice: orange zest

Salt: sea salt in orange juice

Crisp and Chewy #3

MAIN PLATE

Primary element: whole and unbleached white spelt gluten

First-stage method: teriyaki

Cut: very thin strips

Oil: olive

Cooking liquid/sweetener: mirin

Salt: umeboshi

To Pair with a Vegetable Dish

SIDE DISH

Primary element: whole grain spelt gluten

First-stage method: deep-fry

Oil: safflower

Second-stage method: steep

Herb/spice: fresh ginger, fresh garlic

Cooking liquid: kombu stock

Salt: tamari/shoyu

Not Really Sausage

SIDE DISH

Primary element: whole grain and unbleached white spelt gluten

First-stage method: refry

Oil: olive

Herb/spice: dried basil, dried oregano, dried thyme, dried sage, crushed fennel seed, freshly ground black pepper

Salt: vegetable salt, tamari/shoyu

SOYBEANS

In 2853 BCE, this ancient, complex bean from China was honored as one of the five sacred plants, along with rice, wheat, barley, and millet. Through trade routes, soybeans traveled into Japan, Indonesia, the Philippines, Vietnam, Thailand, Malaysia, Burma, Nepal, and India. The earliest Japanese reference to the soybean is in 712 AD. Soybeans arrived in America in the early nineteenth century, not as seed to grow food, but as dead weight to stabilize ships. It took another century to establish soybeans as food for livestock, nutrients for the soil, and a source of oil. Almost half a century later, around 1950, with more than 10,000 varieties to sort through in China, America began to include soybeans as a human food source.

Soybeans have nutritional contributions in the areas of protein, fat, and minerals. The more a soybean is heated, the higher the protein count. For example, sprouted soybeans have 2.5 grams of protein per cup; sprouts that have been steamed have 8 grams of protein per cup. Tempeh, made from soybeans, remains a whole bean dish. To make tempeh, soybeans are inoculated with a culture called rhizopus oligosporus; after this process, the protein level jumps to 18 grams per cup, plus tempeh contains vitamin B_{12}. Tofu, which is not a whole food but an elegantly refined one, is concentrated protein with the fiber removed; the protein content of a cup of tofu is 28 grams. To drive home my point about cooking the beans well, roasted whole soybeans measure 61 grams of protein per cup. Scientists have found that black soybeans prevent stomach fat buildup and lower blood cholesterol levels.

TOFU AND TEMPEH

I have to remember to eat small amounts of tofu. Its refinement is seductive, but eating more than a half-cup serving bloats me.

Tofu emerged as a Chinese staple through the language of cooking around 1000 AD. Its exact origin is not known, but there is reason to believe that the Chinese, who do not cultivate animals for milk, observed their neighbors, the nomadic people of Mongolia, who depended on their animals for milk products. In observing the transformation of Mongolian milk to yogurt and cheese, the Chinese, who considered Mongolians inferior, thought their cooking liquid (milk) was spoiled. They nevertheless became fond of the cultured food, and they applied the same processes to their cooking liquid (soymilk). This resulted in the popular tofu, which means "soybean spoiled."

Tofu is easy to make, but it takes time, attention, and large pots. The process begins with yellow soybeans that are soaked for 12 hours and then rinsed and blended into a mash by adding more water to them. A piece of kombu sea vegetable and the mash go into a large pot filled one-third with water. The mash is added until the pot is about two-thirds full. Headroom is essential. Stir the pot slowly, making sure that a long-handled bamboo rice paddle reaches every corner of the bottom. This is important to prevent soy protein from sticking to the bottom; it is relentless about letting go. This slurry may cook on a medium flame for an entire hour before the foam rises, at which point I immediately turn off the stove. Maybe give it a gentle blow to contain the foam so it doesn't bond to the stove top. This is the point where foam is usually removed when parboiling soaked, long-term beans. Straining the mash through a slightly damp, very large, thin muslin dish towel separates soymilk from the fiber (called *okara*). Before adding an agent to separate the curds and whey, I think about the herb/spice category. Do I want a "designer" tofu? Lemon? Curry? Garlic? Just color? If so, the herb/spice goes into the warm soymilk. Traditional curdling agents, such as natural calcium sulfate (gypsum) and magnesium chloride (*nigari*), have been used for hundreds of years in Japan and China. Nigari, which originates from sea water, is preferred for its better taste and additional nutrients. To my surprise, I have successfully used sea salt, Epsom salts, and either lemon, lime, or pineapple juice to form the curds. This liquid passes through another damp cloth separating the curds and whey. Whey is the clear liquid that I keep in a jar to be used as soap; the curds are the clouds of soy protein that take the shape of whatever form they are put into and which eventually become tofu. The more liquid that is pressed or dripped from this ball of tofu, the firmer the tofu becomes. Curdling agents also control the firm/softness. Although fresh tofu is delicious and laudable on its own, it hasn't cooked as long as most long-term beans. Second-stage methods not only bring culinary interest to a simple first-stage bean dish, they aid digestibility.

The origins of tempeh are sketchy. Most writing on the subject appears in the twentieth century regarding the relationship between Indonesia/Malaysia and the Netherlands. It is believed that Indonesia is the birthplace of tempeh, and that after having received the soybean in trade with China the Indonesians replicated the Chinese fermentation process of making soy sauce with fermented koji rice. They recognized that the fermentation that resulted from this process was similar to the mold that grew on their coconut cakes; as a result, they adapted the inoculation of soybeans by using rhizopus oligosporus, because it was more suitable to their environment. Indonesia developed the cuisine for tempeh and the Dutch brought it to Europe. Later, in the twentieth century, The Farm community in Tennessee developed and promoted the American version of tempeh production.

Tempeh, like tofu, can be made in home kitchens. The transformation is not controlled by appliances as much as by maintaining the temperature of the environment. The greatest challenge is finding a location that has both air flow and maintains an average temperature of 88°F (31°C). To begin, soak the long-term bean whole or use the pulp (okara) from making tofu. The most devoted effort goes to removing skins of the whole bean after soaking. Continued rinsing and massaging of the beans under water separates the skins and they rise to the top for easy removal. Beans without skin will split. There's a difference in opinion on how long to cook the first-stage bean. Okara has already been cooked. Whole soybeans should cook for 30–60 minutes with a touch of vinegar and then cooled to body temperature. After that they are inoculated with a rhizoid starter, moved to a container that has air available, and placed in a warm environment for about 24 hours. The beans form a cake that holds together by a network of fungal filaments (mycelium), the white fuzz. Making tempeh is not difficult, but as a fermented food there are important things to observe. Detailed directions accompany tempeh starters.

Selecting and Storing

The color, smell, and texture are specific in freshly made tempeh. A white fuzzy coat surrounds the cake. Black streaks or spots are good, red ones are not; if red appears, throw the tempeh out. Tempeh should not be slippery and should smell friendly.

Although it freezes well, tempeh is best used within a week if kept refrigerated. Fresh tofu is stored refrigerated or frozen in clean water. Regularly changing the water of refrigerated tofu prolongs its usability. With commercial tofu and tempeh, a "use by" or "sell by" date is stamped on the package; they are usually okay for about a week beyond the date of sale.

TLT

Primary element: tofu or tempeh
Second-stage method: braise
  Oil: toasted sesame oil
  Herb/spice: garlic, ginger
  Cooking liquid: mirin, rice vinegar, pineapple juice
  Salt: tamari
Primary element: toasted whole grain bread, slice or bun
Decorative: lettuce, tomato, onion
Cut: sliced
  Oil: mayonnaise
  Herb/spice: prepared mustard

My Millionaire

Primary element: pressure steamed tempeh or tofu
Second-stage method: blend
Decorative: celery, green onion, pineapple
  Oil: mayonnaise
  Herb/spice: prepared mustard, fresh dill weed, parsley
  Salt: sea salt and/or umeboshi
Decorative: umeboshi roasted cashews

Vegetable Stroganoff

Primary element: tempeh or tofu
Second-stage method: roast
Hot sauce: vegetable/nut
Binders: caramelized mushrooms, caramelized onion, cashew cream
Cut: slivers
  Oil: olive oil or ghee
  Herb/spice: black pepper, dried basil, paprika, garlic
  Cooking liquid: cashew milk (1 part nuts : 6 parts liquid)
  Salt: umeboshi
Primary element: rice
First-stage method: steep or bake
  Cooking liquid: water
  Salt: sea salt

Spicy Lemon Tempeh

Primary element: tempeh
First-stage method: steep
  Cooking liquid/sweetener: water, fresh lemon juice, agave
  Herb/spice: lemon zest oil, bay leaf, crushed red pepper flakes, turmeric
  Salt: sea salt
Second-stage method: roast
Cut: $1/4$-inch-thick triangles
  Oil: safflower
  Herb/spice: lemon oil
  Salt: umeboshi

Horseradish

Primary element: pressure steamed tofu with horseradish slivers in the steaming water

Second-stage method: blend

Oil: hazelnut

Herb/spice: freshly ground horseradish (if using prepared, omit the cooking horseradish in the liquid)

Cooking liquid: cider vinegar

Salt: umeboshi vinegar

Pink Bell Pepper

Primary element: medium tofu; roasted, skinned, and seeded red bell pepper

Second-stage method: blend, dip

Oil: olive

Herb/spice: garlic, soaked and seeded ancho chile

Cooking liquid: bell pepper, fresh lemon juice (accent liquid)

Salt: sea salt, umeboshi

Tofu Piccata

Primary element: medium-firm tofu

First-stage method: braise

Breading: seasoned white spelt flour

Oil: olive

Herb/spice: paprika, garlic granules

Cooking liquid: caper brine, fresh lemon juice, water

Salt: caper brine

Lasagne

Primary element: pressed tofu

Second-stage method: blend, spread

Oil: olive

Herb/spice: fresh garlic, fresh basil

Salt: umeboshi vinegar

Primary element: mushrooms, leeks

First-stage method: slow cook

Oil: olive oil

Herb/spice: garlic, optional herbs: basil, oregano, marjoram

Salt: sea salt, umeboshi

Hot sauce: vegetable

Binder: crushed or puréed tomato

Cooking liquid: Marsala wine and/or water

Herb/spice: garlic granules, dried basil, oregano, fennel seed, marjoram, sage

Oil: olive

Salt: sea salt

Primary element: grain, uncooked pasta

Third-stage method: bake

Decorative: topping, finely ground umeboshi roasted cashews

Layer from the bottom up: sauce, pasta, tofu, vegetable, pasta, tofu. Press and then continue layering pasta, sauce, nut topping, baking paper, foil.

Quick Slabs

Primary element: tofu or tempeh

Second-stage method: teriyaki

Oil: sesame

Herb/spice: none

Cooking liquid/sweetener: agave or rice syrup

Salt: tamari or umeboshi

With Vegetables and Sauce

Primary element: tofu or tempeh

First-stage method: deep-fry

   Oil: safflower

Primary element: pea pods, red bell pepper, onion

First-stage method: stir-fry

Cut: large for stir-fry

   Oil: safflower

   Salt: sea salt

   Cooking liquid: ice water

Hot sauce: clear

   Binder: kudzu (1 tablespoon : 1 cup liquid)

   Herb/spice: pickling spices, beet juice (grated fresh beet)

   Cooking liquid: pineapple juice, cider vinegar

   Salt: sea salt

Decorative: tamari roasted almonds

Multi Taste

SIDE DISH

Primary element: tempeh

First-stage method: steep

   Cooking liquid: Marsala wine, water

   Herb/spice: garlic, bay leaf, paprika

   Salt: sea salt

Second-stage method: teriyaki

   Oil: olive

   Cooking liquid/sweetener: rice syrup

   Salt: tamari

Not Really Bacon

SIDE DISH

Primary element: tofu or tempeh

Second-stage method: refry

   Oil: sesame

   Herb/spice: liquid smoke or smoking as a pretreatment

   Cooking liquid: none

   Salt: tamari

WHOLE-DISH GRAINS

Grain and grasses are staples of almost every cuisine. The variety of choices is stimulating. I classify grain and grasses into two categories: bread grain and dish grain. Different grains have different experiences growing up, as with any family where environment influences outcome. The main distinction is that bread grain grows without a protective hull. A hull is like a house; it offers protection from sun, heat, and cold. Hence bread grains like wheat, rye, and corn have tougher skins than dish grains. The seeds of dish grains grow with the protection of hulls. Once the hull is removed, the seed is soft, as with rice, quinoa, oats, millet, Job's tears, and buckwheat. Pretreatments on bread grains affect the texture so that they may be served whole. For example, dry roasting and soaking whole wheat or spelt berries make them tender enough to be used as a decorative grain in salad or cooked with rice. Soaked whole corn (posole) opens up to be suitable to receive marinade sauces or to be used decoratively in soups after cooking in a first-stage method. Sprouting rye berries softens their hard seed coat so that chewing them whole is easier.

Whole grain dishes provide complex carbohydrates, which are essential for human metabolic functioning. Highly pigmented grain, like wehani, red quinoa, and black forbidden rice, are higher in antioxidants than off-white varieties. The language of cooking supports creativity with a wide variety of whole-dish grains. People are less likely to have grain sensitivities if variety is part of their diet. Because grain requires the enzyme amylase (found in human saliva) to digest starch well, chewing a whole-dish grain until it is wet will enhance the nutritional benefits of these powerful seeds. Like a flat, blank canvas, grains are subtle and sometimes boring in taste. But people who go the distance and take enough time to chew whole grains are rewarded with more than good digestion—they discover hidden sweet flavors. Grain is most often served as a filler, texture enhancer, or background for more dynamic ingredients, like vegetables and sauces. Nevertheless, it is easy to turn grain into the focus of the meal.

> *W*ind moves fields of grain like nature's chorus line, shafts moving in unison. I see each stalk, anchored in earth with its infinite potential to reproduce, standing on its own, reaching upward, peacefully drinking the sun and rain.

I usually eat grain in the morning. It gives me enough slow-burning, steady energy to work through the day. For me, energetically speaking, whole grain is the carbohydrate component of my diet. My body knows the difference between eating a seed so whole I have to chew it, and refined grain carbohydrates like pastry, bread, pasta, and crackers. The former make me feel slim, calm, energized, and centered; while the latter puff me up, slow me down, and help me feel like I'm on vacation. I save them for partying, with myself or others.

Selecting and Storing

Grain sold in one to two pound packages is often cleaner than grain found in bulk bins. I wash whole grains anyway, just for the ritual; it is not unusual to find a few seeds, sticks, or other foreign matter. The biggest concern is grain moths. Their eggs are easily hidden in clumps of grain, looking like they are held together by static. Not to worry; washing and dry roasting cleans the grain and makes it usable, as long as the moths haven't eaten more than their share. Store raw grain in a cool area, in well-sealed glass or food-grade containers. Bay leaves mingled into the grain keeps grain bugs out. Job's tears and millet are best stored in the refrigerator. Brown rice speckled with green-colored grains indicates a young, healthy crop.

AMARANTH (sweet)

Amaranth, a relative of pigweed, is botanically an herb not a grain. Although it contains no gluten, it is glutinous; the longer it cooks the stickier it becomes. The word "amaranth" was derived from the Greek word *amaranthus*, which means "everlasting." Some of the reasoning for why this ancient Aztec food was celebrated in rituals and eaten by royalty might have to do with its loaded nutrient profile that includes high fiber and complete protein. The water-soluble bran makes it easy to digest and gives it a slippery character. Cooked amaranth seeds have a sweet, nutty taste, are light tan, shiny, tiny, and crunchy, reminding me of caviar. Black seeds speckled in the batch of amaranth are its cousin, pigweed. I don't take time to remove them.

Lemon Porridge

Primary element: amaranth

Pretreatment: dry roast (optional)

First-stage method: steep (1 part grain : 5 parts cooking liquid)

> *Cooking liquid:* hot water with vegetable bouillon, fresh lemon juice
>
> *Herb/spice:* lemon zest or lemon oil
>
> *Salt:* sesame salt, or use sea salt as it cooks

Ready to Stuff into Something

MAIN PLATE

Primary element: amaranth

First-stage method: sauté/bake

Decorative: leek, red bell pepper

Cut: small dice

> *Oil:* light sesame
>
> *Cooking liquid:* water
>
> *Herb/spice:* bay leaf, freshly ground allspice
>
> *Salt:* sea salt

Primary element: winter squash

First-stage method: roast

> *Oil:* light sesame
>
> *Salt:* sea salt

Hot sauce: nut

> *Oil:* pecans
>
> *Herb/spice:* fresh garlic
>
> *Cooking liquid:* water
>
> *Salt:* chickpea miso

Orange Amaranth

SIDE DISH

Primary element: first-stage cooked amaranth

Second-stage method: braise

Decorative: green onion, carrot

> *Oil:* toasted sesame
>
> *Salt:* tamari/shoyu
>
> *Cooking liquid:* orange juice
>
> *Herb/spice:* freshly grated ginger juice, orange oil

Decorative: roasted almonds

BUCKWHEAT (odd/bitter)

I've noticed that people are either fond of or repelled by buckwheat. It has a light energy body and strong taste. Botanically, buckwheat is not a grain, it is a wild grass; but my culinary instincts put it into the grain category for cooking and eating. Kasha—dry roasted buckwheat—is so much more delicious than the raw groats (buckwheat seed) that it earned a name of its own. When raw groats are first-stage cooked, they are pale, sticky, and odd tasting, although they are quite delicious sprouted. Buckwheat absorbs liquid like a sponge. Unless it will be sprouted, I don't wash or rinse the grains.

Croquettes

Primary element: buckwheat

First-stage method: steep

   Cooking liquid: cold water

Second-stage method: deep-fry

Decorative: minced green onion

   Oil: safflower

Cold sauce: dipping

   Salt: chickpea miso

   Cooking liquid: mirin, brown rice vinegar

   Herb/spice: fresh ginger juice

Sour Breakfast

MAIN PLATE

Primary element: kasha (dry roasted buckwheat)

First-stage method: steep (water or vegetable bouillon)

Second-stage method: braise

Decorative: green onion, sauerkraut

   Oil: light sesame oil

   Salt: umeboshi

   Cooking liquid: sauerkraut juice

Primary element: tofu or tempeh

Second-stage method: refry

   Oil: light sesame

   Salt: umeboshi or tamari

Primary element: kale

First-stage method: steep

Cut: whole, shredded

Version of Varsnishka

SIDE DISH WITH SAUCE

Primary element: kasha (dry roasted buckwheat)

First-stage method: steep in vegetable bouillon

Second-stage method: refry

Decorative: onion, arugula, cooked bow tie pasta

   Oil: light sesame or ghee

   Salt: tamari

Hot sauce: clear

Binder: kudzu

Major vegetables: caramelized mushrooms, onion

   Oil: ghee or light sesame

   Herb/spice: fresh garlic, thyme

   Cooking liquid: red wine, water

   Salt: sea salt, tamari/shoyu

Living Cracker

SNACK

Primary element: sprouted buckwheat, onion, carrot, parsnip

First-stage method: sprout

Second-stage method: dehydrate

Cut: grate vegetables, food process/blend to combine

   Oil: soaked sunflower seeds

   Cooking liquid: rejuvelac, fresh lemon juice

   Herb/spice: fresh lemon thyme, basil, oregano

   Salt: sea salt

Asian Flavor

Primary element: buckwheat

First-stage method: sprout

Second-stage method: marinate

Decorative: carrot, beet, cucumber

Cut: grated, fine julienne

Oil: toasted sesame

Cooking liquid: fresh lime juice, mirin

Herb/spice: freshly ground coriander, fresh cilantro

Salt: miso

JOB'S TEARS (odd)

Cooked Job's tears look like plump, moist pearls, shiny and somewhat slippery. When I bite into them, a quick aftertaste bites me back. Even after it has been dry roasted, this grain looks wet because, like oats and amaranth, it has a water-soluble bran. I don't expect a crisp crust from this grain. The shape and color read like concepts of individuality and purity. An ornamental variety of Job's tears uses the strong hull as beads. Like beans, this grain has to be picked through to remove any pieces of the sharp hull, dark brown grain, and other foreign objects. Job's tears require more time and cooking liquid than other grains. Pressure cooking Job's tears is the most efficient first-stage method. Boiling, baking, and steeping are good if one has an hour and a half to wait for the grain to move through the first stage.

Fruit and Spice

Primary element: Job's tears

First-stage method: boiled in curry water

Second-stage method: marinate

Decorative: red bell pepper, yellow bell pepper, green onion

Oil: light sesame oil

Cooking liquid: orange juice, pomegranate syrup

Herb/spice: fresh ginger juice, fresh cilantro

Salt: chickpea miso

Cool Elegance

Primary element: Job's tears

First-stage method: pressure cook

Second-stage method: marinate

Decorative: chives, celery, red radish

Oil: hazelnut oil

Cooking liquid: raspberry vinegar, mirin

Herb/spice: orange zest oil, cardamom

Salt: sea salt

Romantic

Primary element: Job's tears

First-stage method: pressure cook (water, sea salt)

Second-stage method: braise

Decorative: parsley

Oil: olive

Herb/spice: oregano, garlic

Cooking liquid: water, red wine

Salt: umeboshi

On Fire

Primary element: Job's tears

First-stage method: bake (water, paprika)

Second-stage method: marinate

Decorative: black olives, cherry tomato,
    cucumber, parsley

Oil: olive

Cooking liquid: fresh lemon juice

Herb/spice: lemon zest, jalapeño chile

Salt: sea salt

Simple and Deep

SIDE DISH

Primary element: Job's tears

Pretreatment: dry roast

First-stage method: boil (bay leaf, clove)

Second-stage method: braise

Decorative: green onion

Cut: diagonal

Oil: sunflower

Herb/spice: garlic

Cooking liquid: Marsala wine

Salt: umeboshi

Green and White

SIDE DISH

Primary element: Job's tears

First-stage method: pressure cook

Second-stage method: refry

Decorative: green onion, fresh fennel

Oil: light sesame

Herb/spice: dill weed

Salt: umeboshi

Persian Style

SIDE DISH

Primary element: Job's tears

First-stage method: pressure cook

Second-stage method: braise

Decorative: onion

Cut: diced

Oil: ghee

Cooking liquid: fresh lemon juice

Herb/spice: saffron

Salt: umeboshi

Pretty in Pink

SIDE DISH

Primary element: Job's tears

First-stage method: pressure cook

Second-stage method: refry

Decorative: beets

Cut: diced small

Oil: light sesame

Herb/spice: ground coriander

Salt: umeboshi

Savory Pearls

SIDE DISH WITH SAUCE

Primary element: Job's tears

Pretreatment: dry roast

First-stage method: pressure cook

Cooking liquid: water, Marsala wine

Salt: vegetable salt

Hot sauce: nut

Binder: pine nuts

Cooking liquid: Marsala wine, water

Herb/spice: garlic, marjoram

Salt: miso

Fruit and Nuts

Primary element: Job's tears

First-stage method: pressure cook

Second-stage method: refry

Decorative: onion, dried currants

> *Oil:* coconut

> *Herb/spice:* rosemary

> *Salt:* light miso

Decorative: roasted pecans, roasted tofu

Primary element: winter squash

First-stage method: roast

Cut: for stuffing, puncture holes with fork

> *Oil:* light sesame

> *Salt:* sea salt

Hot sauce: nut

> *Oil:* cashews

> *Cooking liquid:* water (1 part nuts : 3 parts liquid)

> *Salt:* umeboshi

Thai Memories

Primary element: Job's tears

First-stage method: pressure cook

> *Cooking liquid:* water

> *Salt:* sea salt

Hot sauce: clear

> *Binder:* kudzu

Decorative: gold bell peppers

Cut: medium diced

> *Oil:* light and dark sesame

> *Cooking liquid:* kombu/spice stock, fresh lime juice, coconut milk

> *Herb/spice:* kaffir lime leaf, galangal, lime oil

> *Salt:* sea salt

To Be Used as Stuffing

Primary element: Job's tears

First-stage method: pressure cook

Second-stage method: braise

Decorative: onion, carrot, parsnips

Cut: small dice

> *Oil:* toasted sesame oil

> *Salt:* tamari

> *Cooking liquid:* rice vinegar, mirin

Primary element: tempeh

Second-stage method: teriyaki

> *Oil:* light sesame

> *Cooking liquid/sweetener:* rice syrup

> *Salt:* tamari

Primary element: red bell pepper

First-stage method: roast

Cut: in half for stuffing

> *Oil:* toasted sesame

> *Salt:* sea salt

Primary element: butternut squash, onion

Hot sauce: vegetable

> *Oil:* light sesame

> *Herb/spice:* crushed cardamom

> *Cooking liquid:* cashew milk (1 part nuts : 18 parts liquid)

> *Salt:* sea salt

Sweet Heat

Primary element: Job's tears

First-stage method: boil (cayenne)

Second-stage method: refry

Decorative: red onion, carrot

> *Oil:* olive

> *Herb/spice:* dried basil

> *Salt:* tamari/shoyu

Red Bean and Job's Tears Patty

Primary element: first-stage cooked Job's tears, first-stage cooked red kidney beans

Second-stage method: refry, patty form

Decorative: red onion, red bell pepper

Cut: minced

Binder: finely crushed red corn chips

    Oil: coconut

    Herb/spice: basil

    Salt: salted red corn chips

Primary element: red bell pepper

Hot sauce: vegetable

    Oil: olive

    Herb/spice: fresh garlic, shallot

    Cooking liquid: water, white wine (optional)

Sunset

Primary element: Job's tears

Pretreatment: dry roast, sauté

First-stage method: pressure cook

Decorative vegetables: mushrooms, shallot

Cut: medium

    Oil: light sesame

    Cooking liquid: macadamia nut milk (1 part nuts : 20 parts cooking liquid)

    Salt: sea salt

Primary element: butternut squash, onion

Hot sauce: vegetable

    Oil: light and dark sesame

    Cooking liquid: water

    Herb/spice: ginger

    Salt: sea salt

MILLET (sweet)

A shiny round hull protects this small seed; birds pick it off with their beaks. I have seen two kinds of millet, a small American seed with most of the hulls removed, and another from Japan called kibi millet. Kibi millet is sticky and glutinous, but it does not contain the protein gluten. It is a fatter seed than the standard American version and stays soft with no definable edge after cooking, unlike common millet whose high silica content forms a firm shape after the cooked grain cools. I use millet in ways that others use polenta. Standard millet is particularly good for holding its shape when refrying and deep-frying. Kibi millet is wet like sticky porridge. I wash both of these grains well, two to three times. It heightens their color and sweet taste.

Once Upon a Time

Primary element: millet

Pretreatment: dry roast

First-stage method: boil

    Cooking liquid: spiced water

    Herb/spice: cinnamon, allspice, star anise, curry powder

    Oil: light sesame or olive

Second-stage method: marinate

Decorative: red onion, red bell pepper, golden raisin, cucumber

    Oil: light sesame, olive

    Herb/spice: curry powder, fresh basil

    Cooking liquid: white balsamic vinegar

    Salt: sea salt, light miso

Decorative: roasted hazelnuts

Millet Mash with Celery Seitan Gravy

Primary element: millet

Pretreatment: sauté

First-stage method: pressure cook

Second-stage method: refry

Major vegetables: cauliflower, onion

Cut: diced small

    Oil: light sesame

    Herb/spice: fennel seed, fresh garlic

    Cooking liquid: water

    Salt: sea salt or vegetable salt

Hot sauce: clear

Major vegetable: celery

Cut: thin diagonal

    Oil: light sesame

    Herb/spice: fresh garlic

    Cooking liquid: cashew milk made with water and white wine (1 part nuts : 18 parts liquid)

    Salt: sea salt or vegetable salt

Decorative: seitan

Triangles

Primary element: millet

First-stage method: steep

Second-stage method: refry, patty form

Decorative: green onion, orange bell pepper, fresh cilantro

    Herb/spice: onion powder, freshly ground pink peppercorns

    Salt: vegetable salt, umeboshi

    Oil: safflower

OATS (sweet)

*I*n 1970 I experienced an herb-laden, savory oat dish with a sauce and roasted sunflower seeds for garnish. It shifted my palate from the commonplace sugary oat dishes that I now reserve for holiday breakfasts to everyday savory dishes with oats.

The most significant characteristic about oats is their creaminess. I think of it as natural fat. Fat goes easily with sweet ingredients, but it requires a heavy hand of herb/spice to impact a dense grain. All forms of oats are whole, but by cutting them, as with steel cut oats, the cooked texture becomes both creamy and chewy. Rolled oats have been pressed and steamed, so they cook more quickly. Because they have been heated once, rolled oats do not store well for long periods of time unless refrigerated.

Oat Stuffing #1

Primary element: rolled oats

Pretreatment: sauté

First-stage method: bake

Decorative: yellow onion, butternut squash, celery

Cut: medium dice

    Oil: light sesame

    Herb/spice: thyme, sage

    Cooking liquid: water

    Salt: vegetable salt

Decorative: tamari/shoyu roasted sunflower seeds

Dessert Porridge

Primary element: rolled or steel cut oats

Pretreatment: dry roast

First-stage method: steep (1 part oats : 4 parts liquid)

Decorative: apricots

Herb/spice: cinnamon stick

Cooking liquid: cashew milk made with apple juice and water (1 part nuts : 4 parts liquid)

Salt: sea salt

Middle East Tones

SALAD

Primary element: whole oat groats

First-stage method: pressure cook

Second-stage method: marinate

Decorative: grapes, green onion, red radish

Oil: pumpkin seed oil

Cooking liquid: fresh lemon juice

Herb/spice: rose water

Salt: sea salt

Smoky Sage Stuffing

SIDE DISH

Primary element: rolled or steel cut oats

Pretreatment: smoke, sauté

First-stage method: steep

Decorative: minced shallot

Oil: hazelnut

Herb/spice: fresh or dried sage

Salt: sea salt

QUINOA (bitter)

My favorite question about quinoa was from a lady who called to ask if it was safe to eat because there were curly, wormlike threads in the cooked grain. I told her she didn't have to pick them out; they were the germ of the seed.

Quinoa's germination point is on the outside of the seed coat. It opens into beautiful spirals when it cooks. This grain's light energy body cooks quickly but also benefits from pretreatments. It carries a bitter background taste that is easily balanced with pungent and sour supporting elements and sweet decorative vegetables. Like rice, quinoa varieties come in many colors—creamy white, reddish brown, and black. Red and black quinoa offer distinctly different tastes and textures. Quinoa has been marked as a complete protein. Serving it with dry roasted nuts or a nut sauce anchors its fluffy character.

Feels Like Spring

SALAD

Primary element: quinoa

First-stage method: steep

Second-stage method: marinate

Decorative: celery, grapes

Cut: diagonal

Oil: hazelnut

Herb/spice: dill weed

Cooking liquid: mirin, cider vinegar

Salt: sea salt

Decorative: umeboshi roasted cashews

Living

Primary element: sprouted red quinoa, grated sweet potato

Second-stage method: dehydrate

Decorative: red bell pepper, poblano chile, nutritional yeast

Cut: blend in food processor

 Oil: pine nuts, olive oil

 Cooking liquid: fresh lime juice, water

 Salt: sea salt

Croquettes

Primary element: quinoa

First-stage method: pressure cook (cold–cold)

Second-stage method: deep-fry

 Oil: safflower

Cold sauce: dipping

 Salt: miso

 Cooking liquid: orange juice, raspberry vinegar

 Herb/spice: garlic

Ritual

Primary element: quinoa

First-stage method: boil, loose vegetable soup

Decorative: green onion

 Oil: dark sesame

 Cooking liquid: vegetable bouillon or stock, fresh lemon juice

 Herb/spice: fresh ginger, lemon zest

 Salt: sea salt, umeboshi

Decorative: fresh cilantro

Red Quinoa with Mushroom

Primary element: red quinoa

First-stage method: boil

Second-stage method: marinate

Decorative: mushroom, red onion, red bell pepper, black olives

Cut: small

 Oil: olive

 Cooking liquid: white balsamic vinegar, olive brine

 Herb/spice: fresh marjoram, fresh thyme, truffle oil

 Salt: sea salt

Passion Plate

Primary element: quinoa

Pretreatment: dry roast, sauté

First-stage method: bake

Decorative: red bell pepper, yellow bell pepper, gold bar or green zucchini, onion

Cut: medium dice

 Oil: olive or ghee

 Herb/spice: saffron, chili powder

 Cooking liquid: water

 Salt: sea salt or vegetable salt

Hot sauce: bean

 Binder: white beans

Decorative: shallot

 Herb/spice: fresh thyme, garlic

 Cooking liquid: almond milk made with bean liquid, water, mirin (1 part nuts : 15 parts liquid)

 Salt: white or chickpea miso

RICE (sweet/bitter)

> *O*ne of the things I appreciate most about the language of cooking is that I am no longer bored with rice. Rice was my teacher.

The symbol of the rice plant that is engraved on the Japanese five yen coin inspired the School of Natural Cookery logo. Nine varieties of rice live in my cupboard—wehani, forbidden black lotus, white basmati, brown basmati, sushi, golden rose brown, wild rice, sweet brown, and Arborio. Rice can be divided into two families—short and long. Within the short-grain family there are white, red, black, and brown colors. Short-grain rice is denser and stickier than long-grain rice, which is light, fluffy, and individual in character. The background taste of rice when completely chewed is sweet, except for sweet brown rice, which is bitter.

Red Rice

SALAD

Primary element: wehani rice

First-stage method: boil

Second-stage method: marinate

Decorative: roasted red bell pepper, yellow bell pepper

    Oil: hazelnut

    Cooking liquid: fresh lime juice

    Salt: sea salt

    Herb/spice: mint, lavender, lime zest

Brain Burgers

MAIN PLATE

Primary element: 3 parts sweet brown rice : 1 part adzuki beans

First-stage method: pressure cook

    Herb/spice: fresh ginger slices (remove after cooking)

Second-stage method: braise

Decorative: green onion, red bell pepper, celery, carrot, parsnip

Cut: diced

    Oil: olive

    Herb/spice: fresh basil or cilantro

    Salt: umeboshi, sesame salt (optional)

    Cooking liquid: fresh lemon juice

Almost Greek Lemon Rice

SOUP

Primary element: basmati rice

First-stage method: boil, clear soup (1 part rice : 8–10 parts liquid)

    Cooking liquid: vegetable bouillon, fresh lemon juice

    Herb/spice: lemon oil, freshly ground black pepper

    Salt: vegetable bouillon or sea salt

    Optional: well-beaten and tempered egg

Rice Croquettes

Primary element: short-grain brown rice

First-stage method: pressure cook (cold—cold)

Second-stage method: deep fry

Decorative: minced green onion, lemon zest

    Oil: safflower

Cold sauce: dipping

    Salt: tamari/shoyu

    Cooking liquid: mirin, rice vinegar

Chinese-Style Fried Rice

Primary element: first-stage cooked rice

Second-stage method: braise

Decorative: green onion, carrot, celery, bean
    sprouts, peas

Cut: small dice or diagonal

    Oil: toasted sesame

    Salt: tamari/shoyu

    Cooking liquid: mirin

    Herb/spice: fresh ginger juice

Black Ginger Rice

Primary element: black forbidden rice

First-stage method: pressure cook

    Cooking liquid: water

    Herb/spice: fresh ginger slices (large)

    Salt: sea salt

Black Rice Pudding

Primary element: black forbidden rice or any
    other rice

Pretreatment: soak

First-stage method: steep

    Cooking liquid: almond milk made with
        water, maple syrup (1 part nuts :
        10 parts liquid)

    Herb/spice: whole cinnamon stick

    Salt: sea salt

Classic Persian

Primary element: white basmati rice

First-stage method: steep

    Cooking liquid: water

    Oil: olive

    Salt: sea salt

    Herb/spice: a major amount of dill weed
        steeped in at the end of cooking

Hot sauce: nut

    Oil: walnuts

    Cooking liquid: pomegranate syrup, water

    Salt: sea salt

Paella

Primary element: Arborio or paella rice

Pretreatment: sauté

First-stage method: steep in a paella pan or skillet without a lid for the entire method; steep without a cover until two-thirds of the liquid has evaporated

Second-stage method: roast in medium oven until the liquid is gone

Decorative: green onion, red bell pepper, roasted tofu cubes, first-stage cooked miniature fava or navy beans

> *Oil:* olive

> *Herb/spice:* garlic, thyme, pimenton, saffron

Cooking liquid: kombu vegetable stock

> *Salt:* sea salt

Cold sauce: place in a cross on top of grain before roasting

> *Oil:* olive

> *Cooking liquid:* fresh lemon juice

> *Herb/spice:* major amount of fresh parsley

> *Salt:* sea salt

Note: Mix the dish before serving to integrate the sauce.

Pad Thai

Primary element: rice noodles

Pretreatment: soak in boiling water only to soften, not quite halfway cooked

First-stage method: braise

Primary element: green onion, carrot, bean sprouts

First-stage method: braise

Decorative: shallot

Cut: diagonal, julienne

> *Oil:* sesame

> *Cooking liquid:* kombu-ginger stock

> *Salt:* tamari/shoyu

> *Herb/spice:* garlic, tamarind, cayenne

> *Miscellaneous:* palm or cane sugar

Primary element: extra-firm tofu

Second-stage method: braise

> *Oil:* sesame

> *Cooking liquid:* kombu-ginger stock

> *Salt:* tamari/shoyu

> *Herb/spice:* garlic, tamarind, cayenne

> *Miscellaneous:* palm or cane sugar

Decorative: lime wedges

Appetizer: A selection of primary elements that serves to stimulate the appetite preparing the diner for the next course of the meal. Soup and salad are the most common appetizers.

Arrowroot wash: To replace egg washes, use equal parts arrowroot starch and liquid. This will help breading and encrusted mixtures stick.

Breading: Flour, ground crackers, bread crumbs used to seal the edges of primary elements usually before they go into oil methods. The purpose of breading is to hold in moisture, usually of the protein element.

Caramelize: Sealing, shrinking, and reducing vegetables as much as possible before burning in order to intensify flavor. Caramelizing is a very long and slow process.

Casserole: A term that indicates all three primary elements are present. Most often a sauce is included.

Cold–Cold and Hot–Hot: Indicates the temperature of the cooking liquid and the temperature of the grain at the onset of a first-stage method. Both will be cold, hot, or a combination.

Croquette: A primary element pressed into a firm shape. A croquette is usually deep-fried, distinguished from a patty shape by being a long log or triangle.

Double dip: This term is used to indicate that during the breading process the primary element goes into the dry ingredients twice. Dry first, then wet, and then dry again before going into the pan.

Encrusted: Used like breading, encrusted mixtures are mostly made of ground nuts with some flour.

Glazed nuts: Roasted nuts are tossed in a syrup that becomes a coating. Equal parts sugar and liquid are cooked to a semihard stage.

Hand blend: Indicates using a potato masher, whip/whisk, or molcajete.

Hors d'oeuvres: Refers to party food where all three primary elements are in each bite. Main plates are shaped into finger-food forms.

Long-term beans: Dried beans that must be soaked before any first-stage cooking method.

Medium-term beans: Dried beans that have the option of being soaked but require approximately 50 minutes to cook without soaking.

Primary element: Ingredient category that holds a basic nutrient profile including grain, vegetable, and protein.

Pudding: A soft-textured grain dish. Rice and bread puddings are primary elements and are usually semisweet.

Rejuvelac: A cooking liquid made by fermenting water with whole grain sprouts.

Short-term beans: Dried beans that do not require soaking or long cooking times.

Tempered: A term used for warming eggs and dairy products so they can be added to a hot liquid, such as a soup or sauce, without curdling.

TABLE 1.1 Chart of Tastes: Primary Elements

VEGETABLES	SWEET	SALTY	PUNGENT	BITTER	ODD	NEUTRAL	SOUR
Artichoke				X	X		
Asparagus				X	X		
Avocado	X						
Baby bok choy	X			X			
Beet root	X						
Bell pepper	X						
Broccoli	X			X			
Brussels sprouts			X	X			
Burdock				X	X		
Cabbage	X		X				
Carrot	X						
Cauliflower			X				
Celery		X		X			
Celery root			X	X			
Chicory				X			
Collard greens				X			
Corn	X						
Daikon	X		X				
Eggplant	X			X	X		
Fennel	X						
Green bean	X			X			
Jicama	X						
Kale				X			
Kohlrabi	X					X	
Lotus root	X				X		
Mushroom					X		
Mustard greens			X	X			
Okra	X						

continued

TABLE 1.1 Chart of Tastes: Primary Elements, *continued*

VEGETABLES	SWEET	SALTY	PUNGENT	BITTER	ODD	NEUTRAL	SOUR
Onion	X		X				
Parsley root	X						
Parsnip	X						
Pea	X			X			
Potato	X						
Radicchio				X			
Radish			X				
Rutabaga	X		X				
Sea vegetables		X					
Summer squash	X			X			
Sunchoke	X				X		
Sweet potato	X						
Swiss chard				X			
Tomato	X						
Turnip	X		X	X			
Winter squash	X						
Yam	X						
GRAIN							
Amaranth	X						
Buckwheat				X	X		
Job's tears					X		
Millet	X						
Oats	X						
Quinoa				X			
Rice							
short and long grain	X						
sweet				X			
wild					X		
Sorghum						X	

HERBS AND SPICES	SWEET	SALTY	PUNGENT	BITTER	ODD	NEUTRAL	SOUR
Ajwain				X	X		
Allspice	X						
Anise	X						
Arugula			X	X			
Asafetida					X		
Basil	X						
Bay leaf			X	X			
Caraway			X	X			
Cardamom	X						
Cayenne			X				
Celery seed				X			
Chiles, hot			X				
Chive			X				
Cilantro				X			
Cinnamon	X						
Clove			X				
Coriander				X			
Cumin				X			
Dill				X			
Epazote				X	X		
Fennel	X						
Fenugreek				X	X		
Garlic			X				
Ginger			X				
Kaffir lime leaf	X						
Lemon zest	X						
Lime zest				X			
Marjoram				X			
Mint	X						
Orange zest	X						
Oregano				X			
Paprika				X	X		
Parsley	X			X			*continued*

204

TABLE 1.2 **Chart of Tastes: Supporting Elements,** *continued*

HERBS AND SPICES	SWEET	SALTY	PUNGENT	BITTER	ODD	NEUTRAL	SOUR
Peppercorn, black			X	X			
Peppercorn, pink	X		X				
Rosemary				X			
Sage				X			
Shallot			X	X			
Sorrel				X			X
Star anise	X						
Thyme				X			
Turmeric				X	X		
OIL, SEEDS, NUTS							
Almond	X						
Cashew	X						
Coconut	X						
Corn	X				X		
Hazelnut	X						
Olive	X			X			
Palm					X	X	
Peanut	X						
Pecan	X						
Pine nut	X				X		
Pistachio	X						
Pumpkin				X			
Safflower					X		
Sesame				X			
Sunflower	X			X			
Walnut				X			
COOKING LIQUID							
Beer				X			
Kombu stock		X					
Lemon juice							X
Lime juice							X
Mirin	X						*continued*

TABLE 1.2 Chart of Tastes: Supporting Elements, *continued*

COOKING LIQUID	SWEET	SALTY	PUNGENT	BITTER	ODD	NEUTRAL	SOUR
Orange juice	X						
Tea, green/black				X			
Tea, fruit	X						
Vegetable juice				X			
Vinegar							X
Wine	X			X			
SALT SEASONING							
Miso, dark	X						
Miso, light	X	X					
Pickle brine		X					X
Tamari/shoyu		X					
Umeboshi		X					X

TABLE 1.3 Chart of Forms

PRIMARY ELEMENT	COOKING METHOD	FORM
GRAIN	bake	side dish; casserole
	boil	soup; stew
	braise	side dish; stuffing
	marinate	salad; decorative
	pressure cook	side dish
	refry	side dish; stuffing
	sprout	salad; decorative
	steep	side dish
VEGETABLES	bake	side dish
	blend	soup; sauce; spread; dip
	boil	soup; stew
	braise	side dish
	broil	side dish
	deep-fry	appetizer; side dish *continued*

TABLE 1.3 Chart of Forms, *continued*

PRIMARY ELEMENT	COOKING METHOD	FORM
	dehydrate	garnish
	grill	side dish
	marinate	salad; decorative
	pickle	side dish; garnish; decorative
	press	salad; decorative
	pressure cook	side dish; spread; soup; sauce
	pressure steam	side dish
	refry	side dish; stuffing
	roast	side dish
	slow cook	side dish
	sprout	decorative
	steam	decorative
	steep	side dish
	teriyaki	side dish; garnish; decorative
PROTEIN—All	braise	side dish
	deep-fry	side dish
	marinate	salad; decorative
	refry	side dish
Bean sprouts	dehydrate	crackers
Beans	bake	casserole
	blend	spread; dip; sauce; soup
	sprout	decorative; crackers
Gluten	bake	casserole
Seitan	broil	side dish
	grill	side dish
Soup	boil	soup
Tofu and tempeh	blend	spread; dip; sauce; soup
	broil	side dish
	grill	side dish
	pressure steam	spread; dip
	roast	side dish; decorative

TABLE 2.1 Chart of Cooking Methods

COOKING METHOD	GRAIN	VEGETABLE	PROTEIN
PRETREATMENT			
Blanch		fruit family	nuts
Dry roast	all		
Sauté	all		
Smoke	all	all	all
Soak	all	seeds; sea vegetables	beans; nuts/seeds
NO OIL			
Fermenting	all		nuts/seeds
Pickle		first stage	
Press		first stage	
Pressure cook	first stage	first stage	first stage
Pressure steam		first stage	
Sprout	first stage	first stage	first stage/beans
Steam		first stage; decorative only	
Steep	first stage	first stage	first stage
OIL			
Baking	first/second stage	first stage	second stage
Blending		second stage	second stage
Boiling	first/second stage	first stage	second stage
Braising	second stage	first stage	second stage
Broiling		first stage	third stage
Deep-frying	second stage	first stage	second/third stage
Grilling		third stage	third stage
Roasting		first/second stage	second/third stage
Slow cooking		first stage	
Stir-frying		first stage	
Teriyaki		first stage	second stage

TABLE 2.2 Pressure Cooking/Pressure Steaming Times for Vegetables

VEGETABLE	MINUTES
Artichoke, globe (pretreat by soaking in salt water)	20
Asparagus	1
Beet, medium-small	20–30
Beet, medium-large	35–40
Broccoli	1
Brussels sprouts	7
Burdock	7
Cabbage (cut into large wedges)	5
Carrot, medium	5
Carrot, large	7
Cauliflower	5–8
Celery	$1\frac{1}{2}$
Corn on the cob	$1\frac{1}{2}$
Daikon	5–7
Green beans	1 (firm), $1\frac{1}{2}$ (tender)
Kohlrabi	5
Leek	$1\frac{1}{2}$
Lotus root	7
Onion	12
Parsnip	5
Potatoes, medium (red, yellow, white, sweet)	20
Rutabaga, medium (whole)	30+
Squash, summer (zucchini, crook neck, pattypan)	3
Squash, winter (buttercup, butternut, acorn, spaghetti, Hokkaido, pumpkin), cut in half, seeded	15
Turnip	12–15
Yam, medium	20
Yucca	35+

Notes:
- The larger or more dense the vegetable, the longer it will take to cook.
- Bring the pressure down quickly to check the vegetables. You can return the cooker to full pressure if further cooking is needed.

TABLE 2.3 Grain Chart: First-Stage Cooking Methods

Grain (1 cup dry)	BAKE (350°F) Liquid (cups)	BAKE Min.	BOIL Liquid (cups)	BOIL Min.	STEEP Liquid (cups)	STEEP Min.	PRESSURE COOK Liquid (cups)	PRESSURE COOK Min.	Yield (cups)
Amaranth	2	35+	8	9	2	30	X	X	2
Barley, hulled	2½	90+	10	45	2½	90	2	35–60	3
Barley, pearl	2	60+	8	35	2	60	X	35–60	3
Buckwheat	2	20+	X	X	2	15	X	X	4
Corn, soaked posole	X	X	10	90	2½	80	1½	35–60	3
Cornmeal	1	35	X	X	4	15–40	X	35–60	3
Job's tears	2½	90+	8	40	2½	70	2	50	3–4
Millet	3½	45+	8	10	3¼	40	3	20	3
Oats, rolled	X	X	X	X	2½	10	X	X	2
Oats, whole groats	2	55+	8	20	2	55	1½	30	2
Quinoa	2	25+	8	9–12	2	15+	1½	7	4
Rice, long-grain brown	2	55+	8	25–35	2	45	1½	35–60	3
Rice, short-grain brown	2	60+	8	27–40	2	50	1½	35–60	3
Rice, sushi	2	40+	X	X	2	35	X	X	3
Rice, sweet brown	2	60+	8	25–30	2	50	1½	35–60	3
Rice, wild	2¼	60+	8	45	2¼	50	1½	45+	3
Rye, rolled	2	35+	X	X	2	25	X	X	2
Rye, whole	2	90+	8	40	2	90	1½	30–45	2
Teff	3	30+	8	9	3	20	X	X	2
Wheat, bulgur	2	25+	X	X	2	25	X	X	2
Wheat, couscous	2	15+	X	X	2	10	X	X	2
Wheat, cracked	2	30+	X	X	2	25	X	X	2
Wheat, rolled	2	20+	X	X	2	15	X	X	2
Wheat, whole soft	2	90+	8	30–45	2	90	1½	30–45	2

Notes:

- Times given are approximations in minutes based on cooking at an altitude of 5,000 feet above sea level; lower elevations will require less cooking time and ¼ cup less liquid.
- When cooking over three cups of grain at a time, reduce the liquid by approximately ¼ cup per cup of grain used.
- X means this method is not recommended.

TABLE 2.4 Bean Types Based on Cooking Times

SHORT-TERM		MEDIUM-TERM				LONG-TERM
Adzuki	Lima	Anasazi	Great Northern	Pinto		Chickpea (garbanzo)
Lentil	Mung	Black-eyed pea	Kidney	Red bean		Fava
		Black turtle	Navy	Tongue of Fire		Soy, black and yellow

TABLE 2.5 Bean Cooking Times Based on Type

BEAN TYPE AND ALTITUDE	SOAK	CROCKPOT	PRESSURE COOKER	STEEP
Short-term, -3000 ft.	optional	2–3 hr.	15 min.	25–40 min.
Short-term, +3000 ft.	1 hr.	3–5 hr.	25 min.	1 hr.
Medium-term, -3,000 ft.	optional	4–5 hr.	45 min.	1–2 hr.
Medium-term, +3,000 ft.	4 hr.	5–6 hr.	55 min.	2–3 hr.
Long-term, -3,000 ft.	6–12 hr.	10 hr.	50 min.	X
Long-term, +3,000 ft.	6–12 hr.	12 hr.	1 hr.	X

Notes:

- A well-cooked bean has a smooth, soft texture throughout, without broken skin.
- Never use salt or salted ingredients in the first stage.
- General yield: 1 cup dried beans = $2\frac{1}{2}$ cups cooked.
- Store cooked beans in the refrigerator or freezer.
- Use a one-inch piece of kombu sea vegetable for each cup of dry beans. Kombu sea vegetable is used to expedite the breakdown of secondary compounds in beans, making them more digestible.
- X means not recommended.

TABLE 2.6 Cooking Liquid for Beans

BEANS	COOKING METHOD	AMOUNT OF LIQUID
Soaked	Pressure cooker	cover by $\frac{1}{2}$ to 1 inch
Soaked	Steep	cover by 2 inches
Soaked	Crockpot	cover by $1\frac{1}{2}$ inches
Unsoaked	Pressure cooker	$2\frac{1}{2}$ parts liquid to 1 part beans
Unsoaked	Steep	3–5 parts liquid to 1 part beans
Unsoaked	Crockpot	3–5 parts liquid to 1 part beans

Notes:

- For soaked beans, drain the beans well; then cover them with fresh cool cooking liquid to the level indicated above the top of the beans.
- Use $\frac{1}{4}$ to $\frac{1}{2}$ cup less cooking liquid in moist climates at sea level.

with mustard greens, *145*
with oats, *195, 196*
with parsnip, *103*
with pattypan squash, *124*
with peas, dried, *173*
with peas, fresh, *128*
with potato, *104, 105*
with quinoa, *197*
with radish, *106*
with red onion, *114, 115*
with rice, *199*
with rutabaga, *107*
with sea palm, *134*
with spinach, *145*
with sunchoke, *108, 109*
with Swiss chard, *146*
with tempeh, *186, 187*
with tofu, *186, 187*
with tomato, *158*
with turnips, *109, 110*
with white beans, *177, 179*
with white onion, *116*
with yam, *111*
with yellow onion, *115*
with yucca root, *112, 113*
single-focus dishes, 18, 19, 41
snacks, *95, 96, 101, 107, 190*
soups
   Asparagus, Cream of, *160*
   Bean, *43*
   Borscht, Traditional, *94*
   Borscht with Cabbage, *94*
   Broccoli, Cream of, *148*
   Carrot and Ginger, *97*
   Celeriac, Cream of, *97*
   Celery, Light, *162*
   Clear, *39*
   Cream-Style, *39–41*
   Fennel, Cream of, *163*
   French Onion, *116*
   Lotus Soup, White, *102*
   Miso, *100*
   Mushroom, Cream of, *167*
   Potato Leek, *104*
   Rice, Almost Greek
     Lemon, *198*
   Squash, Cream of, *122*
   Sunchoke, Cream of, *109*
   Tomato, Cream of, *158*
   Vegetable, Loose, *41–42*
   White Bean, Cream of, *178*
   with avocado, *153*
   with beans (dried), *171, 172*

with beets, *94*
with burdock, *96*
with carrots, *97*
with chickpeas, *174, 175*
with corn, *126, 127*
with daikon, *100*
forms of, 24, 25
with garlic, *118*
with head cabbage, *140*
with kale, *143*
with lettuce, *144*
methods for, 39–42
with parsnip, *103*
with quinoa, *197*
with radish, *106*
with rutabaga, *108*
with spinach, *146*
styles of, 37
with turnips, *110*
.with yucca root, *112*
soybeans, 183
spices. *See* herbs and spices
spinach, 136, 145, *145–46*
spreads
   with beans (dried), *170*
   with cauliflower, *150*
   with chickpeas, *174, 175*
   with eggplant, *154*
   with garlic, *119*
   with onion, *116*
   with peas, dried, *173*
   with rutabaga, *107*
   with sweet potato, *111*
   with tempeh, *185*
   with tofu, *185*
squashes, 120–25, *121–25*
stages of cooking, 1, 27
stews
   with burdock, *95*
   with kidney beans, *176*
   method for, 42–43
   with okra, *157*
   with rutabaga, *107*
   with sunchoke, *108*
   with sweet potato, *111*
   with vegetables, *42–43*
string beans, 128, *128–29*
substance, flavor, strength
   (SFS) theory, 5, 17
sugar, 66, 76, 110
sunchoke, 91, 108, *108–9*
sweet potato, 110, *111*
Swiss chard, 136, 146, *146*

tamari, 13, 14
tastes/taste theories, 14–15,
   16–17, 202–6
tempeh, 184–85, *185–87*
   baking, 56–57
   broiling and grilling, 60
   deep-frying, 72
   fermenting not recom-
     mended, 76
   marinating, 68
   pressure steaming, 45
   as protein source, 168
   refrying, 69
   roasting, 59
   smoking, 35
   in soups and stews, 43
   steaming, 48
   steeping, 52
   teriyaki, 66
theories of cooking, 14–19
"to fit" theory, 5, 15–16
tofu, 183–85, *185–87*
   age, 25
   baking, 56–57
   broiling and grilling, 60
   deep-frying, 72
   fermenting not recom-
     mended, 76
   marinating, 68
   pressure steaming, 45
   as protein source, 168
   refrying, 69
   roasting, 59
   smoking, 35
   in soups and stews, 43
   steaming, 48
   steeping, 52
   teriyaki, 66
tomato, 152, 153, 157,
   158–59
tools for cooking, 1–2, 53,
   72, 73
turnips, 91, 109, *109–10*

vegetables, 90. *See also*
   specific types of
   baking, 56, 57
   blanching, 34
   blending, 73
   boiling, 36–37
   braising, 65
   broiling and grilling, 60
   cutting, 19–24

deep-frying, 70–71
dehydrating, 75
dry roasting, 29, 30–31
fermenting, 76
first-stage cooking for, 27
flower family, 146–47
fruit family, 152–53
leaf family, 136–37
liquids for cooking of, 10,
   11
marinating, 67–68
mushroom family, 163–65
pickling, 54–55
pod/seed family, 125–26
pressing/wilting, 53–54
pressure cooking, 44
refrying, 69
roasting, 59
root family, 90–92
round, 20, 21
sealing/sautéing, 31
sea vegetables, 129–30
slow cooking, 61–62
smoking, 35
soaking, 33
soups from, 37, 39, *39–42,*
   41
sprouting, 73–74
stalk family, 159–60
steaming, 48
steeping, 50–51
stew from, 42–43
stir-frying, 63
stock from, 37, 38, *38*
teriyaki, 66
vegetable flowers, 24
vegetable protein, 167–68
vine family, 120–21
washing, 28

wakame, 130, 135, *135*
white beans, 177, *177–79*
white onion, 116, *116*
whole-dish foods, 11
wholeness theory, 14

yams, 91, 110, *110–11*
yellow onion, 115, *115–16*
yucca root, 91, 111–12,
   112–13

zigzag technique, 15–16
zucchini, 125, *125*

BOOK PUBLISHING COMPANY

since 1974—books that educate, inspire, and empower

To find your favorite vegetarian and soyfood products online, visit:

www.healthy-eating.com

The Ultimate Uncheese Cookbook
Delicious Dairy-Free Cheeses
and Classic "Uncheese" Dishes
Jo Stepaniak
1-57067-151-6 $15.95

Raw Food Made Easy
Jennifer Cornbleet
1-57067-175-3 $16.95

More Great Good
Dairy-FreeDesserts
Fran Costigan
1-57067-183-4 $19.95

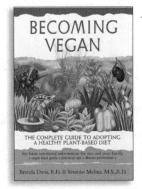

Becoming Vegan
Brenda Davis, RD,
Vesanto Melina, RD
1-57067-103-6 $16.95

The Nut Gourmet
Zel Allen
1-57067-19-5 $19.95

Purchase these health titles and cookbooks from your local bookstore
or natural food store, or you can buy them directly from:

Book Publishing Company • P.O. Box 99 • Summertown, TN 38483
1-800-695-2241

Please include $3.95 per book for shipping and handling.